O9-CFT-090

THE
IMPOVERISHMENT
OF THE
AMERICAN
COLLEGE
STUDENT

THE
IMPOVERISHMENT
OF THE
AMERICAN
COLLEGE
STUDENT

JAMES V. KOCH

BROOKINGS INSTITUTION PRESS

Washington, D.C.

Copyright © 2019
THE BROOKINGS INSTITUTION
1775 Massachusetts Avenue, N.W., Washington, D.C. 20036
www.brookings.edu

All rights reserved. No part of this publication may be reproduced or transmitted in any form or by any means without permission in writing from the Brookings Institution Press.

The Brookings Institution is a private nonprofit organization devoted to research, education, and publication on important issues of domestic and foreign policy. Its principal purpose is to bring the highest quality independent research and analysis to bear on current and emerging policy problems. Interpretations or conclusions in Brookings publications should be understood to be solely those of the authors.

Library of Congress Cataloging-in-Publication data are available.
ISBN 978-0-8157-3261-7 (paper: alk. paper)
ISBN 978-0-8157-3262-4 (ebook)

9 8 7 6 5 4 3 2 1

Typeset in Minion Pro

Composition by Westchester Publishing Services

Contents

Contents

Preface

Higher education traditionally has constituted one of the most important avenues of social and economic mobility in the United States. A university education has been a very important means by which generations of individuals have elevated both themselves and society.

This book reflects my concern that the social and economic mobility provided by our nation's public colleges and universities is declining. Increasing numbers of prospective college students simply cannot afford to attend a public college or university. Headcount collegiate enrollment has fallen six years in a row in the United States, and students and their families have accumulated more than $1.4 trillion in student debt.

Public institutions of higher education, which enroll three-fourths of all American college students, have been a primary ladder by which millions of individuals have improved their own lives and the world around them. How much poorer we would be as a society without the diverse contributions of public university graduates such as Marc Andreesen (the University of Illinois), Warren Buffett (the University of Nebraska), Gerald Ford (the University of Michigan), Nikki Haley (Clemson University), Colin Powell (City College of New York), Tennessee Williams (the University of Iowa), Oprah Winfrey (Tennessee State University), and Steve Wozniak (the University of California, Berkeley). This list of distinguished public college and university graduates could be replicated many times over, but rising costs of public higher education threaten to choke these possibilities in the future.

The problem confronting us is straightforward: if we fail to provide promising individuals with affordable paths to the mobility and success that flow from higher education, then we should anticipate adverse outcomes as a consequence, including stagnant economic growth and crippling social divisions. This might not signal the end of our grand American experiment, but it surely would not bode well for the future.

Those who read this book hoping to discover a single magic solution for our nation's higher education affordability crisis will be disappointed. There are many different reasons why higher education has become less affordable. Parsimonious governors and state legislatures may be the most important cause, but we cannot ignore the reluctance of higher education to innovate, as well as mission creep, curricular bloat, administrative aggrandizement, competition for ratings, the proliferation of expensive student-oriented amenities, governing boards that haven't been doing their jobs, and the student financial aid policies of the federal government.

Because the reasons why we are experiencing a higher education cost crunch are so many and so complex, there does not exist a single, foolproof way to improve the situation. Readers will find that the affordability crisis in higher education has many nuances, some of which are not acknowledged or understood even by college presidents, faculty, and members of governing boards. An example is the role of federal student financial aid in stimulating tuition and fee inflation. Accumulating empirical evidence suggests that more generous federal student financial aid policies stimulate inflationary cost increases in higher education. This flies in the face of much conventional thinking on how to make college affordable.

The first and most important task in front of us is to delineate the nature of the complicated higher education cost beast—what has been happening to higher education costs and why it has been happening. Only then can we devise public policies that will improve the situation. It is my earnest hope that this book will move the proverbial ball down the field in this regard.

Acknowledgments

This book, like virtually all books, would not have been brought to fruition without the support and cooperation of many different individuals and organizations. I cannot list them all, but among the most influential and helpful individuals have been Donna Koch, John Broderick, Jeff Tanner, Helen Dragas, Don Zimmerman, James Toscano, Rich DeMillo, Pat Callan, Dave Harnage, and Ziniya Zahedi. I gratefully acknowledge mentors such as Jim Fisher, David Sweet, Sam Braden, Eleanor McMahon, Bob Bell, John Worthen, George Dragas, Richard Barry, and Arthur Diamonstein, each of whom has shaped my thinking. Skillful direction, editing, suggestions, and patience came from William Finan at the Brookings Institution, and I was the beneficiary of numerous perceptive edits and observations from John Donohue and Kelley Blewster at Westchester Publishing Services.

Not to be forgotten is the support of the Strome College of Business at Old Dominion University and its Department of Economics. The Brookings Institution deserves credit for its willingness to provide a forum for diverse points of view.

Mistakes, errors, and omissions, however, remain mine.

THE
IMPOVERISHMENT
OF THE
AMERICAN
COLLEGE
STUDENT

ONE

The Spiraling Costs of Higher Education

Mind numbing.
> —Chris Jones, Chairman of the Appropriations Committee of
> the House of Delegates in Virginia, after he learned of the
> College of William and Mary's substantial increase in tuition
> and fees, May 16, 2016

The precise causes of this increase are not yet well understood.
> —The President's Council of Economic Advisors, referring to
> the causes of tuition and fee increases, July 2016

When Jackie Krowen, a thirty-two-year-old former college student living in Portland, Oregon, agreed to be interviewed by the venerable Consumers Union, it is unlikely she anticipated that she would crystalize the national predicament facing the United States concerning college pricing and affordability. Ms. Krowen averred dispiritedly, "I kind of ruined my life by going to college."

Having borrowed $128,000 to complete a nursing degree, Ms. Krowen found by 2016 that she owed $152,000 to her creditors because she had not kept up with the mounting interest accumulating on her obligations. Her confessional candor resulted in her words being featured on the August 2016 cover of *Consumer Reports* magazine.[1] By itself, the magazine cover was a signal that higher education had shifted to a new and less favorable position in the public imagination.

Ponder again this unhappy alumna's bleak assessment: "I kind of ruined my life by going to college." To some, her situation represented an indictment of a higher-education system that they believe has gone astray. To others, her problems were self-inflicted and not representative of the mass of students who may borrow, but who graduate with much lower levels of debt and repay those debts after they graduate.[2]

Approximately 30 percent of those who earn a bachelor's degree graduate with no debt at all.[3] Still, if we focus only on those who did borrow, then their total average obligation rose to a bit more than $31,000—not an overwhelming amount,[4] but problematic if the individual has graduated in a discipline such as education, where in 2016 the average salary earned by a graduate was only $34,891.[5]

Reputable economists have demonstrated that the high levels of debt accumulated by some students are inflicting measurable harm on our nation's economy. Among the adverse economic consequences that accrue to the 44.2 million Americans who have student debt are reduced rates of home ownership, smaller or no contributions to retirement savings, poor credit ratings, and lower rates of marriage.[6] Most adults agree that higher education is essential both to individuals and to society, but they also believe that sharply increasing costs of attendance are diminishing or denying collegiate access to promising individuals, especially those from less affluent backgrounds. Even the members of college governing boards are worried; a 2017 survey commissioned by the Association of Governing Boards of Universities and Colleges revealed that 68 percent of them rated the rising price of higher education as one of their top three concerns.[7]

The New York–based public policy organization Demos unabashedly labels this period in the higher-education world "the unaffordable era."[8] The economist Bryan Caplan put an exclamation point on a portion of this thinking by arguing that for many students, college simply "is not worth it."[9]

How did we get to this point? How did higher education lose its sheen?[10] Why does the cost of attending even public colleges today frequently outstrip the ability of students and their families to pay the accompanying costs? Providing carefully considered answers to these questions is the raison d'être of this book. The answers are more complex and interconnected than many believe.

If blame is to be apportioned, then some must reside within colleges and universities themselves. As we will see, presidents, senior administrators, faculty, and members of governing boards have some culpability. But we should not neglect the roles played by state governors and legislators, many of whom prefer that public colleges and universities raise tuition rather than supplying them with state funding. The behavior of state and federal agencies and competition among institutions also emerge as factors.

A typical way to describe the existing situation in American higher education is "broken,"[11] whether the discussion is about higher-education finance, tuition and fee increases, lagging state appropriations, faltering connections between curricula and job markets, or flagging student financial aid. Indeed, the notion that our current approach to higher education is malfunctioning has become so prevalent that one university president authored an op-ed piece with the title "What Isn't Broken in American Higher Education?"[12] South Carolina's Commission on Higher Education warned recently that the predominant business model in public higher education is "not sustainable."[13]

There has been a significant decline in confidence in higher education. In late 2016, the *Hechinger Report* detailed a series of public-opinion surveys that showed "widespread skepticism about how colleges and universities are run, how much they cost, and whether or not they're worth the money."[14] Critics have ranged from President Barack Obama to ordinary citizens. It is time to admit that "Houston, we have a problem."

Implicit in the assertions that the current financial model in American higher education is broken or unsustainable is the reluctant conclusion that *too often, too many colleges and universities have not been acting in the best interests of their students or society.* Consider the 2018 complaint by a top administrator of Minnesota's public colleges and universities that "tuition freezes aren't working." Anne Blackhurst, president of Minnesota State University Moorhead, opined, "Freezing tuition, even when the Legislature replaces that with the allocation, really removes one of our most important tools in accomplishing our other objectives."[15]

One must ask, "Not working for whom?" Total state appropriations to public higher education in Minnesota increased by 21.2 percent after inflation between the 2012–13 and 2017–18 fiscal years.[16] Full-time equivalent enrollment at the seven institutions in the Minnesota State University system has fallen for eight years consecutively and is down more than 20 percent since 2010.[17] And despite the notion that tuition and fees have been frozen, the *Chronicle of Higher Education* discloses that tuition at Minnesota State Moorhead increased 1.73 percent after inflation between 2012–13 and 2017–18.[18]

Controlling student costs and increasing student access do not appear to have been high-priority objectives in the Minnesota State University system. But let's not pick on Minnesota. Too many institutions of higher education have become grasping enterprises that operate primarily to further the interests of faculty and administrators (and in some cases intercollegiate athletic programs) rather than those of students and citizens. As a consequence, *Hechinger* found that 59 percent of adults now believe that "colleges care mainly about the bottom line" rather than educating students and benefitting society.[19]

Unfortunately, this behavior has been aided and abetted—sometimes unknowingly—by governors and legislators who have been overly parsimonious and inattentive; less than optimal federal financial aid policies; co-opted interested parties including governing board members; and alumni and media who seem to lack an awareness of the critical issues.

This book focuses on undergraduate students at four-year public colleges and universities. The rationale for this spotlight is straightforward: 16.30 million of the 19.01 million total college students in the United States in the fall of 2016—more than 85 percent—were undergraduate students.[20] Additionally, public colleges and universities now enroll 75 percent of all students. Further, essential data concerning performance and spending are more readily available for four-year public institutions than for two-year colleges and independent institutions. Finally, in most critical respects, four-year public institutions occupy the epicenter when we discuss adverse tuition and fee pricing trends and our ability to make meaningful changes in public policy.

NAGGING QUESTIONS

Numerous reputable empirical studies inform us that college graduates earn substantially more throughout their lives than high school graduates, and that the "skill differential"—the income premium attached to higher education—usually increased annually between 1980 and 2010. The most common way to measure this income premium has been to compare the earnings of college graduates to those of individuals whose education ended at high school. Researchers at the Federal Reserve Bank of Cleveland are among many who have documented this development.* Claudia Goldin and Lawrence Katz have done the same at the National Bureau of Economic Research.[21]

Though financial comparisons based on skill differentials are commonplace, one should understand that by themselves they are not completely persuasive if one's goal is to ascribe economic value to a baccalaureate degree. Why not? Let's explore four major reasons. First, college graduates comprise a nonrandom and in some ways carefully curated group of individuals. In terms of ability, motivation, and labor market skills, they are on average more favorably endowed than those whose education ended at high school.

Further, a completion of a college degree reveals that the graduate has had some ability to take direction and to complete a range of sequential mental and physical tasks. These are desirable employee attributes. The "economics of signaling" suggests that many employers may not really need or highly value what college graduates have learned in college, but baccalaureate credentials convey to them useful information about recipients' mental abilities and their ability to complete tasks.[22]

College graduates might be expected to excel beyond ordinary high school graduates in earned income even if the individuals who graduated from college had never attended college at all. This follows not only because as a group they are differently endowed and motivated, but also because they are "connected" and are the beneficiaries of more useful social and economic contacts that often have nothing to do with their collegiate educations.

Second, related to the notion of social and economic connections, the college earnings premium is sensitive to the family income background of those who graduate and join the labor force. The Upjohn Institute has provided persuasive evidence that the earnings premium for a bachelor's

---

*A technical point of considerable substance: not only has the wage premium associated with higher education increased, but overall wage inequality has also increased. Even among college graduates, there now is more wage inequality than there was in several previous decades. This may reflect increased levels of underemployment—some graduates taking jobs that do not require four-year degrees—but also may be the result of generally slack demand for graduates in some disciplines. These labor market conditions likely are one cause of falling labor force participation rates among some graduates. San Yoon Lee, Yongseok Shin, and Donghoon Lee, "The Option Value of Human Capital: Higher Education and Wage Inequality," Working Paper 21724 (Cambridge, Mass.: National Bureau of Economic Research, November 2015).

The U.S. Department of Education (USDED) produces a College Scorecard, which attempts to assess the performance of individual colleges and universities. USDED recognizes the possibility of a difference in the ability/motivation of college graduates versus high school graduates by adjusting its estimates of the median earnings of graduates of specific institutions for typical student academic preparation, major course of study, and likelihood of obtaining a graduate degree.[23]

degree relative to a high school diploma declines significantly when the graduate comes from a low-income household. Specifically, the career earnings premium for a bachelor's degree is 71 percent above that of a high school diploma for an individual who comes from a low-income household (defined as an income below 185 percent of the poverty line), but 136 percent for those coming from a household above this line.[24] This warns us that the college earnings premiums we observe reflect a variety of societal, personal, and institutional factors in addition to the education and diploma received.

Third, earnings premiums are sensitive to the institutions students attend and their major courses of study. For example, the lifetime earnings premium for arts and humanities graduates is only about one-half of that for STEM graduates. Thus, a student who majors in a field such as history at a non-elite institution may experience no earnings premium at all.[25]

Fourth, even if earnings premiums exist (and few knowledgeable individuals deny their existence), by themselves they should not determine personal or public decision making until those premiums are weighed against the cost of acquiring them. Affordability ultimately must reflect both the cost of education and its payoffs.

These caveats should inspire caution when inferences are drawn about the productivity of a college education. Nonetheless, figure 1-1 is instructive. It compares the median weekly earnings of college graduate men and women workers age twenty-five or older to the incomes earned by those whose formal educations stopped after they earned their high school diplomas. Figure 1-1 expresses these comparisons as a ratio in which a college graduate's median weekly earnings are divided by a high school graduate's median weekly

FIGURE 1-1

Widening Income Premiums Associated with Higher Education: Ratios of Median Weekly Earnings of College Graduates to Earnings of High School Graduates for Male and Female Full-Time Workers Age 25+, 2001–16

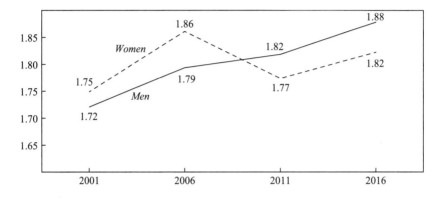

Source: Bureau of Labor Statistics, Median Weekly Earnings, Full-Time Workers, 25+, Years. Series LEU0252921300, LEU 0252822500, LEU0252925300, and LEU0252926500 (www.bls .gov).

earnings. In 2016, for example, the median weekly income of a female college graduate was 1.82 times that of a high school graduate.[26]

One can see that ratios of the earnings of college graduates to those of high school graduates typically rose between 2001 and 2016. Higher education appears to pay off for most individuals if earned income is the measuring stick and we ignore the costs of acquiring degrees. Note, however, that for women, the relative payoff to a college education has been slightly smaller as well as more variable than that for men.

The income premiums depicted in figure 1-1 are averages, and the variability around those averages is substantial. What is true for a STEM bachelor's degree recipient from MIT does not necessarily hold true for an art major from a regional state university.

Of course, enhanced income is not the only factor individuals should consider when they reach decisions about whether they should attend college at all, what college they should attend if they do, and what they will study. There are significant non-economic reasons why an individual might wish to pursue higher learning, and why society might wish to subsidize that individual's attendance. Interpreted broadly, higher education may enhance an individual's personal understanding and development and improve his or her appreciation of the human condition in its many different manifestations. Higher education has been tied positively to individuals' propensity to vote and participate fully in civic society, negatively to the number of crimes they commit, and positively even to their ability to raise children who become successful adults.

Nevertheless, in most current conversations, the income premium between college graduates and high school graduates is the dominant reason cited by the public at large for why earning a college degree is worthwhile. Given the changing nature of job markets for college graduates, one hears less frequently assertions that one should invest in a baccalaureate degree because it will enable one to appreciate Ravel's *Bolero*, or understand why the Russians believe they were the ones who really won World War II in Europe. Conversations concerning public higher education gradually have become more labor market oriented, especially in state legislatures.

The income differentials illustrated in figure 1-1 do not take into account the costs of attending college. Even so, *prima facie*, they have become part of a favorable narrative often presented in support of higher education: college degrees lead to better jobs, lower unemployment rates, higher incomes, and larger tax payments. This narrative is one of the pillars of a very traditional American success story that emphasizes the opportunities and mobility that colleges and universities provide citizens. Bureau of Labor Statistics income and employment data provide empirical support for most of the elements of this plot line, albeit without reference to any costs attached to postsecondary education and without considering the caveats noted above.

The narrative relating to the financial benefits of a college education is widely known and circulated and traditionally has been a central part of the American mythos. Because this is true, it is even more attention-grabbing when individuals suggest otherwise. However, considerable angst is being voiced today among some citizens and decision makers concerning the validity of this narrative. Widely cited has been Goldman Sachs's assertion that graduates of what the firm terms "the bottom twenty-five percent" of collegiate institutions earn less on average than high school graduates. Are they on to something new and important, or is this simply old wine in recycled bottles?[27]

HYPOTHESES AND HESITATIONS

Those who critique higher education today typically rely upon a knotty set of interconnected assertions and hypotheses. Only some of these hypotheses focus directly on rising tuition and fees at four-year public colleges and universities—the principal emphasis of this book. Let's begin with the two most prominent assertions:

- Tuition and fee charges at four-year public colleges and universities have been increasing at rates far in excess of increases in the Consumer Price Index and have dwarfed increases in median household incomes and worker wages.

- Except at a handful of prestigious "Public Ivy" institutions, financial aid available to students with demonstrated need has not kept up with rising costs of attendance at public colleges and universities.

Multiple other hypotheses focus on the same phenomena:

- Reduced state financial support is a major cause, perhaps *the* major cause, of tuition and fee price inflation at four-year public colleges and universities, but reduced state support cannot account for the dramatic increases in tuition and fees we have observed.

- Prices that students pay have been driven up because they are being assessed for nonessential activities such as intercollegiate athletics and accoutrements including upscale dining halls, lazy rivers, exercise facilities, and climbing walls.

- Though well-intentioned, the federal government has made the tuition and fee inflation problem worse via its financial aid programs because its actions essentially ratify the price increases of individual institutions.[28]

- Many colleges and universities have proliferated administrators and administrative complexity, and students end up paying for this.

- Rapidly increasing tuition and fees have not translated into high student graduation rates. Only 48.3 percent of first-time full-time students graduate within six years at the typical four-year public institution.[29]

- Of those students who take out loans to pay for their educations at four-year public colleges and universities, 36.5 percent subsequently do not earn more than $25,000 annually for six years after their enrollment.[30]

- Despite rapidly rising tuition and fee charges, many colleges and universities seem to be stuck in technological mud. Instruction at many public colleges and universities in 2017 often was implemented in ways that do not vary significantly from what would have taken place at the same institutions 50 to 100 years ago.

- Mission creep (regional state colleges' attempt to imitate flagship state universities) and curricular bloat (institutions' offer of excessive numbers of highly specialized courses) have pushed up costs that ultimately are transferred to students.[31]

- Rather than serving as engines that provide opportunity and reduce inequality, many public colleges and universities now perpetuate and even increase societal inequalities. Their tuition and fee pricing policies promote this development.[32]

- Governors, legislators, and members of public institution governing boards too often are co-opted by faculty, administrators, and alumni and no longer either pose critical questions to senior administrators or represent the best interests of students and citizens. Boards no longer act as bulwarks against price increases.

- Too many public colleges and universities now are being operated substantially for the benefit of faculty, staff, and administrators rather than for students and taxpayers. Despite occasional hand-wringing, these campus constituencies advocate policies that require tuition and fee price inflation.

- Redistribution of income from one student to another by means of differential tuition and fee charges and varying levels of financial aid support has become increasingly common and generates higher overall tuition collections.

- Confronted with reduced state financial support, many well-regarded public universities now prefer to enroll out-of-state students because they pay higher levels of tuition than in-state students.

These are powerful and often controversial hypotheses; thoughtful observers such as economists Robert Archibald and David Feldman of the College of William and Mary skewer many of them as "overheated rhetoric."[33] Nevertheless, as we will see, several have proverbial legs and cannot be dismissed as the products of mad scientists. Indeed, there is at least some evidence in favor of each, and substantial evidence in favor of several, though the quality of this evidence varies and therefore must be viewed with a gimlet eye.

Faced with the preceding hypotheses and public consternation about tuition and fee increases, members of the higher-education establishment typically argue either that many students end up paying prices lower than advertised or that it is the fault of parsimonious state governments that have sliced institutional appropriations. They assert that larger societal and economic factors (such as changes in the distribution of income and systematic differences in productivity growth across economic sectors) are at work, and it is these forces beyond the control of institutions of higher education that are pushing up tuition and fees.

The economic behavior one observes in higher education, some argue, is analogous to that which one observes in other professional services markets that are heavily reliant upon well-paid, highly educated providers. Medicine is the most prominent example proffered in this regard. Here, despite a spate of fresh approaches and new technologies, the increasingly expensive services and activities provided by physicians and medical professionals have turned out to be resistant to productivity increases conventionally measured.

As applied to the realm of higher education, proponents of this argument assert that stagnant productivity and skill-based technological change requiring more expensive personnel have translated into price increases in higher education. Archibald and Feldman have skillfully presented this view in a series of publications, several of which have been commissioned by the American Council on Education, an organization that has a legitimate but proprietary interest in the topic. It is not that this argument does not hold some water—it does. Rather, it is that this argument is only a portion of the story and cannot account for or excuse some observed pricing behavior in higher education.

Let us take a quick tour of the evidence that has generated support for the hypotheses noted above. This in turn will lead us to a more lengthy examination of them.

GALLOPING PRICES

Hardly any adult is unaware that the price of attending a college or university has been increasing rapidly. Figure 1-2, which presents average published prices for tuition and fees and room and board at all four-year public

FIGURE 1-2

Published Average Annual In-State Tuition and Fees Plus Room and Board Charges at Four-Year Public Colleges and Universities, Enrollment Weighted, 1997–98 to 2017–18

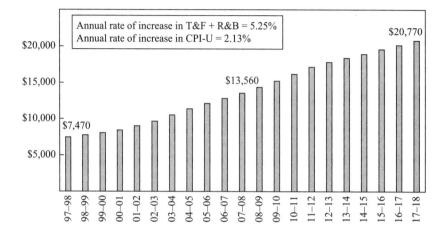

Sources: College Board, *Trends in College Pricing 2017*, table 2 (https://trends.collegeboard .org/college-pricing); Bureau of Labor Statistics, Series CUUR0000SA0 for July of each year (www.bls.gov).

institutions, provides rough and ready support for this notion. No financial aid or loans received by students are considered in the data in figure 1-2, but we will introduce them shortly.

Between the 1997–98 and 2017–18 academic years, the College Board tells us that published enrollment-weighted tuition and fees and room and board at four-year public colleges and universities increased annually by an average of 5.99 percent (compounded). Meanwhile, the average annual increase in the Consumer Price Index for All Urban Consumers (CPI-U) was only 2.13 percent.[34]

Two immediate qualifying comments are in order. First, Archibald and Feldman point out that there have been post–World War II time periods when increases in tuition and fees have been much more moderate and comparable to changes in the Consumer Price Index. The 1990s provide a fairly recent illustration. Second, just as the list price pasted to the window of a new automobile sitting in the showroom of a dealership is unlikely to be the final price a customer pays for that automobile, so also higher-education list prices (the prices

FIGURE 1-3

Annual Percentage Changes in Average In-State Four-Year Public College Tuition and Fees versus the Consumer Price Index (CPI) and the Public Institution Higher Education Price Index (HEPI), 2006–16

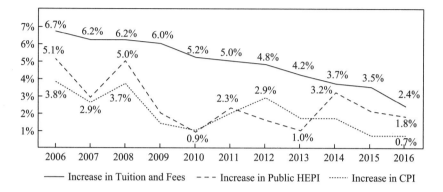

Sources: CPI: Consumer Price Index for All Urban Consumers (June 2006 through 2016), table 2 (www.bls.gov). HEPI: Commonfund Institute, Higher Education Price Index (www.commonfund.org/commonfund-institute/higher-education-price-index-hepi). Tuition and fees: College Board, *Trends in College Pricing 2017*, table 2 (https://trends.collegeboard.org/college-pricing).

that are published in catalogs and brochures) frequently are much higher than the transaction prices students actually pay. I will have more to say about this in the next chapter, but one former member of a college governing board acerbically charged recently that published tuition and fee numbers are "as good as useless now" because they don't tell us the prices many students actually pay.[35]

The growing gap between published tuition and fee prices and prices in other markets has not gone unnoticed. Figure 1-3 zeroes in on the behavior of college tuition and fees, the Consumer Price Index (CPI), and the Higher Education Price Index (HEPI) over the past decade. The Bureau of Labor Statistics of the United States Department of Labor constructs the CPI, which is designed to reflect overall changes in the prices of items a typical consumer purchases, all weighted by frequency of purchase. The CPI is a well-known economic measure that receives wide attention in the media.

The HEPI, on the other hand, is less well known, but was developed by D. Kent Halstead for the United States Department of Health, Education, and Welfare to provide higher-education institutions and decision makers with a more accurate measure of the items they purchase. Colleges and universities often argue that they purchase a different collection of goods and services than the usual consumer, and therefore the CPI is not an accurate reflection of the prices they face.

Today's HEPI is maintained by the Commonfund Institute and examines eight separate higher-education cost factors, including faculty salaries, utilities, and fringe benefits as a basis for generating an overall higher-education price index. The Commonfund has developed useful separate indexes for public, independent, and doctoral institutions. My presentation here relies upon HEPI's public institutions index.[36]

One can see in figure 1-3 that over the past decade, the annual published increases in tuition and fees at four-year public colleges and universities typically have dwarfed comparable annual changes in either the CPI or the HEPI. Thus, in 2010, tuition and fees increased by 5.2 percent, even while the CPI increased only 0.9 percent and the HEPI a mere 0.9 percent. Over an eleven-year time span ending in 2016, the average annual published tuition and fee increase was 4.9 percent, while the CPI increase averaged only 1.94 percent and the HEPI rose an average of 2.61 percent. Tuition and fees rose 98 percent faster than the HEPI and 166 percent faster than the CPI.

Further, when we extend the analysis to a longer period of time (2000 to 2016, as figure 1-4 does), the tuition and fees that institutions advertise in their catalogs and brochures rose more than 90 percent faster than the prices of medical services, and 116 percent faster than the HEPI. Apparel prices actually declined during the lengthy time period.

Only a brief perusal of figures 1-3 and 1-4 is required to understand that many believe that college and university tuition and fee increases have been exorbitant at worst, or only a bit exuberant at best. Nevertheless, as noted above, some argue that the buoyant behavior of tuition and fees simply mirrors what has been happening in several other service sectors of the economy where it has been difficult to generate productivity increases similar to those experienced in other sectors such as manufacturing and agriculture. Symphony orchestras supply an immediate illustration. Should we mandate an increase in their productivity by ordering them to play faster? This analogy has some validity, but turns on the relative inability (or unwillingness) of public colleges and universities to introduce innovations that would increase their measured productivity. We will examine this argument in greater detail in chapter 9.

FIGURE 1-4

Comparing the Percentage Increase in Tuition and Fees at Four-Year Public Institutions to Percentage Increases in Prices for Other Items, June 2000–June 2016

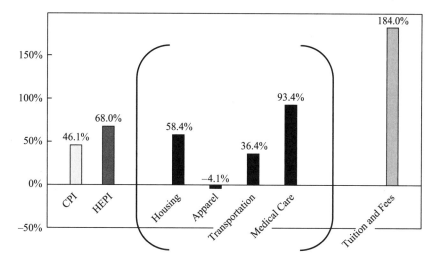

Sources: HEPI: Commonfund Institute, Higher Education Price Index (www.commonfund .org/commonfund-institute/higher-education-price-index-hepi). CPI: Bureau of Labor Statistics (www.bls.gov). Components of the CPI: Federal Reserve Bank of St. Louis (https:// fred.stlouisfed.org/). Tuition and fees for four-year public institutions: College Board, *Trends in College Pricing 2017* (https://trends.collegeboard.org/college-pricing.)

TUITION AND FEE INCREASES OUTSTRIP GROWTH IN INCOMES

Few among us worry very much about prices that we find easy to pay. We smile when the prices of computers fall, and most of us do not worry very much about the price of a burrito at Taco Bell. Rising prices of certain things, however, do give us pause and stimulate us to ask, "Can I really afford to buy this item?" This is particularly true when the item whose price is rising carves out a substantial portion of our income.

What has been the relationship between tuition and fee increases and changes in median household income—a broad measure of the ability of a student or family to pay college bills? Figure 1-5 illustrates this for us by tracing four-year public institution tuition and fee increases between 2000 and

FIGURE 1-5

Comparing Annual Average In-State Tuition and Fee Increases at Four-Year Public Colleges and Universities to Annual Changes in Median U.S. Household Income, 2000–16

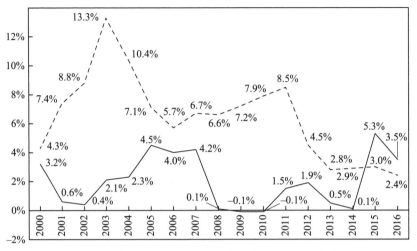

—— Annual Change in Median HH Income   – – – Avg. Annual Increase in Public 4-Yr. T&F

Sources: Tuition and fees: College Board, *Trends in College Pricing 2016*, figure 3 (https://trends
.collegeboard.org/sites/default/files/2016-trends-college-pricing-web_0.pdf). Median household
income: Federal Reserve Bank of St. Louis, Table MEHOINUSA646N (https://fred.stlouisfed
.org). 2016 median household income is estimated.

2016 and changes in the median (fiftieth percentile) incomes of households
in the United States during the same period. One can see that tuition and fee
increases easily outstripped increases in median household income every year
between 2000 and 2014. Indeed, what only can be described as a huge
7.1 percent gap between the average percentage tuition and fee increase and
the change in median household income appeared in 2009, and this was followed by an 7.8 percent gap in 2010 and a 7.0 percent difference in 2011. The
persistent gaps between the behavior of tuition and fees and median household
income help explain why many students and households have found it difficult to pay the rising tuition and fee charges of colleges and universities.

Figure 1-5 also helps us understand why even modest rises in student
indebtedness have become burdensome. Stagnating incomes have made it

TABLE 1-1

The Ratio of Median Household Income to Average In-State Tuition and Fee Charges at Four-Year Public Institutions, 2000–01 to 2016–17

Year	Median HH Income	Enrollment-Weighted Average Tuition and Fees at Four-Year Public Institutions	Ratio of Median HH Income to Average Tuition and Fees
2000	$41,990	$3,508	11.97
2001	$42,228	$3,766	11.21
2002	$42,409	$4,098	10.35
2003	$43,318	$4,645	9.33
2004	$44,334	$5,126	8.65
2005	$46,326	$5,492	8.44
2006	$48,201	$5,804	8.30
2007	$50,233	$6,191	8.11
2008	$50,303	$6,599	7.62
2009	$49,777	$7,073	7.04
2010	$49,276	$7,629	6.46
2011	$50,054	$8,276	6.05
2012	$51,017	$8,646	5.90
2013	$53,585	$8,885	6.03
2014	$53,657	$9,145	5.87
2015	$56,516	$9,420	6.00
2016	$59,000	$9,650	6.11

Sources: Annual median household income data: Federal Reserve Bank of St. Louis (https://fred
.stlouisfed.org). Tuition and fees: College Board, *Trends in College Pricing 2016*, figure 3 (https://
trends.collegeboard.org/college-pricing). 2016 median household income is an estimate.

increasingly difficult for students and households to service even small increases in debt.

Table 1-1 elaborates on the data used in figure 1-5 and provides additional perspective on the financial vise that is clamping typical American students and families. The ratio of median household income to average annual published four-year public college and university tuition fell from 11.97 in 2000 to 6.11 in 2016. Holding constant increases in financial aid, this represents a 49.0 percent decline in four-year public college and university affordability— if median household income is the criterion. Only in 2015 and 2016 did this deterioration moderate as the United States substantially emerged from the Great Recession.

Notably, this measured decline in college affordability occurred while head-count enrollment at degree-granting postsecondary institutions in the United States shifted from an expansionary mode to one of stagnation or decline. In the fall 2017 semester, for example, the unduplicated head count of college students nationally fell by 1.0 percent—the seventh year in a row that headcount enrollment declined.[37] Whether economic times have been bad (during the Great Recession) or good (in 2016 and 2017), head-count enrollment has wilted. While the causes of declining enrollment undoubtedly are several, a reasonable supposition is that the rising gap between household incomes and the cost of higher education was one factor discouraging college enrollment.

To provide context, let's consider how these trends have affected a typical production or nonsupervisory worker in the United States such as a machinist. In 2016, the median wage rate paid him/her was $20.05 per hour. In the same year, the College Board reported that the average published tuition and fee charge at a four-year public college or university was $9,650. This tells us that it took 481.3 hours of labor in 2016 for this typical worker to pay the average four-year public college or university tuition and fee charge, which represents a 110 percent increase over the 228.7 hours required in 2000.[38] Recognize also that this 481-hour computation does not taken into account taxes that might be paid on the $20.05 per hour, or deductions for benefits, etc. Hence, a much larger number of hours of work likely would be necessary to pay the $9,650.

The key takeaway from figure 1-6 is this: there has been a *continuous, unabated increase in the number of hours of work required from a typical private-sector worker for him/her to be able to pay the average student's published tuition and fee charges at one of our nation's public institutions of higher education.* This tells us that unless tuition and fee increases have been matched by equivalent increases in financial aid (which has not occurred), the affordability of a college education to most families has declined.

It comes as no surprise, then, that many argue that public higher education is in the process of pricing itself out of the reach of prospective middle class and poor students and their families. The *Washington Post* prominently published a ten-part series of critiques of college and university pricing practices in 2013 under the provocative title "The Tuition Is Too Damned High."[39] Additionally, critics ranging from Thomas Frank and the *New York*

FIGURE 1-6

Number of Hours of Work Required for the Average Private-Sector Employee to Earn Income Sufficient to Pay the Average In-State Annual Tuition and Fee Charge at a Four-Year Public College, 2000–16

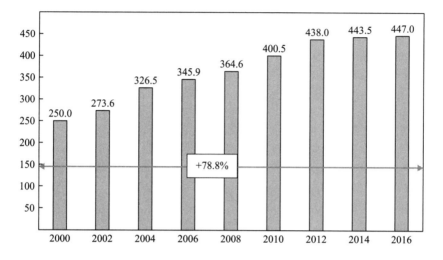

Sources: For hourly earnings: Bureau of Labor Statistics, Series CES 500000003 (www.bls.gov). For average four-year public tuition and fees (weighted by enrollment): College Board, *Trends in College Pricing 2016*, table 3 (https://trends.collegeboard.org/college-pricing).

Note: Year 2000 tuition and fees are for the 2000–01 academic year, etc.

Times on the left to Rich Vedder of Ohio University and the Martin Center for Academic Renewal on the right have questioned the current operational and pricing patterns of institutions of higher education. They have chorused almost in unison that the existing model cannot persist if higher education is to remain accessible to qualified students.[40]

FINANCIAL AID HAS NOT KEPT PACE

Fortunately, the published tuition and fee and room and board charges that public colleges and universities advertise are not the prices that end up being paid by a majority of individual students. From these published prices must be deducted grants and scholarships that accrue to students from federal, state, and private sources as well as from the colleges and universities themselves.

Federal grants (not including loans) to students come from three major programs: (1) Pell Grants, which go to students from lower-income families for a maximum of twelve semesters and could not exceed $5,920 annually per student in 2017–18; (2) Federal Supplemental Education Opportunity Grants (SEOGs), which typically go to students who already have Pell Grants and substantial financial need; and (3) veterans and military grants, which may or may not focus on financially needy students. Pell Grants dominate this mixture and in 2014–15 accounted for 68.0 percent of total federal grants, followed by grants to veterans and members of the military at 30.4 percent. However, the total dollar amount of Pell Grant expenditures declined from a high of $39.4 billion in 2010–11 to $26.6 billion in 2016–17, and the percentage of undergraduates receiving Pell Grants fell from 37 percent to 32 percent over the same period.[41]

Figure 1-7 demonstrates that the total dollar value of federal grants to undergraduate students increased dramatically through the first decade of this century, but then began to tail off. We need to place this expansion in context. Much changed during the twenty-five-year period portrayed in the figure. Two of the more significant changes in the higher-education environment were increases in the Consumer Price Index and fluctuations in the total enrollment at four-year public colleges and universities. The Consumer Price Index rose 76 percent during this period, while full-time equivalent enrollment at four-year public institutions increased 52 percent. Figure 1-7 recognizes these variations by deflating total federal student grant largesse to recognize this price and enrollment growth. The $43.25 billion in federal student grants in 2015–16 declines to $24.6 billion after we adjust for increases in the Consumer Price Index and further to $16.2 billion when we consider increases in public college and university enrollment.

This illuminates the college affordability challenge. Federal financial grants (until recently) increased on a per student basis even after adjusting them for price inflation. The problem is that tuition and fees and other expenses rose even more rapidly.

What really counts in terms of college affordability is the amount of money a student must actually pay to attend an institution after deducting any grants and scholarships received. *Net price* is the term most often used to describe the residual, actual price students pay their college or university after their grants and scholarships have been deducted from the institutions' published prices. It is a term we will utilize often.

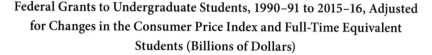

FIGURE 1-7

Federal Grants to Undergraduate Students, 1990–91 to 2015–16, Adjusted for Changes in the Consumer Price Index and Full-Time Equivalent Students (Billions of Dollars)

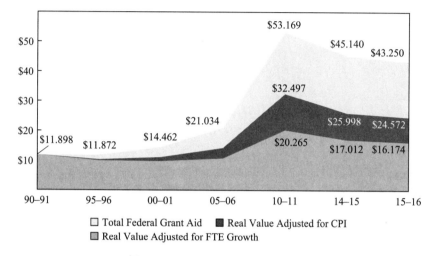

Source: College Board, *Trends in Student Aid 2016*, table 2 (https://trends.collegeboard.org/student-aid).

The College Board has computed and kept track of the actual net prices paid by students for approximately three decades. Between the 2000–01 and 2017–18 academic years, average published tuition and fees for in-state undergraduates at four-year public institutions, adjusted for inflation, rose 93.5 percent. If financial aid grants had risen comparably, affordability challenges would have been minimized. However, this is not what occurred. Even after taking financial aid grants from all sources into account, the College Board found that *the average inflation-adjusted net price at four-year public colleges and universities rose an eye-opening 71.7 percent between 2000–01 and 2017–18*. Figure 1-8 displays these data.

Students and families might have been able to handle even a 93.5 percent increase in the real net price of attending the typical four-year public college or university if their wages and incomes had grown commensurately. Unfortunately, as we already have seen, median household income has stagnated or declined in many years since the turn of the century. Students and their

FIGURE 1-8

Published Average Four-Year Public Undergraduate College and University In-State Tuition and Fees (T&F) Compared to the Average Net Price at the Same Institutions

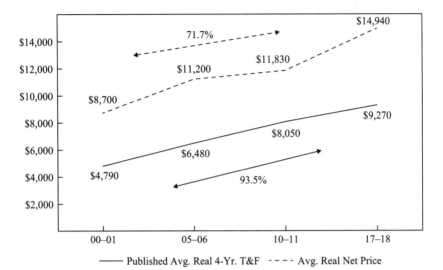

—— Published Avg. Real 4-Yr. T&F   - - - - Avg. Real Net Price

Source: College Board, *Trends in College Pricing 2015*, table 7 (http://trends.collegeboard.org /sites/default/files/2015-trends-college-pricing-final-508.pdf).

Note: All dollar values are expressed in constant 2015 dollars.

families have had to cope with higher net prices at the same time median household income has remained constant or declined.

The bottom line? The net price of student attendance (after considering grants and scholarships) at four-year public colleges and universities has risen significantly at the very time when the ability of a typical student and his or her family to pay these prices has declined. The consequences? Some students who clearly could benefit from college now cannot afford to attend. Many have had to take loans and, in some cases, accumulate substantial amounts of debt to complete their degrees; others have opted to attend part-time; still others have dropped out.

We will examine the phenomenon of rising student loans and debt in detail in the next two chapters. However, figure 1-9 may pique your interest in this topic. It shows that households indeed are assuming increasingly large

FIGURE 1-9

Total Student Debt of Households (Trillions of Dollars) and the Percentage of Total Household Nonhousing Debt That Is Student Debt

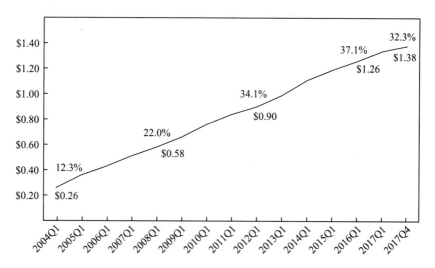

Source: New York Federal Reserve Bank, *Quarterly Report on Household Debt and Credit (Fourth Quarter, 2017)* (www.newyorkfed.org/microeconomics/databank.html).

amounts of debt to send their members to colleges and universities. Student debt held by households rose 430 percent between first quarter 2004 and fourth quarter 2017. In real terms (taking account of price inflation), the increase remained a substantial 322 percent, and this occurred at a time when real household median income was declining.[42] This is one of the reasons why some observers argue that higher education's current business model is not sustainable.

TWO

The Student Fallback Options
Loans and Debt

Here's something you don't hear every day: It's a good time to be taking out student loans.

—Christine DiGangi of Credit.com, 2016

or is it . . .

They have placed themselves in a financial stranglehold for unmarketable degrees.

—Charles Sykes, *Fail U.: The False Promise of Higher Education*, 2016

The picture I've painted thus far has been a bit dour because it questions the ability of many students and their families to pay the rising prices being charged by four-year public colleges and universities. Even after growing dollar amounts of grants and scholarships to students have been considered, a typical student from a typical family can struggle to pay the cost of attending a four-year public college or university.

The key variable to consider in evaluating this scenario is the net price that undergraduate students pay after any grants and scholarships they have received have been deducted from their bill. *The net price associated with attending a typical four-year public institution has been rising far more rapidly than median household income, a rough and ready measure of the ability of students and families to pay higher-education costs.*[1] After upward turns in 2015 and 2016, real (price-adjusted) median household income finally climbed above its 1999 value.[2] This means that the ability of the typical household to pay for the rising costs of higher education stagnated for almost two decades. Grant-based financial aid, while swelling in amount, has been quite insufficient to match the rapidly increasing prices that students have had to pay.

In chapter 1, we saw that the number of hours of work required from the average private-sector employee to generate income sufficient to pay the average published annual tuition and fees at a four-year public institution had almost doubled between 2000 and 2016. Mathematical gymnastics are required to avoid concluding that many current and prospective undergraduate students now find it increasingly difficult to come up with the financial resources necessary to attend a four-year public college or university. To the extent this is true, they face some combination of the following alternatives:

- *Don't attend college*, or delay attendance until they can afford to pay the net price that applies to them.

- *Drop out or attend part-time*, presumably while simultaneously working at a job that will generate income sufficient to cover their part-time attendance.

- *Lower the net price* they must pay by attending a less expensive institution. For example, they can opt for a community college rather than a four-year public college or university.

- *Reduce out-of-pocket expenses* by living at home rather than on campus. The danger, however, is that this may simply redistribute rather than reduce their costs. Living at home may require the use of an automobile, and the American Automobile Association estimates that the average annual cost of owning an automobile exceeds $8,800.[3]

- *Negotiate a loan* for which either the federal government or a private lender is the banker. In 2014–15, the federal government was the lender for more than 90 percent of the value of all new student loans.[4]

It is the last alternative—taking out a loan—that is the major focus of this chapter.

FIGURE 2-1

Total Federal and Nonfederal Loans to Undergraduate Students, 1995–96 to 2016–17 (Billions of Dollars)

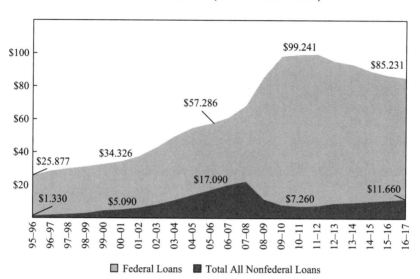

Source: College Board, *Trends in Student Aid 2017*, table 2 (https://trends.collegeboard.org /student-aid/figures-tables/student-aid-nonfederal-loans-current-dollars-over-time).

FEDERAL LOANS

The federal government has assumed a huge role in providing loans to American college students. Figure 2-1 illustrates the expanding federal presence in funding undergraduate education. In 2016–17, 95.4 percent of all loans taken out by college students were financed by the federal government, according to the College Board. The annual volume of federal loans of all types to American undergraduates increased 283 percent between the 1995–96 and 2010–11 academic years. The most dramatic expansion in federal loans to undergraduate students began in 2007–08 and continued through the 2009–10 academic year, roughly coincident with the Great Recession. Since then, the pace of the federal presence has slackened noticeably, though the annual volume of loans extended by the federal government still is more than triple what it was two decades ago.

The federal undergraduate student loan data presented in figure 2-1 are nominal and not adjusted for the change in prices that occurred over the

FIGURE 2-2

Nominal versus Real Value of Federal Student Loans to Undergraduate Students, 1995–96 to 2016–17 (Billions of Dollars)

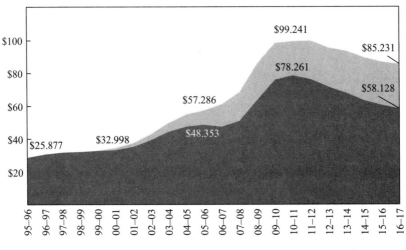

□ Nominal Value, Federal Loans   ■ Real Value Federal Loans, 2016 Prices

Source: College Board, *Trends in Student Aid 2017*, table 1A (https://trends.collegeboard.org /student-aid).

twenty-one-year period. Figure 2-2 makes this adjustment by valuing each year's student debt in terms of 2016 prices. This presents a different, less terrifying picture. Total federal undergraduate student debt still grew 125 percent over the two decades, but this indebtedness represented a larger number of students. Undergraduate student head count nationally grew 42 percent during this period.

Thus, by the numbers, the overall economic burden of student debt today is less than it seems at first glance. The problem is that while this debt was being accumulated, household incomes were stagnant. Over these twenty years, real median household income grew only 9.1 percent, and a scant 2.9 percent over the past decade.[5] Even these paltry gains disguised internal changes in the distribution of income that resulted in only marginal gains for the average family. Worse yet, there were discouraging economic reversals for those households in the bottom one-half of the income distribution.

A 2016 Congressional Research Service study found that between 1967 and 2015, the average price-adjusted household income of the bottom 40 percent of households barely moved, grew slightly for the middle quintile, rose nicely within the fourth quintile, and surged upward by more than 80 percent for the top quintile.[6] These statistics reflect the reality that over the past half century, the distribution of household income has become less equal in the United States. To wit, between 2007 and 2015, the average real income of a bottom-quintile household actually fell by 5.7 percent, while it grew 5.4 percent for the average highest-quintile household. The bottom 60 percent of American households collectively lost ground and ended up with lower real incomes in 2015 than they had in 2007.*

The moral to the story is that what at first might appear to be workable increases in student debt have become problematic because income growth has languished for the bottom 60 percent of households. Students coming from these households are the individuals who most often have been affected adversely by rapidly rising college costs and burdensome student debt. It is they whose presence at many flagship state universities is becoming less common, as the *New York Times* recently reported.[7] Hence, what may at first appear to be manageable debt challenge for higher education overall turns out to be a much more pressing problem when viewed in the context of students who come to campuses from middle-income or lower-income households.

FAFSA is the acronym applied to the Free Application for Federal Student Aid. Applicants for federal student financial aid must complete a FAFSA to qualify for a federal loan or grant; this involves supplying information about their incomes, savings, and wealth. FAFSA forms and processes have been simplified in recent years, but still may intimidate some applicants.[8]

---

*These data exclude capital gains and losses, which would accentuate the inequalities noted.

FEDERAL LOAN PROGRAMS

Approximately two-thirds of all undergraduate students receive some kind of federal financial aid at some time during their college careers.[9] This financial aid often involves loans. Three federal loan programs dominate the financial worlds of undergraduate students: (1) subsidized Stafford loans from the federal government, which go to undergraduate students with demonstrated financial need, and on which the U.S. Department of Education pays the interest while students are in school and for the first six months after they leave school;* (2) unsubsidized Stafford loans from the federal government, which do not require any demonstration of financial need, and on which interest begins to accumulate immediately; and (3) Parent PLUS loans from the federal government, which go to parents without negative credit histories who have dependent students† and which do not necessarily require a demonstration of financial need. Interest on Parent PLUS loans (the rate currently is 7 percent) begins to accumulate immediately. Parent PLUS loans also carry with them an up-front 4.276 percent origination fee.

Figure 2-3 shows the comparative size of each of these loan programs in the 2016–17 academic year as well as the much smaller *Perkins loan* program, which involves loans made by institutions supported with federal funding. These go to students who have exceptional financial need. The current Perkins interest rate is 5 percent.

How much may be borrowed by an individual student? Figure 2-4 discloses the annual loan size limitations that applied either to subsidized or unsubsidized loans that undergraduate students received from the federal government in any combination of programs in 2016–17. Separate maximums applied to students who were legal dependents for tax purposes as opposed to students who were independent for tax purposes. The indepen-

---

*According to the U.S. Department of Education, "There is a limit on the maximum period of time (measured in academic years) that you can receive Direct Subsidized Loans. This time limit does not apply to Direct Unsubsidized Loans or Direct PLUS Loans. If this limit applies to you, you may not receive Direct Subsidized Loans for more than 150 percent of the published length of your program. This is called your 'maximum eligibility period.'" U.S. Department of Education, "Federal Student Aid" (https://studentaid.ed.gov/sa/types/loans/subsidized -unsubsidized#subsidized-vs-unsubsidized).

†They are dependent for financial aid purposes, though not necessarily for income tax purposes.

FIGURE 2-3

FIGURE 2-3

Federal Undergraduate Student Loan Programs, 2016–17 Academic Year

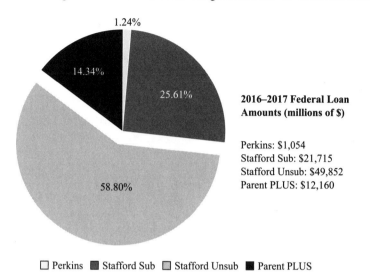

2016–2017 Federal Loan Amounts (millions of $)

Perkins: $1,054
Stafford Sub: $21,715
Stafford Unsub: $49,852
Parent PLUS: $12,160

□ Perkins ▣ Stafford Sub ▢ Stafford Unsub ■ Parent PLUS

Source: College Board, *Trends in Student Aid 2017*, table 2 (https://trends.collegeboard.org/student-aid/figures-tables/student-aid-nonfederal-loans-current-dollars-over-time).

dent loan maximums were considerably larger because they allowed students to take out substantial unsubsidized loans.

The annual loan constraints depicted in figure 2-4 did not apply to loans received from nonfederal sources such as private lenders or even from the institution students were attending. Finally, the total loan restrictions did not diminish any *grant* funds that students received from the federal government (Pell Grants being the most prominent example). In contrast to loans, grants do not need to be repaid.

Note that an undergraduate student dependent on his or her parents for financial aid purposes (though not necessarily on an income tax return) could have borrowed up to $31,000 over four or more years via the federal government's direct Stafford loan programs, but no more than $23,000 of that sum could have been subsidized loans offering more relaxed repayment terms, delayed interest payments, and lower interest rates.

One of the major differences between subsidized and unsubsidized federal student loans is the size of the interest rate that the student debtors pay (or don't pay). Between July 1, 2016, and June 30, 2017, subsidized loan

FIGURE 2-4

Annual Limits on the Amounts of Money That Dependent- and Independent-Status Students Could Borrow from the Federal Government, 2016–17

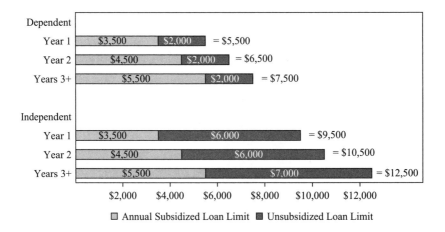

Source: U.S. Department of Education, "Federal Student Aid" (https://studentaid.ed.gov/sa/types).

recipients paid an annual 3.76 percent rate of interest on their unpaid balances, though they paid no interest while pursuing their undergraduate degrees full-time, and their interest payments could have been deferred under a variety of circumstances. Direct Stafford unsubsidized loan interest rates also were 3.76 percent, but recipients started paying this interest immediately.[10]

Undergraduate "career" loan limits also exist. The total amounts of money that dependent- and independent-status students could have borrowed from the federal government during their undergraduate careers are $31,000 and $57,500, respectively. Neither dependent nor independent students, however, could have exceeded $23,000 in subsidized loans.

AN INSTRUCTIVE EXAMPLE

The student financial aid world is complicated, almost surely more so than necessary. An example may help dispel some of the fog. Let's look at a medium-sized, predominantly undergraduate state institution, Illinois State University, as an example. Institutions such as Illinois State enroll approximately 60 percent of four-year public college and university students today.

TABLE 2-1

Financial Aid Received by Beginning Undergraduate Students at Illinois State University, 2016–17

Type of Aid	Number Receiving Aid	Percentage Receiving Aid	Total Amount of Aid Received	Average Amount of Aid Received
Any student financial aid	3,179	86%	—	—
Grant or scholarship aid	2,370	64%	$21,620,000	$9,124
Federal grants	1,123	30%	$5,190,000	$4,624
Pell grants	1,115	30%	$5,000,000	$4,624
Other federal grants	173	5%	$200,000	$1,128
State/local government grants and scholarships	1,178	32%	$5,760,000	$4,895
Institutional grants and scholarships	2,012	55%	$10,660,000	$5,300
Student loan aid	2,324	63%	$18,190,000	$7,828
Federal student loans	2,277	62%	$12,400,000	$5,444
Other student loans	420	11%	$5,800,000	$13,800

Source: College Navigator, Illinois State University (https://nces.ed.gov/collegenavigator/?q =Illinois+state+university&s=all&id=145813#netprc).

Note: Overlap exists in several categories above and therefore the subcategories do not sum to the category totals.

Table 2-1 details the most common sources of financial aid for beginning undergraduate students at Illinois State, which has 21,039 students (18,643 undergraduates). It has an 81 percent retention rate for all full-time under-graduate students, a 72 percent six-year graduation rate, and an average enrolled freshman composite ACT test score of almost 24. (The national average ACT composite score is 21.0, and the Illinois average is 20.7.)[11]

Thus, Illinois State is a public institution more selective in admissions than most regional state colleges and universities that began their lives as teacher's colleges, but less selective than Public Ivies such as the University of Michigan, the University of Virginia, or the campuses of the University of California. It resides solidly in the upper-middle rung of four-year public institutions in the United States and provides a useful comparator that occupies a middle ground between the most selective elite public universities and those much less selective that typically occupy a regional geographic slot.

The College Navigator at the National Center for Education Statistics website is a valuable resource. It informs us that Illinois State advertised a $28,197 total cost of attendance for in-state undergraduates living on campus in 2016–17. Immediately apparent in table 2-1 is the multiplicity of sources of financial aid that Illinois State students received. More than one-half (64 percent) of all incoming freshmen received some form of grant or scholarship, and 63 percent received some form of loan. The average size of the federal loan to each student was $5,444, worth an aggregate $12.40 million. Even so, with 30 percent of these freshmen receiving Pell Grants, their financial need was substantial. They also took out $5.80 million in loans from other sources.

Earlier, stress was placed upon the importance of "net price." What was Illinois State's net price—its tuition and fees and room and board less grants and scholarships (but still including loans that must be repaid)? Illinois State, like most public universities, features a price discriminatory* net price structure that is highly dependent upon the household incomes of its students (see figure 2-5). Thus, students coming from households with incomes of $30,000 or less paid an average net price (after grants and scholarships) of $14,083, while those with incomes of $110,000 or more paid an average of $25,937—about 90 percent of the institution's list price.

The Illinois State freshmen who did receive federal loans borrowed an average of $5,444. Were an exemplary Illinois State freshman to replicate his or her borrowing for three additional years and graduate on time in four years, then this individual would owe $21,776 upon graduation—below the 2017 national average of $27,975 for students who borrow.[†] This national average, however, included independent institutions in addition to public colleges and universities.

---

*The word *discrimination* in the economics term *price discrimination* does not carry a pejorative meaning equivalent to what the word often connotes in legal and social circles. Economic price discrimination refers to a situation in which the prices charged different consumers are not proportional to the individual marginal costs of producing for, and serving, each. Intelligently implemented price discrimination can increase the profits of sellers, most often by charging higher prices to customers with less elastic demand curves and lower prices to customers with more elastic demand curves. Price discrimination is commonplace and much of it is banal—for example, charging matinee movie goers a lower price than those attending in the evening. Some firms could not survive if they did not engage in price discrimination.

[†]The Student Loan Report, "Student Loan Statistics 2018" (https://studentloans.net/student-loan-debt-statistics/).

FIGURE 2-5

Average Net Price Paid by Undergraduate In-State Students at Illinois State University, Categorized by Their Household Incomes, 2016–17

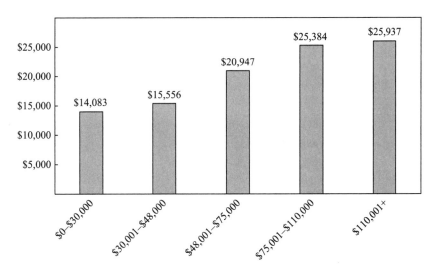

Source: College Navigator, National Center for Education Statistics (https://nces.ed.gov/college navigator/?q=Illinois+state+university&s=all&id=145813#netprc).

If the loan interest rate were 3.76 percent (the 2016–17 direct subsidized loan rate) and the loan were paid off in ten years, then this would have required our representative Illinois State student to make a $217.88 monthly loan repayment. Likely this would not have proven problematic if our student were earning the national annual average $61,321 that computer science graduates enjoy, but more challenging if he or she were earning only the $34,891 national annual average for a new K–12 teacher.

Within the domain of four-year public colleges and universities, Illinois State is an expensive institution. Substantially, this reflects the dolorous financial condition of the state of Illinois, which in recent years has sent its institutions only a small fraction of their approved state funding. Illinois State's 2017–18 annual undergraduate in-state tuition and fee charge of $14,061 was 41 percent higher than the national four-year public institution average of $9,970.

It is here that we can identify some of the challenges and paradoxes inherent in the current collegiate financial aid system. Illinois State is relatively expensive, and 30 percent of its students received Pell Grants, compared to the national average of 32 percent in 2016–17. It is not a well-endowed institution (its 2014 endowment value was $140.6 million) and therefore cannot provide scholarship aid that many flagship public institutions offer. Further, it does not enroll large percentages of out-of-state students, who typically provide substantial tuition revenue that is used to cross-subsidize in-state students. Hence, its average in-state 2016–17 net price of $19,227 was approximately 20 percent above the four-year public institution average.

But, here's the rub. Illinois State's retention and graduation rates are well above four-year public institution averages, and its graduates also tend to find productive employment. Later, high proportions of its alumni repay their federal loans; the institution's loan default rate is low (only 2.8 percent as opposed to the 7.8 percent four-year public college average). This is one reason why a recent study based upon data contained in the U.S. Department of Education's College Scorecard ranked the institution 66th among 535 public institutions in terms of the ultimate financial rate of return that a representative student would earn on his or her investment if he or she attended Illinois State.

Thus, while net price is important, it is not the only relevant variable for students and families to consider. Low net cost institutions that are dropout factories could lead to disastrous results for students who choose to attend them. On the other hand, some higher net cost institutions such as Illinois State could be worth the substantial investment they require if they provide a high-quality education that leads to high levels of life satisfaction and remunerative employment. *Economically speaking, costs must be weighed against benefits. In this regard, much depends upon what students choose to study as well as the institutions they attend, not simply net price.*

A BRIEF INTERINSTITUTIONAL COMPARISON

To provide context, let's briefly look at institutions in addition to Illinois State. Figure 2-6 provides net price information by household income class for a selection of six public institutions. The University of California, Berkeley (UC-B) offers a visible demonstration of the sometimes cavernous gap between published list prices and the prices students actually pay. UC-B's published annual cost for an in-state undergraduate student living on campus was a very healthy $35,894 in 2016–17, but the average net price paid by students coming from households with annual incomes of $30,000 or less was

FIGURE 2-6

Average Net Prices Paid by In-State Undergraduate Students Living on Campus at a Selection of Public Institutions, Sorted by Annual Household Income, 2015–16

Annual household income

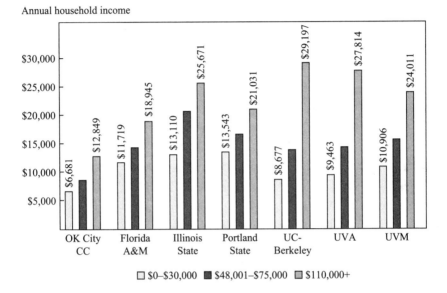

□ $0–$30,000 ■ $48,001–$75,000 ■ $110,000+

Source: College Navigator, National Center for Education Statistics (http://nces.ed.gov/college navigator).

only $8,602. This was only about $2,000 more than the average net price paid by students coming from the same household income bracket at Oklahoma City Community College.

One can see in figure 2-6 that the University of Virginia (UVA), a prestigious Public Ivy, reported a relatively modest average net price of $9,463 for the $0–30,000 annual household income group, which was thousands of dollars less than that reported by a Historically Black institution, Florida A&M. *Indeed, despite their hefty published prices, both UC-B and UVA offered lower costs of attendance to lower-income students than many public institutions located farther down the prestige totem pole, including the aforementioned Florida A&M, Illinois State, Portland State, and the University of Vermont (UVM).*

FEDERAL EDUCATION TAX CREDITS

Analyses of the net prices students pay to attend specific institutions almost never take account of federal education tax credits that students and their families can claim, because the amounts of these credits are unknown to the institutions. There are two education tax credits available: the American Opportunity Tax Credit (AOTC) and the Lifetime Learning Credit (LLC).[12]

The AOTC credit (which reduces one's federal income tax obligation dollar for dollar) is $2,500 per year and can be used for each of a student's first four years of higher education. However, it only is available to a taxpayer whose modified adjusted gross income is $80,000 or less ($160,000 or less for joint filers). Above these income levels, the size of the credit is reduced until it disappears at the $90,000 ($180,000 joint) level.

The LLC is available for all types of postsecondary education and can be used by students to offset higher-education expenses once they have exhausted their AOTC credit eligibility. It provides up to $2,000 per annual tax return (not per student), but one's modified adjusted gross income cannot exceed $66,000 ($132,000 joint) to be eligible for this credit.

In addition, students and/or parents can deduct the interest they pay on student loans and thereby reduce their taxable incomes up to a limit of $2,500 annually. Full eligibility here is restricted to modified adjusted gross incomes less than $65,000 annually ($135,000 joint) and phases out completely at the $80,000 ($165,000 joint) annual modified adjusted gross income level.

Figure 2-7 discloses the amount of federal education tax credits claimed by undergraduate students, 1997–98 through 2016–17. One can see that the real annual volume of these credits hit its maximum in 2010–11 and since then has declined every year to $16.07 billion in 2016–17. However, this is hardly to be sneezed at; these credits total approximately three-fifths of the value of Stafford unsubsidized loans in the same year. This further ameliorates the burden of higher-education price increases and student debt.

CROSS-SUBSIDIES TO IN-STATE AND LOWER-INCOME STUDENTS

"Low-cost" institutions by reputation are not necessarily low cost when net prices are the measure. Well-established, prestigious institutions with price-making power such as the University of California, Berkeley, the

FIGURE 2-7

Real Total Education Tax Credits Received by Undergraduates,
1997–98 to 2016–17 (Billions of Dollars and 2016 Prices)

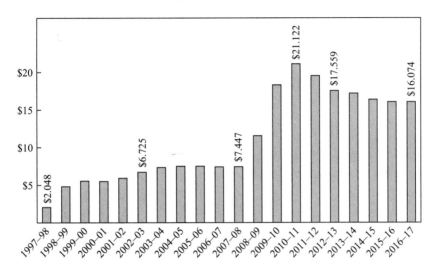

Source: College Board, *Trends in College Student Aid 2017*, table 1B (https://trends.collegeboard
.org/student-aid).

University of Michigan, and the University of Virginia generate funds they
use to cross-subsidize lower-income students. They accomplish this in several different ways. One is to charge out-of-state students much higher
prices than in-state students. Another is to charge students from higher-
income households much higher net prices than those from lower-incomes
households and by this process effectively redistribute costs from upper-
income households to lower-income households. I will have much more to
say about these practices in chapter 4.

However, the current trend toward redistributing costs toward higher-
income students and households and away from lower-income students and
households has not always been the case in public higher education. Almost
fifty years ago, Lee Hansen and Burton Weisbrod of the University of
Wisconsin examined the much lauded public higher-education system of the
state of California and concluded that it redistributed income away from
lower-income students and households toward upper-income students and
households. This was the era of low tuition rates, and talented students
from upper-income households flocked into the high-quality, low-cost, and

high-state-support-per-student campuses of the University of California. Meanwhile, students from lower-income households tended to distribute themselves more heavily among the state colleges (the California State University system) and community colleges, where the state's expenditures per student were substantially lower. This behavior redirected differentially large amounts of state higher-education funding toward higher-income households in California. As such, it represented an unintended consequence.[13]

Some argue that very much the same financial dynamic exists today. The *Hechinger Report* has been particularly vocal in arguing that "rich kids go to elite private and flagship public campuses while poor kids—including those who score higher on standardized tests than their wealthier counterparts—end up at community colleges and regional public universities with much lower success rates, assuming they continue their educations at all." *Hechinger* argues that what it terms "the gap" has been widening at an accelerating rate since the Great Recession began in 2008. The logical consequence, *Hechinger* and others claim, is that public higher education no longer can legitimately claim to be "the equal-opportunity stepping stone to the middle class" that it once was.[14]

Approximately one dozen states have moved in recent years to reduce the relative share of scholarship dollars going to students from lower-income families and to increase funding going to students from upper-income families. The HOPE scholarship programs funded by the state of Georgia since 1992 provide an excellent example.[15] The most prominent HOPE program is a merit-based scholarship award available to Georgia residents who have graduated from high school with a minimum grade point average of 3.0 and who maintain a 3.0 grade point average while attending an eligible college or university in Georgia. Financial need is not considered.

Georgia also awards Zell Miller merit-based scholarships, which currently require a 3.7 high school grade point average and a minimum score of 1,200 on the math and reading portions of the SAT, or a composite 26 on the ACT.

Few would disagree with the premise that the HOPE and Zell Miller programs have been very important reasons why the University of Georgia*

---

*A 2005 study found that the University of Georgia was receiving almost one-quarter of all HOPE funds expended. Matt Thompson, "The HOPE Scholarship and the Law of Unintended Consequences" (www.educationlawconsortium.org/forum/2005/papers/thompson.pdf).

and Georgia Institute of Technology have vaulted into the ranks of the Top 25 public institutions in the country (as ranked by *U.S. News and World Report*). The HOPE and Zell Miller programs also can be credited with increasing the proportion of talented Georgians who have chosen to stay in the state to pursue their higher educations. These are laudable results that taken by themselves bode well for the state of Georgia. Yet it also is true that HOPE scholarship funds have gone differentially to students coming from middle- to upper-income households.

The same state dollars, however, cannot be spent two places; therefore, need-based financial aid for college students in Georgia has withered in relative terms. A National Bureau of Economic Research study by Susan Dynarski found that the HOPE programs reduced aid going to students from the lowest-income families almost on a dollar-for-dollar basis.[16] Additionally, the HOPE programs widened the gap in college attendance between African Americans and whites by 7 to 8 percent* even as they also widened the gap between students coming from upper-income families and lower-income families. The rate of college enrollment for white students in Georgia, for example, was 12.3 percent higher than for white students in neighboring states. Subsequent studies have found somewhat lower percentage impacts, but there is general agreement that taken as a whole, the HOPE scholarship programs have redistributed income away from lower-income families to upper-income families, primarily because financial need is not taken into consideration. At the University of Georgia, 98 percent of all entering freshmen in fall 2016 were either HOPE scholarship or Zell Miller scholarship recipients.[17]

It also appears that the HOPE scholarship programs redirected students toward four-year institutions and away from two-year institutions. This is an understandable reaction from students facing financial constraints that are loosened by the HOPE scholarship programs.

Georgia's HOPE programs initiated a trend that now includes at least fifteen states. Frequently the funds for these programs come from lotteries. A 2014 report by Kati Lebioda produced for the American Association of Colleges and Universities found that in nine states that funded scholarship

---

*The percentage of African Americans attending college in Georgia did increase, however. The presence of multiple Historically Black Colleges and Universities (HBCUs) in Georgia appears to have been a factor. Nevertheless, the HOPE program may have had a net negative influence upon African American enrollment at the state's flagship institutions.

programs with lottery proceeds, financial aid based solely on merit (with no consideration of financial need) accounted for more than 81 percent of scholarship expenditures.[18]

Open-ended scholarship programs can turn out to be expensive, however, and many states have had to diminish the size of the awards they make to scholarship recipients. In Georgia, for example, in 2012–13, more than 117,000 students received financial awards worth $463 million, while Florida spent $312 million on a similar program. Fully 1.7 million students in Georgia had received HOPE scholarships by 2016.[19] Both the rising number of qualifying students and the unpredictability of lottery revenues have caused problems for these states.

Ironically, rising tuition and fees at four-year public colleges and universities has been one of the primary drivers of higher costs for programs like HOPE. If state governments compensate institutions for their tuition increases, then this provides an incentive for the institutions to impose larger increases than they would have otherwise. This in some ways is a state-focused version of the now famous Bennett hypothesis: in 1987 then Secretary of Education William Bennett asserted that federal financial aid policies were significantly responsible for driving up tuition and fees at institutions of higher education.[20] It is an assertion we will examine in greater detail later, but multiple studies have found this effect to be present where Georgia's HOPE programs are concerned. This implies that even though HOPE scholarships have

The *Hechinger Report* asserts that the state of Georgia eliminated all its need-based tuition financial aid in 2012 and now focuses its attention on its HOPE scholarship program. Already by 2013, Georgia had expended more than $6.4 billion on 1.5 million HOPE scholarship recipients. Florida (Bright Futures) and Tennessee (HOPE) operate similar scholarship programs disconnected from financial need. Tennessee, however, also supports the Tennessee Promise Program, which offers the state's high school graduates two years of tuition-free attendance at the state's community and technical colleges. *Hechinger* states that 30 percent of Florida's Bright Futures scholarship funding went to students with family incomes of $100,000 or higher in 2011. Kentucky also supports a financial aid program that does not consider financial need; *Hechinger* reported that the program provided $23.9 million in scholarship aid to students from families who earned more than $100,000 in 2013.[21]

reduced net prices for students who receive them, they probably have increased net prices for students who do not receive them.

The culture of cross-subsidies that dominates the net price structure in public higher education today may diminish the redistributive effects of higher education documented fifty years ago in California by Hansen and Weisbrod.

There are two major factors that must be considered when one attempts to pin down the extent to which public higher education today may subsidize the affluent. First, as noted by the *New York Times* and others, students from upper-income families are disproportionately represented at flagship state universities and especially so among the elite state universities. Students from lower-income families are relatively scarce. For example, the *Times* reported in 2017 that only 12.1 percent of undergraduate students at the College of William and Mary came from households in the lowest 60 percent of income distribution. Table 2-2 provides comparable data for the twenty-eight public colleges and universities ranked by *U.S. News and World Report* as Top 25 institutions in 2017 (several institutions were tied for twenty-fifth), plus a selection of twenty non-elite public four-year institutions and ten community colleges.[22]

One lesson to be drawn from table 2-2 is that higher education in the United States tends to be sharply defined by institutional type. One of the defining characteristics is the incomes of the students who attend different types of institutions. As table 2-2 discloses, only 25.04 percent of the students at *U.S. News and World Report's* Top 25 institutions came from the bottom 60 percent of the income distribution. For twenty less elite flagship institutions, urban institutions, and state colleges, it was 40.52 percent. For ten community colleges, it was 60.6 percent. One can criticize the selection of institutions, but the message is clear. Students, knowingly or not, tend to sort themselves in terms of the incomes of the households from which they

TABLE 2-2

Percentage of Undergraduate Student Bodies Coming from the Top
1 Percent and Bottom 60 Percent of Income Distribution, 2013

Institution	Percentage of Undergraduates from Top 1% of Income Distribution	Percentage of Undergraduates from Bottom 60% of Income Distribution
1) UC Berkeley	3.8%	29.7%
2) UCLA	4.1%	33.5%
3) U Virginia	8.5%	15.0%
4) U Michigan	9.3%	16.5%
5) UNC Chapel Hill	6.0%	20.7%
6) College of W&M	6.5%	12.1%
7) Georgia Tech	3.2%	21.9%
8) UC Santa Barbara	3.4%	33.1%
9) UC Irvine	1.3%	34.2%
9) UC San Diego	1.8%	43.0%
9) U Florida	3.2%	30.1%
12) UC Davis	2.4%	37.6%
13) U Wisconsin	1.6%	27.3%
14) Penn S U	2.3%	29.5%
14) U Illinois UC	2.5%	29.5%
16) Ohio S U	2.0%	27.1%
16) U Georgia	5.1%	21.5%
18) Purdue U	3.1%	21.1%
18) U Connecticut	2.1%	23.1%
18) U Texas Austin	5.4%	27.7%
18) U Washington	2.9%	26.8%
22) U Maryland CP	N.A.	N.A.
23) Clemson U	N.A.	N.A.
24) U Pittsburgh	2.0%	23.5%
25) Rutgers U	1.3%	31.7%
25) Texas A&M	4.2%	21.8%
25) U Minnesota	1.9%	23.0%
25) Virginia Tech	2.8%	15.0%
Top 25 Average	**3.43%**	**25.04%**
Illinois S U	<1.0%	19.6%
Colorado S U	2.8%	20.2%
Keene S C	<1.0%	21.3%
Miami U (O)	7.0%	23.7%
California S U Chico	2.6%	27.8%
U Nevada Reno	1.9%	28.1%

TABLE 2-2 (CONTINUED)

Institution	Percentage of Undergraduates from Top 1% of Income Distribution	Percentage of Undergraduates from Bottom 60% of Income Distribution
Ball S U	1.2%	29.6%
Central Washington U	<1.0%	29.8%
Slippery Rock U	<1.0%	33.6%
Florida Gulf Coast U	2.3%	33.7%
U North Texas	1.1%	36.7%
U Montana	1.9%	37.2%
Nicholls S U	1.3%	37.8%
U Central Missouri	<1.0%	41.6%
Rhode Island C	<1.0%	42.3%
Morehead S U	<1.0%	50.0%
Shawnee S U	<1.0%	62.6%
Eastern New Mexico U	<1.0%	67.4%
North Carolina Central U	<1.0%	76.1%
Mississippi Valley S U	<1.0%	91.3%
Other Average		**40.52%**
Western Wyoming CC	<1.0%	35.8%
Salt Lake CC	<1.0%	43.9%
Illinois Central CC	<1.0%	50.8%
Northwest Iowa CC	<1.0%	52.9%
Tidewater CC	<1.0%	53.3%
Glendale CC	<1.0%	67.3%
Nashville State CC	<1.0%	69.7%
Northwest Mississippi CC	<1.0%	70.8%
Miami-Dade CC	<1.0%	77.7%
Borough of Manhattan CC	<1.0%	84.4%
Community College Average		**60.6%**

Source: Gregor Aisch and others, "Some Colleges Have More Students from the Top 1 Percent than the Bottom 60," *New York Times*, January 18, 2017.

come. That is, the student bodies of our public institutions of higher education tend to be stratified on the basis of household incomes.

This student sorting and stratification by institutional type would matter little if it were not also true that expenditures per student (which can be interpreted as subsidies) also vary by institutional type. To no one's surprise, the average Top 25 institution spends far more on each of its students than do the middle-rung institutions, and dramatically more than the community colleges. Hence, the disproportionate representation of students from upper-income families at the elite institutions means they are receiving more financial attention than students attending other types of institutions.

This brings us to the second important factor to consider: the redistributive effects of most public colleges' pricing structures. While all students are quoted the same sticker prices (tuition and fees, room and board), only some pay the full price. Most others receive grants that lower the effective net price they pay. What is not clear is whether this financial redistribution away from upper-income students outweighs the difference in expenditures per student just noted.

An important 2016 Brookings Institution study by Jason Delisle and Kim Dancy concluded that higher-education subsidies today actually decline on average as student and family incomes increase.[23] That is, the redistribution effect just noted is larger in absolute size than the student sorting effect. They argue that the composition of the student bodies of flagship state universities has been democratized in recent years and no longer is dominated by students from upper-income households. Thus, in 2011–12, Delisle and Dancy found that 25.1 percent of all students at "very selective admission" public universities came from families with incomes $0–30,000, while 30.0 percent of the students at "selective admission" state universities came from the same lower-income group.

The Delisle-Dancy income data appear to be inconsistent with the *New York Times* family income data cited in table 2-2. If we regard the *U.S. News and World Report* Top 25 public universities as "very selective," then on average they enrolled only 25.04 percent of their undergraduate student bodies from the entire bottom 60 percent of the income distribution. Delisle and Dancy say that 25.1 percent of the student bodies at very selective public institutions came from families with annual incomes of $0–30,000, which would place most of them in the bottom quintile (much more restrictive than the bottom 60 percent) of household income distribution. The Tax Policy Center reports that the upper limit of the bottom household income quintile in 2015 was $22,800, while the mean was $12,457.[24] It is difficult to reconcile the divergent *Times* and Delisle-Dancy income measurements.

Delisle and Dancy also argue that the differential net prices quoted by institutions to students of varying financial circumstances have gutted the less discriminatory pricing and subsidy structure that reigned in California when Hansen and Weisbrod conducted their study in 1969. Delisle and Dancy report that at the very selective public institutions, students from the lower-income class received 28.5 percent of financial subsidies granted, while they received 35.2 percent of all subsidies at the selective institutions. Overall, in all public institutions, they accounted for 37.4 percent of all students and received 38.8 percent of all subsidies.

These results are, however, sensitive to Delisle and Dancy's measures of the subsidy received by any student. They approximate it by the average dollar amount a student's college or university spent per student minus the tuition and fees a typical student paid after institutional grants had been deducted. They did not consider Pell Grants.

As expected, Delisle and Dancy found that both "very selective" and "selective" public institutions provided the largest financial subsidies per student, and the "least selective" institutions provided the smallest subsidies per student. The more selective institutions had (and have) more money to spend, and this is reflected in the subsidies they offer.

The Brookings researchers utilized two separate measures of institutional spending. The first included expenditures specifically related to instruction plus some spending on academic and student services. The second encompassed *all* spending by the institution per student and therefore incorporated spending on research, public service, and other activities in addition to the factors listed in their first measure.

Delisle and Dancy discovered that the "average indirect subsidy among each income group declines as income rises." But this finding was based upon their narrower definition of spending that did not include research and public service expenditures. Their conclusion almost reversed, however, when they utilized the more expansive definition of institutional spending. Here, a mild positive relationship emerged between student income levels and the per student subsidy received. As student incomes rose, so also did the size of the average subsidy they received.

The Delisle and Dancy evidence is best interpreted as telling us that the often-hypothesized positive relationship between higher-education subsidies and the incomes of students may not be as large as some believe. This is an argument worth hearing, but should be interpreted with the cautions just noted. More research is needed.

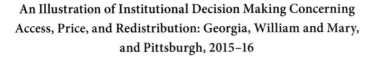

FIGURE 2-8

An Illustration of Institutional Decision Making Concerning Access, Price, and Redistribution: Georgia, William and Mary, and Pittsburgh, 2015–16

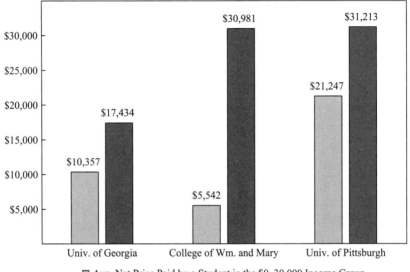

□ Avg. Net Price Paid by a Student in the $0–30,000 Income Group
■ Avg. Net Price Paid by a Student in the $110,000+ Income Group

Source: College Navigator, National Center for Education Statistics (www.nces.ed.gov/college navigator).

A TOP 25 PUBLIC INSTITUTION COMPARISON

Let's clarify several of the critical issues and choices by examining three public institutions, each of which is ranked by *U.S. News and World Report* among its Top 25 public universities. At the University of Georgia (UGA), Pell Grant recipients constituted 22 percent of its undergraduate student body in 2016–17. Only 21.5 percent of its undergraduate student body came from the bottom 60 percent of the household income distribution for its class of 2013 (see table 2-2). As figure 2-8 illustrates, the average net price paid by individuals in the $0–30,000 income class at UGA was $10,357, while the average net price paid by individuals in the highest income class ($110,000+) was a bit less than 1.7 times that amount, or $17,434.[25]

Meanwhile, at William and Mary, where only 11 percent of the undergraduate student body was composed of Pell Grant recipients in 2015–16, the price paid by the students coming from the lowest income class was only $5,542, while students coming from the highest income class paid more than five times as much, or $30,981. While William and Mary did not admit very many Pell Grant recipients overall (only 12.1 percent of its student body came from the bottom 60 percent of the household income distribution in 2013), clearly it committed institutionally to reducing their cost of attendance.

The University of Pittsburgh (Pitt) presented a visible contrast. Pitt's undergraduate student body in 2015–16 included only 16 percent Pell Grant recipients, and in 2013 only 23.5 percent of its students came from the bottom 60 percent of the household income distribution. The lowest-income students at Pitt paid an average of $21,247 to attend in 2015–16. Pitt (like its counterpart institution, Penn State) has not placed a high priority either on enrolling large proportions of Pell Grant students or on providing need-based student financial aid.

One can see from figure 2-8 that UGA falls between William and Mary and Pitt in terms of accessibility to lower-income students. Further, its net prices were comparatively low across all student income groups. The HOPE scholarship program is an important reason why the upper-income students

States and institutions of higher education often develop narratives (sometimes approaching mythology) that portray them the way they would like to be seen. These narratives ultimately have an impact on higher-education policies. The HOPE scholarship programs have become part of the Georgia narrative, just as tuition-free public institutions once were part of the California narrative. Once narratives become entrenched, it becomes very difficult to change policy direction. It would take decades, for example, for Pennsylvania to move away from its current high-net-price, low-financial-aid model, or for many flagship state universities such as Alabama and Michigan to reduce their financial dependence upon out-of-state students.

at UGA paid an average net price of only $17,434, well below the prices charged by the Berkeleys, Michigans, and UVAs of the academic universe.*

The contrasting data for these three institutions underline that both states and institutions are not simply helpless prisoners of fate. In the long run, states and many individual colleges and universities have the ability to make choices about general-fund tax support, tuition and fees, access, and subsidies. A more detached view reveals that there is much less inevitability attached to current pricing, aid, and access situations than states and individual institutions might wish outsiders to believe. The differing models followed by UGA, William and Mary, and Pitt illustrate this. Habit does not constitute destiny.

---

*The nature and size of the HOPE scholarship program are decided by the Georgia legislature, not the University of Georgia, though the university has actively lobbied a succession of governors and legislatures concerning HOPE details. Hence, it is more accurate to say that many of the underlying factors in UGA pricing are decided off campus, and the university reacts accordingly.

THREE

A Rising Flood of Student Indebtedness

Americans now owe more on student loans than on credit cards.
—David Wessel, *Wall Street Journal*, October 12, 2016

T he cost of attending college has increased significantly over the past quarter century. Even after one adjusts for additional financial aid grants that students do not need to repay, and after one additionally adjusts for effects of price inflation, the real net cost of attending a four-year public college or university has increased dramatically. Figure 3-1 shows that the inflation-adjusted net price of attending a typical four-year public institution remained roughly constant for about five years at the tail end of the last century, but then increased about 68 percent between 2000–01 and 2017–18.

When students and their families find themselves unable to pay these rising costs, they have limited options. The student can move to a less expensive institution, or change to part-time status, or simply drop out. Or the student and his or her family can borrow money to pay the rising costs.

Many students and families choose to go into debt to pay for college expenses. They can do so because the federal government has made it relatively easy for them to borrow money. Nearly 40 percent of all individuals between ages twenty and forty now have some student debt.

FIGURE 3-1

Average Real Net Price: Average Tuition and Fees Plus Room and Board Less Grants for Full-Time Undergraduate Students at Four-Year Public Colleges and Universities, 1996–97 to 2017–18

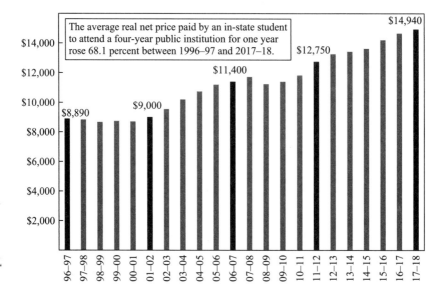

The average real net price paid by an in-state student to attend a four-year public institution for one year rose 68.1 percent between 1996–97 and 2017–18.

$14,940

$12,750

$11,400

$9,000

$8,890

Source: College Board, "Average Net Price over Time for Full-Time Students, by Sector," table 7 (https://trends.collegeboard.org/college-pricing/figures-tables/average-net-price-over -time-full-time-students-sector).

Note: All dollar values are stated in 2015–16 prices and therefore are comparable in real terms over time.

The total volume of student debt continues to rise, though at a decelerating rate in recent years. The influences driving this upsurge have been the escalating real price of public higher education and stagnant household incomes.

Rising real net prices per student at four-year public colleges and universities are analogous to the mercury in a thermometer. The rising mercury of net cost (see figure 3-2) discloses that real, after-inflation prices per student at four-year public institutions rose 48.1 percent between 2003 and 2017. This translated to 2.8 percent annual growth, after inflation.

Students and families responded by borrowing money—lots of it. *Real (after-inflation) accumulated student debt increased 307.7 percent between the first quarter of 2003 and the fourth quarter of 2017.*

FIGURE 3-2

Real Total Student Debt and Real Net Prices at Four-Year Public Colleges and Universities, 2003–17 (Indexed to 100 in 2003)

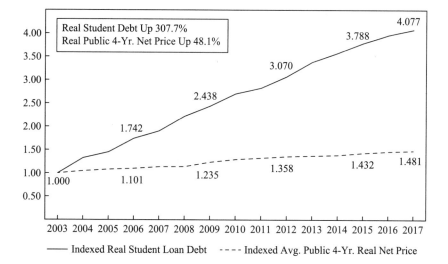

Sources: Center for Microeconomic Data, "Household Debt and Credit Report," New York Federal Reserve, February 2018 (www.newyorkfed.org/microeconomics/hhdc.html), updated May 2018; College Board, "Average Net Price [defined as T&F + R&B – Grants] for Full-Time Students, by Sector," table 7 (https://trends.collegeboard.org/college-pricing/figures-tables /average-net-price-over-time-full-time-students-sector); Bureau of Labor Statistics, Series CUUR0000SA0 (http://data.bls.gov/cgi-bin/surveymost).

IS STUDENT DEBT DIFFERENT?

One of the distinctive things about student debt is that in recent years it has been increasing much more rapidly than other kinds of household debt. In 2003, household credit card debt was much larger (2.88 times) than student debt. By the first quarter of 2018, things had almost reversed: student debt was almost 65 percent larger than credit card debt (see figure 3-3) and had risen to $1.407 trillion.

THE FEDERAL GOVERNMENT AS CREDITOR

The federal government (as opposed to private lenders) has become visibly more flexible in its dealings with student loan debtors. By June 2016, nearly

FIGURE 3-3

Household Debt Balances by Category, 2003–18 (Trillions of Dollars)

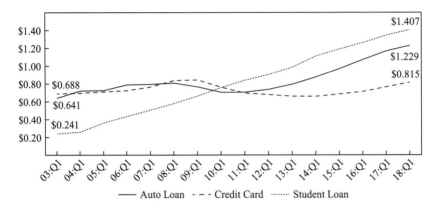

Source: Center for Microeconomic Data, "Household Debt and Credit Report," New York Federal Reserve, first quarter 2018 (www.newyorkfed.org/microeconomics/hhdc.html).

5.3 million student debtors were enrolled in a variety of programs that permitted them either to delay paying interest, or to have portions of their loan forgiven because they were working in public service–related occupations, or to have their payments capped at a certain percentage of their postgraduation incomes.[1] These income-based repayment plans currently also forgive all federal direct loans after the student debtor has made twenty years of payments in good standing.

Once again, however, the profusion of different federal loan repayment programs based upon income has confused many student and post-student debtors. At least five different federal student debt repayment plans exist. Their complicated nuances have given rise to a new microindustry that helps guide debtors through the maze of programs.

LOAN REPAYMENT PROBLEMS AND RISING DEFAULTS

More-lenient federal repayment programs notwithstanding, the truth is that large numbers of student debtors are not paying off their loans and subsequently find themselves in default status. In third quarter of 2017, only about 57 percent of all individuals who held a student loan with the federal government were making payments on that loan. Even so, only 22 percent of individ-

In 2015–16, students who borrowed from the federal government received the following average loan amounts from the three largest federal student loan programs. Private-sector loans are not included:

Direct subsidized loans $ 3,748

Direct unsubsidized loans $ 4,125

Parent PLUS loans $14,752

Source: National Association of Student Financial Aid Administrators, *National Student Aid Profile: Overview of 2016 Federal Programs*, June 2016 (www.nasfaa.org/uploads/documents/2016_National_Profile_2.pdf).

uals required to make payments were in default (defined as not having made any payment in the past year).[2] The remainder had negotiated some type of forbearance with the federal government, or perhaps still were in school.

Some student debtors fail to take the steps necessary to emerge from their debtor circumstances. Recent data published by the Federal Reserve Bank of New York revealed that more than 12 percent of baccalaureate degree recipients age thirty-three who were student debtors were in default status with respect to their student loans. This rose to more than 26 percent if the individual was an arts/humanities graduate of what the Fed termed a "nonselective" college.[3]

One can see in figure 3-4 that the percentage of the total value of outstanding student loans that were seriously delinquent (ninety days or more) rose steadily from 6.13 percent of all loans in the first quarter of 2003 to almost 12 percent in the third quarter of 2013, but since has leveled off. The rising loan delinquency rate reflects a variety of factors, including the deleterious effects of the Great Recession, deterioration in job markets for college graduates, and of course the rising cost of attending a college or university.

The important lesson conveyed by figure 3-4 is that student debt has not been behaving like other debt. Many student loan debtors (whether the students themselves, parents, or other loan guarantors) are choosing not to meet their student debt obligations in the same way they service their other debts. It is revealing that 10.96 percent of outstanding student debt balances were

FIGURE 3-4

Comparing Student Loan Delinquency Rates to Delinquency Rates for Other Types of Household Debt, 2003–17 (90+ Days)

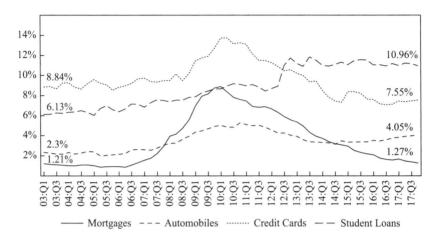

Source: Center for Microeconomic Data, "Household Debt and Credit Report," New York Federal Reserve Bank, February 2017 (www.newyorkfed.org/medialibrary/interactives/house holdcredit/data/xls/HHD_C_Report_2016Q2.xlsx).

ninety days or more delinquent in the fourth quarter of 2017, but only 7.55 percent of outstanding credit card balances and 4.05 percent of automobile loans were similarly delinquent.

This may seem paradoxical because except in narrow circumstances, a debtor cannot escape an outstanding student loan obligation by declaring bankruptcy. Therefore, one might expect debtors to service their student debts first. Though the courts recently have become somewhat more lenient, non-dischargeable student debts can follow a former student for the remainder of his or her life and involve more than momentarily acquiring a lower credit score. As Judith Scott-Clayton put it in June 2018:

> When a student loan enters default, the entire balance becomes immediately due, and borrowers lose access to options that might otherwise have applied, such as deferment and forbearance. If the borrower does not make arrangements with their servicer to get out of default, the loan may go to collections. Fees of up to 25% of the balance due may be added as a result. Defaulting on a student loan can also lower

credit scores, making it harder to access credit or even to rent an apartment in the future. In some states, default can lead to revocation of professional licenses, and credit histories may be evaluated as part of employment applications, making it harder to find or keep a job. Also, students cannot receive any additional federal student aid while they are in default, making it more difficult to return to school.[4]

On the other hand, student debtors do not have to post collateral for their loans. If they default on an automobile loan, their financial lender will take that automobile. There is nothing comparable for a student loan.

One might be tempted to write off or minimize the subpar loan repayment performance of student loan recipients by asserting that rising indebtedness is a problem characteristic of most households. In this view, many households are encountering economic distress (remember the rhetoric in the 2016 presidential campaign) and as a consequence, are diving deeper and deeper into debt of all kinds. This story does not match up well with the facts. As figure 3-4 reveals, delinquency rates on other forms of household debt generally have been declining since 2010.

Daniel Pianko has written in detail about federal student loan repayment rates. He points out that the federal government's treatment of student debtors who have fallen behind in their payments often has been extremely lenient. Further, he argues that some colleges and universities reduce their debt repayment default percentages by convincing their former students to make a minimal monthly payment (perhaps as low as $5) in order to remove them from the list of those in absolute default. Pianko believes that realistic debt default percentages are much higher than those being reported by the federal government and talks of a "tsunami of nonpayment."[5]

Recent data also suggest that increasing numbers of student debtors are escaping some or all of their debt obligations by alleging successfully to the

No collateral: While student loan debt is not dischargeable in a bankruptcy, student debtors seldom if ever supply the federal government with any collateral when they take out their loans. Hence, compared to most loans, especially those received from private lenders, there are reduced consequences.

> **Questionable debt facilitation activities by institutions:** 40 percent of all students nationally attend colleges and universities that have signed agreements with financial institutions that encourage students to open college-sponsored and -logoed credit cards accounts. A December 2016 report issued by the Consumer Financial Protection Bureau commented dryly that "students' interests may be an afterthought in many marketing agreements."[6] This is because the credit card arrangements encourage additional student debt and often feature high fees and unfavorable terms. Institutions, or surrogates such as their alumni associations, however, earn revenue from these agreements and, in the fashion of college bookstores, may not always behave in the best financial interests of students.

U.S. Department of Education that they were defrauded by the collegiate institutions they attended. This has become especially common where for-profit institutions are concerned. By March 2018, 84,362 student debtors had lodged claims that Corinthian Colleges defrauded them and hence some or all of their student loans should be forgiven.

The Brookings Institution has devoted considerable resources to analyzing the phenomenon of student debt and has published several studies on the subject. At first glance, these studies appear to promote contradictory conclusions. Former Brookings scholars Beth Akers and Mathew Chingos argued in a 2014 Brookings study and later in a well-argued book in 2016 that the notion that a widespread student debt crisis exists has been overdone.[7] They point out that college remains a good investment for a typical student who does not drop out and earns a degree. Further, large student debt balances are unusual, most students eventually pay off their student debt (or have that debt forgiven), and high default rates are confined to certain categories of students.

However, Brookings subsequently published two reports in 2018 by economist Judith Scott-Clayton, one of which was titled, "The Looming Student Debt Crisis Is Worse Than We Thought."[8] The title obviously suggests urgency and Scott-Clayton provided data showing how and why.

Credit to Brookings for thoroughly airing student loan and debt is-

FIGURE 3-5

Default Rates on Federal Loans, Organized by Types of Institutions and Ethnicities of Undergraduate Students

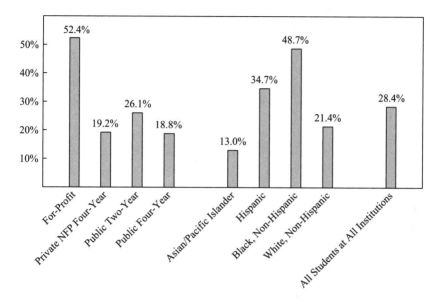

Source: Judith Scott-Clayton, "What Accounts for Gaps in Student Loan Default, and What Happens After" (Brookings Institution, June 21, 2018).

sues. On closer inspection, the views of these scholars are not as far apart as they might initially seem.

Figure 3-5 is based on data taken from a June 2018 study authored by Brookings economist Judith Scott-Clayton.[9] The data reflect a very large sample of students who entered college in 2003–04 and outline their federal student loan status in 2015. Note that more than one in four undergraduate students experienced default during the twelve-year period. The very high rate of default for black, non-Hispanic borrowers (48.7 percent) commanded Scott-Clayton's attention. She found that about one-half of the default gap between black, non-Hispanic borrowers and white, non-Hispanic borrowers could be explained by family circumstances such as income and employment. Students' standardized test scores and their grade point averages also helped explain some of the gap.

Interestingly, in her most developed predictive model, Scott-Clayton found that default was negatively associated with the size of a student's borrowing.

Each additional $10,000 of federal student debt reduced the probability of default by 4 percent. Presumably some of the willingness of students to assume additional debt reflects their perceptions about their later ability to repay that debt. Scott-Clayton found that the lower the ratio of students' debt to their incomes, the lower the probability they would *not* default. Students who believe they will earn more money after they graduate assume more debt. If they actually do earn high incomes, then they are quite likely to pay off their loans.

Scott-Clayton also analyzed what happens to students who do default. Their lives can be difficult. She found that 54 percent of defaulters were able to resolve at least one of their defaults by the end of the twelve-year period, and this did not vary by race. Fourteen percent of defaulters found a way to return to college.

Other studies also have found that defaulters:

- attended college in a high-net-cost state[10]

- are college dropouts[11]

- are individuals who have not fared well in job markets, often because they majored in a low-demand discipline at a non-elite institution[12]

- accumulated significant debt in graduate school (in 2012, students who earned medical degrees and borrowed money owed an average of $162,000 compared to $27,000 in that year for undergraduates who borrowed).[13]

Additionally, women student debtors appear to take on about 20 percent more debt than men and take about two years longer on average to repay their debt than men. Women also are more likely to be in default status with respect to their student debt than men (these data come from a 2018 American Association of University Women report).[14]

In fiscal year 2017, 78 percent of all student debtors owed less than $40,000. Counterintuitively, the highest rates of loan default belonged to students who owed smaller amounts of money: $10,000 or less. Almost two-thirds of all student loan defaults in 2011 came from loans with outstanding balances less than $10,000. Even so, a recent Brookings study reported that 17 percent of student debtors owed more than $50,000 in 2014 and many of them, while not in default, were not reducing their debt balance.[15]

Where federal student loans are concerned (and they account for about 62 percent of all outstanding student loans), about 55 percent of the approxi-

TABLE 3-1

Characteristics and Amounts of Direct Federal Student Loans, FY 2017

	Percentage of Dollars	Percentage of Recipients
In school	13%	19%
Repaying	53%	45%
Deferment	11%	10%
Forbearance	10%	7%
Grace	2%	4%
Default	10%	16%

Source: College Board, *Trends in Student Aid 2017*, figure 10B (https://trends.collegeboard.org/student-aid).

Notes: If the federal government grants a loan deferment, then the student debtor need not make any payments on the outstanding balance and may not be required to pay interest.

Loan forbearance means that although the student debtor does not qualify for deferment, he/she does not have to make loan repayments. Interest continues to accrue.

After graduating or moving to part-time status, student debtors do not have to begin to repay their loans for six months (sometimes extendable to three years if military service is involved). Interest does not accrue.

mately 28 million direct student loan debtors were not making payments on their loans in fiscal year 2017. This number, however, perhaps is deceptively high because it includes currently enrolled students whom we would not expect to be making loan payments. Of all federal student loan recipients, 16 percent were in default on those loans (see table 3-1).

In 2000, only one of the twenty-five highest aggregate student debt schools in the country was a for-profit institution, but by 2014 this number had grown to thirteen.[16] Revised federal financial aid regulations, however, put a serious crimp in the ability of for-profit institutions to participate as fully in federal loan programs as they have in the past. ITT Technical Institute's demise in August 2016 provides a powerful illustration. ITT received 79 percent of its cash flow from the federal government—56 percent from the federal direct student loan program and 23 percent from Pell Grants.[17] Tightened federal scrutiny of for-profit colleges was the primary factor in causing it to close its doors even though it still enrolled 40,000 students in thirty-eight states.*

---

*Apollo Educational Group's for-profit University of Phoenix supplies an additional example of significance. Between 2010 and 2016, its enrollment fell more than 70 percent, and in 2015 alone it

In 2018, however, the tide appears to have turned: federal regulatory oversight is waning, and for-profit institutions are among the beneficiaries of this relaxed approach. Experience suggests this is likely to lead to increased loan defaults.

Loan defaults are not the exclusive province of for-profit institutions. Two-year public institutions also exhibit high student loan default rates. Students at Indiana's public Ivy Tech, a community college system with campuses located through the Hoosier State, recorded a 23 percent default rate during the 2011–14 period.[18]

Thus, a version of a "student debt crisis" does exist. If I have accumulated $100,000 in student debt, but do not have a job that will enable me to pay off this debt, then I might well believe we are in the midst of a student debt crisis. Or even if I graduate with only $30,400 in debt (close to the 2016–17 average for undergraduates), but I have not fared well in job markets, then I too will feel I am in difficult straits. As we will see in the next section, these are not idle musings. Student debt changes behavior.

Even so, it is important that we recognize that the problems that do exist are not uniform across all classes of borrowers. The situation is nuanced, and certain groups of students are much more likely to acquire student debt and be less likely to repay that debt.* This means that "one size fits all" national solutions may miss the mark because a student debtor's circumstances and ability to repay depend so much on the affluence of that student's family, her major course of study, the institution she attends, and a prosperous, growing economy that generates attractive jobs that support timely debt repayment.

---

lost more than 50,000 students. The three-year federal student loan default rate for Phoenix students who either graduated or dropped out between 2011 and 2014 was 19 percent. Katie Lobosco, "University of Phoenix Owner Gets Out as 50,500 Students Flee" *CNNMoney*, February 8, 2016.

*The Federal Reserve Bank of New York has shown that approximately 75 percent of student debtors end up better off financially, even having borrowed the average amount—if their higher education increases their earnings by $401 per month or more. These are among the reasons why Akers and Chingos of the Brookings Institution concluded that the typical student borrower is no worse off today than he or she was a generation previous and that there is no generalized student debt problem today. Rajashri Chakrabarti, Nicole Gorton, Michelle Jiang, and Wilbert van der Klaauw, "Who Is More Likely to Default on Student Loans?," *Liberty Street Economics* (blog), Federal Reserve Bank of New York, November 20, 2017; Beth Akers and Mathew M. Chingos, "Is a Student Loan Crisis on the Horizon?" (Brookings Institution, June 24, 2014).

Debt repayment numbers might change for the worse if the United States plunges back into economic recession, or if the federal government alters its current tendency to find ways to forgive the student indebtedness of large numbers of borrowers. However, these numbers might change for the better if the long-standing stagnation in household income comes to an end, or we see a deceleration in increases in the net prices paid by students.

As this is being written, the United States is enjoying the second-longest economic expansion since World War II, and unemployment rates are historically low. Eventually, however, this economic expansion will come to an end. When this occurs, student debt problems that now seem a minor irritant will become major problems. As the next section reveals, student debt is associated with a wide variety of suboptimal economic outcomes.

THE IMPACT OF STUDENT DEBT ON THE ECONOMY

Abundant economic evidence is available demonstrating that having meaningful amounts of student debt changes the behavior of debtors. As touched on in chapter 1, empirical studies have tied substantial amounts of individual student debt to reduced rates of home ownership, diminished retirement savings, lower credit ratings, negative net worth, choice of college major, whether students complete a degree program they start, and even reduced marriage rates. *For some former students, their outstanding student debt burden has become the defining characteristic of their lives.*

The New York Federal Reserve Bank reported in 2017 that 40 percent of individuals who had earned a baccalaureate degree or more, but had no student debt, were homeowners. This fell to 33 percent if they had student debt.[19] An earlier study by Brown and Caldwell found a 5 percent absolute difference in the home ownership rate for the average thirty-year-old with student debt compared to a thirty-year-old with no student debt.[20] A 2014 review and extension of the literature on this topic by Cooper and Wang of the Federal Reserve Bank of Boston concluded that "the homeownership rate for households with student debt is always below the rate for households without student debt," as exemplified by a 3 percent differential for individuals aged thirty to thirty-four.[21] Akers, however, issued what might be termed a "not so fast" warning with respect to these conclusions by providing a set of methodological criticisms of these past studies.[22]

Another New York Federal Reserve Bank study (2016) found that "the steady growth in student debt and borrowing, combined with the very slow rate of student loan repayment we have documented elsewhere, has materially contributed and will continue to contribute to negative household wealth and wealth inequality."[23] The aforementioned Boston Federal Reserve Bank study reached the same conclusion.[24]

Student debt also appears to diminish saving for retirement. Studies by Yuh and colleagues and by Cavanagh and Sharpe found that a variety of kinds of debt (including, by implication, student debt) reduce saving for retirement.[25]

Predictably, there is a connection between an individual student's debt obligations and that individual's credit score. Brown and Caldwell's 2013 study revealed that the average thirty-year-old with student debt had a credit score that was twenty-four points lower than that of a student without debt.[26]

Economists located at the Board of Governors of the Federal Reserve System connected student debt to the inability of young adults to leave home and form their own households.[27] These Washington economists found that the observed rise in debt-holding between 2005 and 2013, which was driven significantly by a rise in student loan debt, could explain 32 percent of the increase in numbers of young adults living with their parents, and 26 percent of the increase in median time spent living with one's parents.

New businesses often require that the founders go into debt; if they already have student debt, they are less likely to attempt to form a new business. Philadelphia Federal Reserve Bank economists found that a one standard deviation increase in student debt reduced by 14 percent the number of new businesses with one to four employees between 2000 and 2010.[28]

Rothstein and Rouse are among several researchers who have examined the impact of student debt on student choice of major course of study; they found that student debt causes students to shy away from low-paying and public-sector jobs.[29] The duo reported that each incremental $10,000 in student debt made graduates 6 percent less likely to take a job in the government, nonprofit, or education sectors. Separately, it has been found that student debtors also are less likely to apply to graduate schools.

Dew and Gicheva have uncovered a connection between student debt and marriage rates. Gicheva found that one out of seven student debtors delayed marriage because of their student loans.[30] Separately, Baum and O'Malley found that couples say they delayed having children because of their student debt.[31]

Millett found that undergraduate debt reduces the probability that student will pursue graduate degrees.[32]

Hence, even when students can pay off their debts in a timely fashion (and most do), their debt alters their behavior. None of the behavioral changes I have just reported are surprising because each conforms to what basic economic intuition predicts. The uncertainty relates to the size of the effects.

There are opportunity costs associated with incurring and servicing student debt. Dollars spent dealing with student debt cannot be spent on other goods and services. Further, student debt affects the balance sheets of individuals and therefore not only influences how they behave and choose to bear risks, but also how creditors and lenders evaluate them if the former students wish to obtain credit or loans for any purpose.

INNOVATIONS

Income-share agreements are one oft-mentioned way to make it easier for students to assume and pay for debts they accumulate in college. Purdue University's "Back a Boiler" program provides the most prominent example. The program utilizes endowment funds typically raised from alumni to help students pay their college expenses. The students subsequently pay back the provided funds by means of paying Purdue a percentage of their future earned income.[33]

The Progressive Policy Institute (PPI) has utilized Purdue's easily accessible financial software to generate two hypotheticals to illustrate how the income-share agreements work.[34] First, consider a computer science major who will graduate in 2020 and earn a salary of $68,000. She utilized $26,000 in Back a Boiler funding. To repay this support, she will pay Purdue 7.31 percent of her future salaries for eighty-eight months. Second, consider an English major who likewise graduates in 2020, but earns $30,000. He utilized $20,000 in Back a Boiler funding and will be obligated to pay 7.46 percent of his future salaries for 116 months.

Note that students are protected from possible future income volatility (for example, if they become unemployed), but Purdue also benefits if a Back a Boiler student strikes it rich. Necessarily, it also means that Purdue has a strong interest in helping Back a Boiler students find and maintain lucrative employment. Students from lower-income households also benefit because questionable family or student credit records and incomes no longer are barriers to college attendance.

There are several concerns related to income-share agreements. One is that they might distort the majors that students choose, though this remains to be seen. Another is that less well-endowed public colleges and universities simply do not have the resources to mount programs similar to Back a Boiler. It takes large endowments and highly successful alumni to make the program viable.

Further, where institutions are concerned, a long-term motivational problem is associated with income-share agreements because they do nothing to discourage growth in college costs. If Flagship U inflates its costs, then its foundation (with the valuable support of Flagship U alumni) will validate those increases by enabling students to pay the higher costs. This dynamic bears resemblance to the one associated with federal student loans (usually labeled the Bennett hypothesis, about which we will talk much more in chapter 8). What incentive does an institution have to control costs if it can successfully pass those costs on to employers via the students it graduates?

FINAL THOUGHTS

Some student debtors have found themselves in proverbial dire straits because of their debt obligations. Approximately three-quarters of all student debtors, however, are not overburdened by their debts and can service them until they disappear. More generous federal loan forgiveness programs in recent years and an improving economy are the primary reasons for this.

Still, as we have seen, student debt does affect the behavior of student debtors—even those who pay off their loans in a timely fashion. Most of these effects are negative, and they put a damper upon economic growth.

On the other side of the ledger, there are documentable positive economic spinoffs that are generated by loan-financed higher education. Student debt is an investment that often produces better, more productive citizens, at least as measured by their earned incomes. Arguably, because of their educations, they can live more satisfying lives, be superior citizens, raise better children, lead healthier lives,* and (not to be forgotten) pay more taxes than someone who has not attended college.

---

*Many of the benefits attributed to higher education are difficult to measure. The assertion that a college education leads the recipient to live a healthier, longer life, however, is measurable and a recent *Journal of Health Economics* article did just that. Buckles and colleagues estimate that an additional year of college decreases mortality rates by 15 to 16 percent. If so,

Because student debt problems are not generalized across all students, common solutions that apply to all student debtors often will miss the mark. Difficulties and debt defaults are concentrated primarily in certain student and demographic categories. What would benefit virtually all concerned, however, would be to:

- require greater transparency on the part of academic institutions in terms of the job prospects associated with major courses of study, and the provision of vital information such as retention and graduation rates (tasks that many institutions eschew)

- disclose to students precisely what their debts will mean to them once they leave their institution (including provision of some of the empirical results cited above, because there is evidence that many students do not understand the burdens they have assumed)

- ensure that students understand that student debt seldom is dischargeable in a bankruptcy proceeding

- expand income-based debt repayment possibilities at the federal level and encourage innovative state and institutional programs such as that at Purdue University

- enhance state general fund support for higher education, including relatively more emphasis on need-based financial aid and relatively less on non-need-based scholarship programs

- restrain tuition and fee increases so that eventually they roughly match the long-term growth in the Consumer Price Index and median household income (perhaps a pipe dream, but vitally important)

- reduce state and federal mandates that virtually require institutions to employ additional administrators and staff

- pay less attention to external university ranking systems that push institutions into competitive expenditures for which students must pay

- recognize and control cost-inflating amenities such as climbing walls and lazy rivers that students ultimately finance

---

this would increase the rate of return on any investment in higher education. Kasey Buckles and others, "The Effect of College Education on Mortality," *Journal of Health Economics* 50 (December 2016), pp. 99–114.

- beware of institutional mission creep that requires cost-inflating expenditures

- encourage increased use of university endowments and accumulated reserve funds to moderate cost increases

- focus attention upon net prices as opposed to published prices to obtain a more accurate reading of what campus pricing actually is

It is not an oversimplification to observe that to the extent we achieve success in one or more of these endeavors, we will diminish the negative effects associated with rising student debt. This "we," however, is inclusive of many different parties, certainly beginning with students and families, but also embracing Congress, governors, legislators, university governing boards, the media, administrators, and faculty members. The access and affordability issues that have emerged in higher education in the United States are multifaceted and not easily addressed because so many different entities are involved.

Further, we should acknowledge that many of the problems we face relate to our overall economic and social landscape. Stagnant household incomes and increasing economic inequality influence the amounts of debt students incur and their later abilities to repay their debts. They are among the reasons why even moderate increases in net college costs prove problematic for some students and families.

These economic realities do not absolve parties such as legislatures, governing boards, college presidents, and faculty for their actions, but they are circumstances that should not be ignored.

FOUR

Cross-Subsidies and Affordability in Public Higher Education

Advertised tuition prices should thus be interpreted akin to the charges listed on a health-care billing statement, meaning they bear little relationship to what many people actually pay.
　　—Keith Humphreys in the *Washington Post*, September 13, 2016

Student fees at public institutions are of particular concern due to both the magnitude of the fees in many states and their rapid growth.
　　—Robert Kelchen in the *Review of Higher Education*,
　　　Summer 2016

The extent to which a public institution of higher education is (or is not) affordable depends upon many different factors, one of which is a complex set of subsidies that flow into public colleges and universities from governmental and private sources. The majority of public university students are subsidized because they do not pay tuition and fees as high as the cost expended educating them. However, in some states, out-of-state tuition and fee charges are required to reflect the "full cost" of educating out-of-state students.*

---

*Nevertheless, many states have negotiated tuition exchange programs with neighboring states that either give students from those states "in-state" tuition status, or limit their

By whatever methods colleges or universities accumulate revenues, they invariably then engage in cross-subsidization behavior whereby some students and programs receive or send financial support to other students and programs. Two psychology majors taking identical course schedules may pay different net prices based upon their household incomes. Or an engineering-student brother may pay a higher net price than his history-major sister even though both come from the same family.

The subsidies and cross-subsidies in four-year public colleges and universities are sufficiently complex that it will take two chapters to describe them in detail. While most citizens aren't accustomed to thinking of higher education in this way, the financial world of public higher education teems with subsidies and cross-subsidies. It is a situation in which some students and citizens support other students and citizens, albeit often without either party being aware of the situation. The reader should not infer that cross-subsidization is either bad policy or illegal. My intent is to clarify rather than to damn.

The moral to this story is that whether college is affordable to a particular student often depends upon which subsidies and cross-subsidies they receive, and how much they receive. Not all students are treated the same, even if they are pursuing the same major in the same institution.

The best place to start is to do a quick analysis of the major sources of revenue that public colleges and universities receive.

SOURCES OF HIGHER-EDUCATION REVENUE

If there is a college or university that does not receive financial subsidies from the outside, primarily from governments and private donors, then they have escaped public notice. Virtually all institutions, and especially those that are public, receive state general fund tax support, tax preferences, gifts from private donors, and grant support for specific activities—including research—from government agencies and private foundations. Institutions also operate revenue-generating auxiliary enterprises that range from residence halls

---

out-of-state tuition charge to no more than, say, 150 percent of the in-state level. Two examples of these types of agreements are the Midwest Student Exchange and the Western Interstate Commission for Higher Education.

FIGURE 4-1

Percentage Distribution and Sources of Total Revenue at Public Degree-Granting Postsecondary Institutions of Higher Education, 2014–15

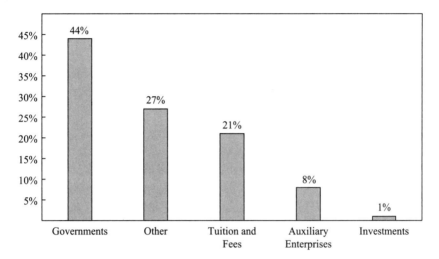

Source: "Postsecondary Institution Revenues," National Center for Education Statistics, figure 1 (https://nces.ed.gov/programs/coe/indicator_cud.asp).

Note: Does not sum to 100 percent because of rounding.

to intercollegiate athletics. Figure 4-1 illustrates the typical revenue sources of public institutions of higher education in 2014–15. The 44 percent contribution from governments predominantly represents a public subsidy to institutions of higher education from state governments, even while the federal government has become an increasingly important source of funds in recent years.

The idiosyncratic domain of subsidies can be likened to the proverbial briar patch of folklore—a thorny acreage that is difficult to penetrate and understand, and powerfully resistant to outsiders who have the temerity to cast doubt on the size, direction, or effects of the subsidies. The nearest analog to what one sees in higher education is the federal income tax system, which (like higher education) contains a welter of subsidies, preferential tax rates, protections from competition, and attempts to improve perceived equity. In economic terminology, both the federal income tax system and public higher education often reflect "rent-seeking" behavior: attempts by individuals and groups to insulate themselves from the discipline of the marketplace so that they can earn higher wages or returns than they would in a freely operating, nonmonopolized market.*

Just as the federal income tax system has proven to be strongly resistant to change—even modifications that a clear majority of Americans say they prefer usually go nowhere—the public higher-education establishment often stoutly resists attempts to alter the peculiar universe of subsidies that has been established on campuses. Entrenched special interest groups (such as those who promote intercollegiate athletics) energetically defend their subsidized benefits, often mobilizing vocal off-campus constituencies on their behalf. Imitating Brer Rabbit in the Uncle Remus fable, once inside the briar patch and earning their rents, faculty, administrators, alumni, and friends tend to scoff at those who venture to suggest changes or improvements.

Gordon Winston encapsulated this topsy-turvy world years ago when he noted that "virtually all U.S. colleges and universities sell their primary product—education—at a price that is far less than the average cost of its production." A for-profit business that consistently sold nearly all of its products at prices well below its fully allocated costs of production eventually would go out of business.[1] Not so in higher education. The data in figure 4-1 reveal that only about one-fifth of the revenue of a public college or university is derived from tuition and fees. The message is that the education of a typical public in-state undergraduate is highly subsidized. Further, because of interstate tuition compacts and local options, the same holds true for many out-of-state students as well. Thus, it is fair to conclude that only a small minority of American public college and university students pays the full costs of their educations, and virtually no student pays more than this.[†]

---

*The cherished academic institution of faculty tenure provides an illustration. One can build a plausible rationale for faculty tenure that is based upon the need to provide and protect academic freedom. Nevertheless, in today's colleges and universities, faculty tenure often functions as an employment security device that effectively enables its beneficiaries to avoid the marketplace competition of other faculty who might take their places.

†Even this judgment, however, is subject to qualifications. Should we be talking about the average cost of educating a student, which would include fully allocated overhead costs, etc., or the marginal cost, which would include only the incremental costs of educating a student and would pay attention to class sizes, use of equipment and facilities, etc.? It is difficult enough to calculate average cost. Estimating marginal costs is beyond the competence of most institutions of higher education.

THE MOST SIGNIFICANT HIGHER EDUCATION SUBSIDIES

A nonexhaustive list of the subsidies and cross-subsidizes in public higher education includes the following:

Revenue Subsidies

- Governments (local, state, federal) provide financial and resource support and tax exemptions that allow higher-education institutions to offer prices per student that are below their actual operational costs per student.

- Private support comes from individuals and organizations in the form of gifts and grants that similarly support prices that are lower than actual operational costs per student.

Cross-Subsidies

- Nonresident students pay higher tuition and fees that enable resident students to pay lower tuition and fees.

- Undergraduate students pay prices that generate revenues large enough to enable institutions to shift some of those revenues to support graduate programs and students.

- Undergraduate students pay prices that generate revenues sufficient to shift some of those revenues to support faculty research.

- Freshmen and sophomore students pay prices that generate revenues that are transferred to support the educational programs of junior and senior students.

- Students in the humanities and social sciences subsidize those in the sciences and engineering.

- Most international students subsidize students from the United States.*

- Nonathletes pay prices (often in the form of fees) that go directly to intercollegiate athletic programs and athletes.

---

*About 80 percent of international students pay the full published, out-of-state price, according to Jon Marcus, "Student Subsidies of Classmates' Tuition Add to Anger over Rising College Costs," *Hechinger Report*, August 29, 2012.

- Younger faculty perform duties that often are identical to those of older faculty, and are equally productive, but are paid lower salaries.

- Faculty in low-demand academic disciplines perform duties that may be identical to those of faculty in high-demand disciplines, but are paid lower salaries than faculty in the high-demand disciplines.

- Part-time faculty usually are paid much lower prices for teaching the same course at the same time as full-time faculty.

- Faculty who teach hundreds of students receive no more remuneration than those who teach a handful of students.

- Students living off-campus (sometimes hundreds or thousands of miles away from the home campus) pay fees for programs and services that realistically they never will be able to access.

- Students taking courses in the evening or on weekends may pay different prices for the same course than a student who takes the course during the day or the regular week.

Public colleges and universities often are reluctant to talk about this welter of cross-subsidies that exist on their campuses because such discussions frankly prove to be divisive.[2] The notion that students majoring in disciplines such as psychology actively subsidize chemistry majors is likely to promote unhappiness among psychology majors and their families and perhaps most students majoring in most disciplines in the humanities and social sciences. Nevertheless, intuitively most individuals accept the notion that it is more expensive to produce chemists and engineers than psychologists and historians. The salient question is whether the chemists and engineers should pay premium tuition and fee rates as a consequence.

DIFFERENTIAL FEES

At Purdue University, in the 2017–18 academic year, majors in computer science and engineering paid an extra $2,050 in tuition on top of the basic in-state tuition and fee charge of $10,002 that all students paid. Management students paid $1,436 extra. Honors College students paid an additional $200. These fees presumably reflected the higher costs associated with educating majors in those disciplines.[3]

Does the incremental tuition revenue raised by these fees go to these programs? Probably in a formal sense, yet it would be very difficult to tell in actuality because wily administrators are capable of counteracting such budget increases by reducing other budget allocations to the units they know will benefit from dedicated fees. In such cases, the special incremental tuition is simply another way for the institution or program to earn more revenue that they can deploy elsewhere.

Interestingly, a variant of the special fee rationale often is used by state legislators when they reduce university budget allocations. They believe (with some validity) that in contrast to many other state agencies, state colleges and universities have the ability to raise tuition and fees and thereby avoid significant injuries because of budget cuts. Thus, if budget cuts must be made, higher education should soak up more than its proportional share because institutions have the ability to defend themselves from such cuts by means of tuition and fee increases.

Do the incremental tuition charges at Purdue fully account for differences in the cost of educating students in various disciplines? We would need to see precise Purdue numbers to know, but data from other institutions suggest that it is even more costly to educate engineers, for example, than is accounted for by the $2,050 surcharge.

CROSS-SUBSIDIES BASED ON STUDENT/HOUSEHOLD INCOMES

Cross-subsidies of students based upon the incomes of the students and their families often are not perceived in the same way as are cross-subsidies by discipline. Eyebrows sometimes furrow when someone openly suggests that public universities are a mechanism whereby well-to-do families subsidize less financially fortunate families. However, redistribution practices similar to this are not unusual in markets outside of higher education. The prices paid by Medicare recipients for prescription drug coverage are tailored to recipients' incomes—higher-income individuals pay more than lower-income individuals for the same coverage. Further, most individuals are neither surprised nor appalled when parties selling homes, jewelry, or automobiles guesstimate the incomes of prospective customers before quoting them a price.

Even so, imagine the reaction if McDonald's began to charge its customers different prices for identical hamburgers, with the price differentials depending upon the customers' incomes. Or consider a world in which Apple began to require customers to supply the equivalent of a FAFSA (Free Application for Federal Student Aid) prior to the purchase of a new iPhone7, and this were followed by Apple quoting each customer a unique price for the phone based upon that customer's FAFSA.

We don't live in a world that requires FAFSAs when we purchase iPhones, groceries, or virtually any other good or service, but the primary reason may be that sellers have not figured out quick, inexpensive ways to estimate customers' incomes with accuracy. By contrast, at least fifteen states have adopted written policies that explicitly approve of tuition and fee policies that redistribute funds from students coming from upper-income households to students coming from lower-income households. The remaining thirty-five states may not officially have adopted such policies, but they and their public colleges and universities implement them all the same. *Today, it is widely understood, if not accepted, that the effective net price paid by public college and university students will reflect the incomes of the households from which the individual students emanate. Only occasionally does one encounter naysayers or doubters on this issue.*

The magnitude of the price differentials paid by students based upon household incomes is surprisingly large on some campuses (the University of Michigan and the University of North Carolina at Chapel Hill provide prime examples) and revealingly small on other campuses (for example, Historically Black Colleges and Universities (HBCUs) such as Delaware State University and Jackson State University). As we shall see, the point is that the affordability of a college education to a specific student rises and falls on the basis of such differentials. Let's look at the evidence.

NET PRICE RATIOS

Recall from chapter 2 that in 2016–17, the average net price paid by an undergraduate student at Illinois State University was $19,227. However, students coming from households earning $110,000 or more annually paid an average net price of $25,937, while the average net price for students emanating from households with annual incomes between $0 and $30,000 was only $14,083. Thus, the ratio of the higher-income group's net price to the lower-income group's net price was $25,937/$14,083 = 1.84. Keep that ratio—1.84—in mind as we look at other institutions.

In reality, Illinois State engages in less financial redistribution among its student body than many public colleges and universities. Let's verify this.

Consider table 4-1, which reports similar ratios for the Top 28 public colleges and universities in *U.S. News and World Report's* fall 2017 annual ranking.* (*U.S. News* seeks to report a Top 25, but ties in rankings that year resulted in a Top 28.) Within this sample of twenty-eight prestigious public institutions, in 2016–17 the average ratio of the net price paid by students from the highest-income households to the overall average net price paid by students from lower-income households was 3.16—substantially higher than Illinois State's 1.84. After seeing these data, a senior administrator at one of the elite twenty-eight averred to me, "We soak our upper-income students more than Illinois State because they can afford it and within reason will pay whatever we choose to charge them."

Table 4-1 reveals that the elite public institutions redistributed substantial income away from their upper-income students to their lower-income students. Indeed, the highest ratios were 7.69 at the University of Michigan's flagship Ann Arbor campus and 5.59 at the College of William and Mary. At the other end of the spectrum, Pittsburgh recorded a 1.47 ratio, followed by Penn State at 1.59. The latter institutions are not so heavily involved in redistributing income via their tuition and financial aid systems.

What do such differentials amount to in terms of actual dollars? At Illinois State, the difference between the net price paid by students from the highest-income households and the net price paid by students from the lowest-income households was $11,854 in 2016–17. At the typical Top 28 institution, it was $16,034 per student, including $21,060 per student at *U.S. News's* top-ranked UCLA, $21,752 at the University of Michigan Ann Arbor, and $19,752 at the University of North Carolina at Chapel Hill (see figure 4-2).

Nevertheless, other institutions are even more actively engaged in redistribution, led by the College of William and Mary (which exhibited a $25,439 differential between the average net price it charged students coming from $110,000+ annual income backgrounds and the average charge it assessed those coming from $0–30,000 annual income backgrounds). William and

---

*The rankings effectively reflect the 2015–16 academic year.

TABLE 4-1

Net Price Ratios for the Elite 28: *U.S. News and World Report*'s Highest-Ranked Public Universities, Resident Students, 2016–17

Institution	Ratio of $110K+ Net Price to $0–30K Net Price	Pell Grant Percentage
UC Berkeley	3.63	28%
UC Davis	2.85	39%
UC Irvine	3.34	42%
UCLA	3.56	34%
UC San Diego	3.25	38%
UC Santa Barbara	3.04	36%
Clemson U	1.61	17%
U Connecticut	2.39	21%
U Florida	2.66	26%
U Georgia	1.68	22%
Georgia Tech	2.43	15%
U Illinois CU	3.34	21%
U Maryland CP	2.65	19%
U Michigan	7.69	15%
U Minnesota	3.13	19%
UNC Chapel Hill	5.75	22%
Ohio S U	2.53	20%
Penn S U	1.59	15%
U Pittsburgh	1.47	16%
Purdue U	4.22	17%
Rutgers U	2.39	29%
Texas A&M	2.21	21%
U Texas Austin	2.10	24%
U Virginia	3.05	12%
Virginia Tech	1.92	16%
U Washington	3.41	21%
College of W&M	5.59	11%
U Wisconsin	3.35	13%
Averages	**3.10**	**22%**

Source: College Navigator, National Center for Education Statistics (http://nces.ed.gov/college navigator).

FIGURE 4-2

**Difference in Net Prices Paid by Resident Students Coming from
Households with Annual Incomes $110K+ and from Households with
Annual Incomes $0–30K at the Elite 28:** *U.S. News and World Report*'s
Top 28 Public Institutions, 2016–17

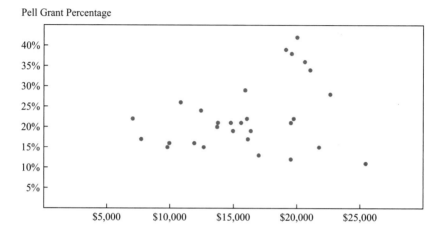

Source: College Navigator (http://nces.ed.gov/collegenavigator).

Mary's ability to redistribute in this fashion reflects in part the reality that it enrolls the smallest percentage of Pell Grant students (11 percent) of any public college or university in the country. Strategically, the institution has made the decision to enroll a small number of lower-income students, but then to support them very well. Institutions that choose to enroll larger proportions of Pell Grant students would be stretched mightily to pursue the same approach.

The University of Georgia's $7,077 differential between the net prices paid by the highest-income students and the lowest-income students was the smallest among the Top 28 institutions, followed by Clemson at $7,740. Pell Grant students accounted for 17 percent of Clemson's undergraduate student body in 2016–17, while they were 22 percent at Georgia. Both percentages are at or below the national average (which is slightly more than 38 percent) and the Top 28 average of 22 percent.* Consciously or not, Clemson and Georgia

---

*A 2006 Lumina Foundation report found a 22 percent Pell Grant recipient average at fifty flagship state universities compared to the then 35 percent Pell Grant recipient average for all of

A tuition and fee caveat. In 2011, the Cornell Higher Education Research Institute found that 11 percent of all master's-degree-level institutions and 41 percent of all doctoral-degree-level institutions have differential tuition policies whereby students in some disciplines (most commonly business, engineering, and nursing) pay higher tuition rates than the institution's published rate for undergraduates. This means that published tuition rates and computed net prices often underestimate actual student expenses.[4]

appear to have decided not to enroll large numbers of Pell Grant students as well as not to engage in large-scale redistribution of income.*

The Commonwealth of Pennsylvania provides an interesting exception to the general tendency of the Top 28 institutions to redistribute their tuition collections in favor of students from lower-income households. Not only are Penn State and Pittsburgh high-tuition institutions, but also they do not enroll significant proportions of Pell Grant recipients (only 15 percent at Penn State and 16 percent at Pittsburgh). Additionally, as can be seen in table 4-1, the two institutions' ratios of the average prices they charge their highest income students to those they charge their lowest income students were 1.59 and 1.47, respectively.†

Students from lower-income households in Pennsylvania do not lack for opportunities to attend public colleges and universities. The state as a whole, however, operates high-tuition public colleges and universities that do not

---

higher education. Danette Gerald and Kati Haycock, "Engines of Inequality: Diminishing Equity in the Nation's Premier Public Universities" (Washington, D.C.: Education Trust, 2006).

*Institutions occupying market positions similar to those of Clemson and Georgia Tech might observe that they would have to admit less-qualified students if they were to admit more Pell Grant students. Additional Pell Grant students could exert downward pressure on retention and graduation statistics and require significant institutional financial aid. Hence, many institutions facing this situation choose admissions and financial aid policies that effectively limit Pell Grant students.

†An important reason why Penn State and Pitt are high-tuition institutions is that the levels of state general fund tax support per student they receive are rather low in a national context.

receive high levels of tax support per student. Pennsylvania has not placed a high priority on providing access to students from lower-income households. As a consequence, its two flagship state universities (the main Penn State campus and the main University of Pittsburgh campus) enroll high proportions of students from upper-income households. IPEDS (Integrated Postsecondary Education Data System) data suggest that approximately 67 percent of Penn State's undergraduates come from the top two College Navigator income classes; it is approximately 61 percent at Pitt. The Top 25 average is 45 percent, with the University of California, Irvine's 20 percent being the lowest among the Top 25.*

A bipartisan movement has begun to emerge in the U.S. Congress that would require colleges with relatively few low-income students to enroll higher percentages of such students if the campuses wish to continue their participation in federal loan programs. Institutions failing to do so would pay the equivalent of a fine to the federal government. Were some variant of this policy to be implemented, it likely would encourage institutions with brand magnetism to increase their out-of-state tuition as well as to engage in additional redistribution of costs by charging higher net prices to students from upper-income households. These tactics would generate the additional funds needed to meet the demands of the increasing number of lower-income students for financial aid. Actions such as these, though predictable, no doubt would be classified as unintended side effects by the uninitiated.

THE RANKINGS DEMON

Espeland and Sauder's *Engines of Anxiety* (2016) captured much of the frenzy associated with the chase for rankings by focusing on the impact of those rankings and related reputation cultivation on institutional decision making.[5] Though their primary interest was law schools, the duo documented the distorting impact of national rankings on admission standards, faculty salaries and research, fundraising, job placement—indeed, virtually everything—in today's colleges and universities. Espeland and Sauder wrote, "Nearly everyone we spoke with lived in dread of the inevitable day when the new

---

*A reviewer noted (accurately) that IPEDS household income data for financial aid recipients may not be precise.

rankings would come showing that the school had dropped to a worse number or tier." They concluded that the rankings have evolved from an attempt to measure what *is* going on into a motivating influence that determines what *will* go on.

Approvingly, Espeland and Sauder cited Leon Botstein, the president of Bard College, who lamented, "An entire industry that's supposed to be populated by the best minds in the country—theoretical physicists, writers, critics—is bamboozled by a third-rate news magazine"—an indelicate reference to *U.S. News and World Report*. *New York Times* columnist Frank Bruni has argued that a ranking system such as that of *U.S. News and World Report* "shortchanges certain gems."[6] "Gaming" the rankings—finding ways to massage the student body or the data in order to improve one's rankings—has become the unspoken task of many a dean or vice president. Nonetheless, the pursuit of rankings has become such an ingrained part of American higher education that National Public Radio now ranks the rankings.

To be sure, the admissions tradeoffs that campuses confront do not present them with a torturous academic equivalent of Sophie's choice. Even so, most campuses and their faculties struggle mightily with the alternatives they must face. Many institutions place a high value on equity and inclusion even as they also covet rankings and prestige. Nonetheless, putting lofty rhetoric aside, the actions of many public campuses reveal that when the proverbial rubber hits the road, they are more concerned about their rankings and prestige than they are about their accessibility to the public.

Arizona State University (ASU) under its president, Michael Crowe, is one of a handful of national public research university exceptions. ASU consciously has adopted admissions and outreach policies that are not conducive to high rankings. Its main Tempe campus in 2017 was ranked 115th among national universities and 53rd among public national universities by *U.S. News and World Report*.[7]

TRADEOFFS EVERYWHERE

Table 4-2 highlights several of the admissions and financial tradeoffs that college administrators, boards of trustees, and, implicitly, legislators and governors face. To be a "state university" that is a portal of mobility and opportunity to all segments of a state's population requires institutions to admit and support some talented students who have great financial need as

TABLE 4-2

**Net Price Ratios and Pell Grant Percentages for the Typical 49:
Resident Students, 2016–17**

Institution	Ratio of $110K+ Net Price to $0–30K Net Price	Pell Grant Percentage
Alabama A&M U*	1.29	71%
U Alaska Anchorage	1.69	22%
Northern Ariz U	1.73	35%
U Cent Ark	1.47	40%
Cal S Chico	2.22	45%
Adams S U	1.78	52%
Central Conn S U	1.56	34%
Delaware S U*	1.53	49%
Fla Gulf Coast U	1.60	30%
Ga Coll & S U	1.34	19%
U H Hilo	1.72	48%
Lewis-Clark S C	1.25	35%
Western Ill U	1.62	48%
U So Ind	2.15	26%
U No Iowa	1.72	26%
Pittsburg S U	1.53	36%
Morehead S U	1.60	32%
Nicholls S U	1.60	38%
U So Maine	1.93	36%
Morgan S U*	1.47	52%
Westfield S U	1.72	31%
Grand Valley S U	1.81	31%
Bemidji S U	1.80	31%
Jackson S U*	1.35	61%
U Central Missouri	1.81	32%
MSU Billings	1.40	32%
Chadron S C	1.36	35%
Nevada S C	1.43	40%
Keene S C	1.36	23%
William Paterson U	1.06	47%
E New Mex S U	1.79	33%
SUNY Potsdam	2.14	50%
No Car Central U*	1.77	65%
Dickinson S U	1.68	22%
Wright S U	1.46	34%

(continued)

TABLE 4-2 (CONTINUED)

Institution	Ratio of $110K+ Net Price to $0–30K Net Price	Pell Grant Percentage
U Cent Okla	0.90	34%
E Oregon S U	1.61	45%
Indiana U Pa	1.57	37%
RI College	2.32	42%
SC S U*	0.99	74%
Northern S U	1.59	17%
Tenn S U*	1.28	56%
Sam Houston S U	1.88	35%
So Utah U	1.23	33%
Johnson S U	1.61	48%
Radford U	1.84	33%
Central Wash U	2.19	36%
West Va S U*	1.15	30%
U Wisc Platteville	2.02	24%
Averages	**1.64**	**39%**

Source: College Navigator, National Center for Education Statistics (http://nces.ed.gov/college navigator).

Note: The asterisks refer to Historically Black Colleges and Universities.

well as some whose standardized test scores may not meet the institution's usual standards, but who clearly exhibit exceptional promise. The problem is that as laudable as the notion of "portals of opportunity" might be, moving in that direction is not a free good. Admitting such students requires that additional resources be devoted to admissions offices, generous on-campus support for such students, and incremental financial aid.

An institution's choice concerning how many Pell Grant recipient students it decides to enroll carries with it racial and ethnic implications. Larger proportions of Pell Grant recipients are members of minority groups than is true for non–Pell Grant recipients. *Thus, when the Top 25 limit the proportions of their student bodies that are Pell Grant recipients, implicitly they also have made a decision that will limit their enrollment of minority students.*[8]

Many institutions and their faculties are willing to bear the higher financial costs of enrolling more Pell Grant students. However, they often exhibit less willingness to pay the *reputational* costs associated with actions such as enrolling larger proportions of Pell Grant undergraduates. And reputational costs there are. The weight of evidence is unambiguous: higher proportions of Pell Grant students at an institution are associated with lower student retention and graduation rates, reduced standardized test scores, and lower incomes subsequently being earned by its graduates. Perceived deterioration in these variables translates to lower national rankings and reduced prestige, which in turn may well translate into fewer admissions applications from less qualified applicants.

Which college president wants to become known as the prexy who oversaw a noticeable decline in his or her institution's national rankings? In his or her dreams, such a president might hope that understanding faculty, alumni, donors, the media, and the public would focus upon the greater accessibility of the institution as well as its role in supporting societal demographic transition and producing the next generation's leaders. Yet it is unlikely to be so. National institutional rankings have joined football teams in acquiring larger-than-life status on many elite or aspiring elite state university campuses.

PRACTICAL POLITICAL CONSIDERATIONS

Not to be ignored is a collateral effect often associated with less inclusive admissions strategies that do not include high proportions of Pell Grant students. Students from upper-income families who present excellent high school records and high standardized test scores have much greater influence and political clout than Pell Grant students. These "ideal" students can make more noise and apply more pressure than Pell Grant students, who may not even understand the appropriate power levers to pull. They know and provide financial support to state legislators, whom they can pressure to ensure that "not too many" admissions slots are devoted to Pell Grant recipients or nonresident applicants. Squeaky wheels invite the application of grease. Legislators and members of boards of trustees respond by adopting policies and guidelines that ensure generous admissions access for their friends, supporters, and clients. Note that this particular dynamic does not develop because many, or even any, of the participants have strong objections to more-inclusive admissions policies or to Pell Grant recipients. Indeed, they likely admire students from lower-income households who struggle to find a way to attend college and graduate. Instead, it is the logical outcome of political processes that are as old as representative government. The result, however, generally is reduced access and affordability for students coming from lower-income households.

A VERY DIFFERENT PERSPECTIVE: INTRODUCING THE TYPICAL 49

Readers may regard the elite public institutions as a narrow and unrepresentative sample, and they are correct, though they constitute a highly influential group that often sets the pace for all other institutions. More than 600 accredited four-year public colleges and universities exist in the United States. Most are members of the American Association of State Colleges and Universities (AASCU), and some are Historically Black Colleges and Universities (HBCUs). Some are both. Non-flagship four-year public colleges and universities enroll about five times as many head-count students as the flagships. Let us label this forty-nine-institution sample the "Typical 49" and examine their behavior in the tuition and fee arena.*

Table 4-2 reveals that the Typical 49 institutions do not engage in as much income redistribution as either the Top 25 or Illinois State, and they enroll much larger percentages of Pell Grant students. Their average ratio of the net price paid by students coming from the highest-income class to those coming from the lowest-income class in 2016–17 was only 1.64, compared to the Top 28's 3.10 and Illinois State's 1.84.

California State University, Chico, recorded the largest "highest to lowest" net price ratio in the Typical 49 sample: 2.22 However, twenty-one of the twenty-eight elite institutions reported comparable ratios larger than this. This underlines the extent to which nearly all of the Top 25 (or 28) institutions are strongly committed to redistributing their tuition collections on the basis of the reported household incomes of their students. Whether they actively publicize their activities in this regard is another matter.

Table 4-2 supplies some of the reasons why the Typical 49 members do not redistribute income as actively as the Top 25. In 2016–17, the Typical 49 members enrolled far more Pell Grant students (39 percent) than either the

---

*The Typical 49 sample contains one four-year public institution from every state except Wyoming. That state contains only one four-year public institution, the University of Wyoming, and it is a flagship university that does not belong in this group.

Top 28 (22 percent) or Illinois State (28 percent), and the premium they charged students coming to them from the highest-income households compared to the lowest-income households was much smaller (only $8,888 compared to the Top 25's $16,065 and Illinois State's $11,854). Put simply, the Typical 49 institutions do not have significant price-making power and hence cannot impose substantially higher net prices on students who come to them from the highest-income households. Roughly two of every five of their students are Pell Grant recipients, and the great majority of Pell Grants are awarded to students who come from households with annual incomes less than $30,000. These are not students who are capable of paying premium prices.

HISTORICALLY BLACK COLLEGES AND UNIVERSITIES (HBCUs)

The eight HBCUs in the Typical 49 sample (they are starred in table 4-2) display the group's major tendencies, but do so in a more pronounced fashion. They are not as heavily involved in redistributing income; the average ratio of the net price paid by their highest-income students to that paid by their lowest-income students is only 1.35. One HBCU president told me, "We can't redistribute income because we have so few upper-income students." On average, 60 percent of this sample of HBCU undergraduate students were Pell Grant recipients.

HBCUs occupy a distinctive higher-education niche. They exert a magnetism that causes many African American students to prefer them to majority institutions. Nevertheless, HBCUs usually possess very little pricing power because so many of their students emanate from lower-income households. Practically, this means that the HBCUs have relatively little ability to charge the elevated prices to students from higher-income households that would generate the revenues required to offer reduced net prices to students from lower-income households. They simply do not enroll large numbers of students who come from upper-income families.

Further, a perusal of tables 4-1 and 4-2 reveals that in many cases, flagship state universities underprice both HBCUs and members of the Typical 49. In South Carolina, for example, the average net price paid by a student coming from a household with a $0–$30,000 annual income at the University of South Carolina (Columbia) in 2016–17 was $12,386, while the same student would pay $21,094 at South Carolina State University, an HBCU, or $13,918 at Coastal Carolina University. In Florida, the comparable net prices were $6,594 at the University of Florida and $12,459 at Florida A&M, an HBCU. The comparable price at Florida Gulf Coast University, a Typical 49 institution, was $11,681.

These differences underline the difficult competitive challenges that HBCUs and members of the Typical 49 face and help explain why some of them have been experiencing declining enrollments.

ARE FEES A PROBLEM?

"Tuition and fees" is a phrase that rolls easily off the tongue, and many abbreviate it to "tuition." Nevertheless, the "fees" portion of that equation has garnered increased attention in recent years because some assert that rampant increases in mandatory student fees are at least partially responsible for the upward spiral that has occurred in tuition and fees. Fees support activities that range from building construction, libraries, intercollegiate athletics, health insurance, campus safety, student government, parking, information technology, once-surging energy prices, and semi-political activities such as public interest research groups, to providing campus amenities such as exercise and wellness facilities, big-name entertainment, and climbing walls.

The state auditor in Missouri issued a report in 2016 that focused on special fees paid by students at Missouri's public campuses: the fees neatly avoid the state's current ban on tuition increases that exceed the growth of the Consumer Price Index.[9] Fees often are not subject to the same legislative controls as tuition, and they even maintain a degree of popularity with students. A 2013 National Bureau of Economic Research (NBER) study concluded that investments in campus amenities frequently paid off for the campuses making them. NBER economists found evidence that many students were willing to pay more for campus amenities and that they were attracted by them when considering where to enroll.[10]

The most comprehensive analysis of student fees has been conducted by Robert Kelchen, who found that fees add approximately 21 percent to the price of tuition at public institutions. The median fee in 2016–17 among four-year public institutions was $1,885 for first-time, full-time students.[11]

Kelchen examined 532 four-year public institutions between 2001–02 and 2012–13. Among other things, he found that amenity-related fees were limited to a small percentage of colleges, but that fees tended to be higher at institutions with lower freshman applicant yield rates and at those dealing with legislative or central board tuition caps. Fee increases were lower when unemployment was high and when gubernatorial or legislative approval were required. However, his explanatory regressions could explain only about one-quarter of the variance in campus fee levels.

Kelchen argues that fees have been rising faster than tuition. However, Delta Cost Project data do not encourage this view where flagship institutions are concerned. Between 2001–02 and 2013–14, only twenty-nine of sixty-four flagship state universities for whom comparable data were available increased the percentages of their tuition and fee revenue that were derived from fees rather than tuition. For these sixty-four flagships, the percentage of their total tuition and fees accounted for by fees declined from 21.19 percent to 17.68 percent.[12]

For the Typical 49, the story was much the same. Comparable data were available for thirty-six institutions; between 2001–02 and 2013–14, seventeen of them increased the proportion of their tuition and fees that emanated from fees rather than tuition. As a group, however, they were more dependent upon fees than the flagship institutions, earning 23.05 percent of their total tuition and fee revenues from fees as compared to 17.68 percent for the flagships. This is consistent with Kelchen's surmise that institutions with less selective admissions policies rely more on fees to pay for amenities and other improvements that they perceive will improve their admissions competitiveness.

It is well to remember, however, that the decision to call something a fee rather than tuition often reflects local quirks and history. On University of California campuses, for example, historically there was no tuition charge, with everything that we ordinarily regard as tuition and fees being classified as a fee. This practice changed several years into this century. On the other hand, during the same time span, the opposite was true at the University of Alabama, where to this day no part of tuition and fees is labeled a fee unless it is connected to a specific academic program such as engineering. In Massachusetts, tuition is minimal, but fees are substantial. Local custom dictates.

In any case, students as a group at flagship institutions in general and on the elite public campuses have price inelastic demands for the higher-education products they consume; that is, they are not very sensitive to price increases. Price sensitivity increases as institutional prestige and selectivity decline. Virtually every student of price sensitivity has found the demand for higher education to be price inelastic, meaning that a given percentage increase in tuition and fees at a specific institution will elicit a smaller percentage decline in enrollment.[13] As a consequence, total tuition and fee revenue increases at that institution. Thus, tuition and fee increases pay off for the institution, at least in the short run.

Several qualifying comments are in order, however. With few exceptions, price sensitivity increases as time passes because consumers are better able to find and utilize alternatives. Second, the higher-education world of 2018 is very different than that addressed by previous studies. Head-count collegiate enrollment has fallen for a half decade, at least partially because of the unfavorable demographic trends that confront institutions in many states and the less than robust job markets many graduates face. A reasonable inference is that these developments have made students more price sensitive at institutions that do not enjoy high levels of brand magnetism (which is the majority of public institutions, especially those located in rural areas).[14] Nevertheless, until recently, few public college and university presidents and board members ever had to worry excessively about the reactions of student consumers to price increases.

FINAL THOUGHTS

Individuals newly appointed to public university governing boards who are not previously experienced in that capacity invariably are astonished at the sheer number of different activities and enterprises with which public universities are involved. Similarly, they express surprise at the variety of revenue sources and expenditures (most with accompanying restrictions) that characterize the financial life of their institution. Even new board members with significant business experience often find the finances of a large public university surprisingly complicated.

Many trustees (new or not) of governing boards have given little thought to the welter of subsidies and cross-subsidies that routinely distinguish public colleges and universities today. Virtually every institution is actively involved in redistributing income by means of financial aid systems that at some institutions (for example, the University of Michigan's flagship campus at Ann Arbor) charge effective net prices to students coming from upper-income families that are more than nine times as high as the prices charged students coming from low-income households.

Further, only some trustees focus intently on the accessibility of their institutions to academically qualified students from the lowest-income families in their states. If members of governing boards at the elite public universities are aware that on average only 22 percent of their undergraduates receive Pell Grants (compared to almost 40 percent nationally), then they typically say little about this. Nor do most trustees at the elite public institutions seem to understand that not all of the elite tread the same path. The six University of California campuses that are members of the Top 28 enroll a minimum of 28 percent of their undergraduates as Pell Grant students, and one (University of California, Irvine) enrolls 42 percent. Contrast this to the University of Virginia's 12 percent and the University of Michigan's 15 percent.[15]

It will suffice to note that relatively few members of public university governing boards raise access and affordability questions at board meetings, or in more private meetings with university administrators. Or if they do, these are not concerns that lead to soul searching, hand wringing, or action. *Instead, what emerges from nearly all board members are unanimous decisions to increase tuition and fees substantially faster than increases in the Consumer Price Index, median household income, and (critically) need-based financial aid. Pragmatically, this is the higher-education world in which we live.*

FIVE

A Closer Look at Redistributive
Student Pricing

Over the last decade, colleges have gotten very good at price discrimination.

—Kevin Carey, *Chronicle of Higher Education,*
November 26, 2012

C hapter 4 provided data showing the surprisingly large differences that exist between the net prices paid by students. Huge discrepancies also exist between the net prices students pay at one institution and another. For example, in 2016–17, the average net price paid by a low income, in-state undergraduate student living on the campus at the University of North Carolina at Chapel Hill was only $4,155, whereas it was $18,628 at the University of Alabama and $21,514 at Penn State.[1]

Net price differentials inside the same institution can be equally as dramatic. At the University of Michigan, students coming from the lowest-income households paid an average net price of only $3,249, but students coming from the highest-income bracket paid an average net price of $25,001. At Purdue, the comparable net prices were $5,019 and $21,323.

These net price differentials are considered instances of price discrimination by economists. The typical reason a for-profit firm engages in price discrimination is to increase its profits. It sizes up its customers and charges higher prices to those who are willing and able to pay them and lower prices to customers who plausibly would not otherwise have purchased anything at all, or who now will purchase more units because of the lower prices.*

As noted earlier, there is nothing inherently evil about price discrimination. It is widely practiced in virtually all economies of the world and much of it is mundane—for example, a movie theater charging a higher price per ticket in the evening than in the afternoon for the identical movie. Some price discrimination is applauded, as when a public utility charges higher prices for those who use electricity during peak load times, or who use water when there is a drought.

In the context of public higher education, a very important question concerning the price discriminatory activities of colleges and universities is what they do with the incremental revenues they generate from those activities. Subsequent chapters focus on that question, while this chapter documents the size of these revenues.

REDUCED NET PRICES OFFERED TO LOWER-INCOME STUDENTS

Figure 5-1 reports the average net prices paid by students who came to the Top 28 campuses in 2016–17 from households with annual incomes ranging between $0 and $30,000. Once again, Penn State and Pittsburgh are outliers. Neither campus enrolls a large proportion of Pell Grant recipients. Both campuses charged students from lower-income households a net price significantly higher than those offered by the other members of the Top 28. In fact, their net prices for the typical lower-income student were more than twice as high as the elite universities' average. By way of contrast, Michigan, William and Mary, North Carolina at Chapel Hill, and Purdue all offered their lowest-income students net prices below $5,100 annually.

Many higher-education advocates give lip service to the notion that public colleges and universities should occupy spots located in the southeast quadrant of figure 5-1. For example, the University of Florida, with 26 percent of its undergraduates with Pell Grants and an average net price of $6,544 for low-income students, meets this southeast quadrant standard by enrolling a

---

*That is, it charges higher prices to customers with less elastic demands and lower prices to customers with more elastic demands.

FIGURE 5-1

Average Net Price Paid by Undergraduate Students Coming from Households with Annual Incomes between $0 and $30,000: The Top 28, 2016–17

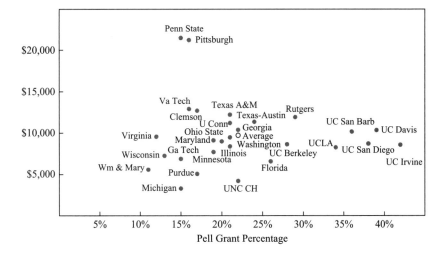

Source: College Navigator, National Center for Educational Statistics (http://nces.ed.gov /collegenavigator).

significant percentage of Pell Grant students and offering them a net price below the elite average.

Some candidates for elected office advocate that tuition and fees should be zero. This means that public colleges and universities would enroll significant percentages of Pell Grant recipients and offer them low net prices. Perhaps the six University of California campuses in the elite group fulfill this criterion. Each enrolls an above-average percentage of Pell Grant students and offers those students net prices that hover around the Top 28 average.[2]

Nothing of economic value ultimately is free, however. Institutions that aspire to be in the southeast quadrant of figure 5-1 must enjoy a combination of state support plus institutional resources that makes it possible for them to do so. This requirement immediately eliminates virtually every one of our Typical 49 institutions from consideration.

Inevitably, tradeoffs emerge. Enrolling more Pell Grant students usually exerts downward pressure on retention and graduation rates, on standardized

FIGURE 5-2

Comparing the Top 28 and the Typical 49 in Terms of the Net Prices Paid by Their Lower-Income Students and Pell Grant Percentages, 2015–16

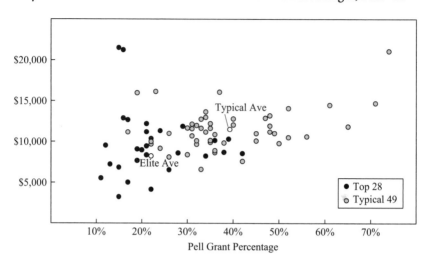

Source: College Navigator, National Center for Educational Statistics (http://nces.ed.gov/college navigator).

test scores, and on institutional rankings. These tendencies discourage institutions from enrolling larger percentages of Pell Grant students.

Figure 5-2 underlines the huge differences that often arise between the worlds inhabited by the Top 28 and the Typical 49. The black dots represent the Top 28 institutions. The gray dots denote institutions in the Typical 49, only two of whom enroll a lower proportion of Pell Grant students than the Top 28 average of 22 percent.

However, contrary to what some may believe, and Typical 49 institutions often advertise, frequently they are not the least expensive institutions for students from lower-income households to attend. Indeed, the average price paid by a lower-income student at a Top 28 institution in 2014–15 was only $9,696, 19 percent below the Typical 49 average of $11,516.[3] Simply put, the Top 28 have greater resources available that they can use to diminish the net price paid by their lower-income students. The question is whether they wish to do so.

INSTITUTIONAL CHOICE MAKING

Institutions repetitively make choices both about the nature of their student bodies and to what extent they will price discriminate, that is, how they will adjust the net prices paid by students coming to them from households with differing incomes. An institution's choices in this regard and its ability to offer lower net prices to lower-income students depend on several factors that provide it with critical incremental, discretionary revenues, including:

- its overall financial resources, including especially the volume of its state general fund support and private gifts;
- its brand magnetism, which has the potential to provide it with price-making power that translates to many students being willing to pay a net price equal to or near the institution's full published price;
- its ability to enroll nonresident students who pay tuition and fees substantially higher than those paid by in-state students.

We will delve into each of these revenue sources.

FINANCIAL RESOURCES: STATE GENERAL FUND SUPPORT

The net price that a student pays ultimately represents the interaction of supply and demand forces in an economically imperfect market characterized by many barriers to entry and strong product differentiation. On the supply side, the financial resources available to an institution play an important role in determining net price. Central to this for public colleges and universities is the size of the general fund tax support they receive from their state governments.

Within higher education, the most popular explanation of why tuition and fees have risen so rapidly focuses on the deleterious effects of falling state general fund support on net prices. We will examine this argument in greater detail in chapter 7 and find that it can explain much, but far from all, of the tuition and fee increases we have observed in public higher education. For now, it is sufficient to note that state general fund tax support for public higher education clearly has fallen if the measure is the real value of those funds per student. Figure 5-3 demonstrates this.

FIGURE 5-3

Nominal and Real State General Fund Support for Public Higher Education, FY 1999, FY 2008, and FY 2016 (Billions of Dollars)

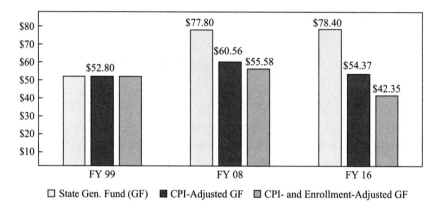

☐ State Gen. Fund (GF) ■ CPI-Adjusted GF ☐ CPI- and Enrollment-Adjusted GF

Sources: Grapevine, College of Education, Illinois State University (https://education.illinois state.edu/grapevine/tables) for state general fund support; the Bureau of Labor Statistics (www.bls.gov) for the Consumer Price Index; and the National Center for Education Statistics, Digests of Education Statistics (https://nces.ed.gov/programs/digest/), various years, for enrollment.

Note: The data do not include Illinois and Pennsylvania in any year because of comparability problems in FY 2016.

Figure 5-3 reports total dollar values for nominal, real, and real enrollment-adjusted state general fund support for public higher education in fiscal year 1999, fiscal year 2008, and fiscal year 2016. All values are expressed in 1999 prices. One can see that even though nominal state general fund support for public higher education increased by 47 percent from $52.80 billion to $77.80 billion in fiscal year 2008, its price-adjusted value was only $60.56 billion, and this fell to $55.58 billion after a further adjustment for the increased number of students being served. By fiscal year 2016, nominal state general fund support had increased slightly to $78.40 billion, but its real value had sunk to $54.37 billion and the enrollment-adjusted amount to only $42.35 billion.

The import of figure 5-3 is difficult to miss. While states are providing more total financial support for public higher education than ever before, the real, enrollment-adjusted value of that support has declined significantly—19.8 percent between fiscal year 1999 and fiscal year 2016. When public colleges and universities argue that they have been forced to

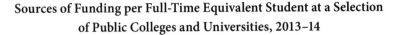

FIGURE 5-4

Sources of Funding per Full-Time Equivalent Student at a Selection of Public Colleges and Universities, 2013–14

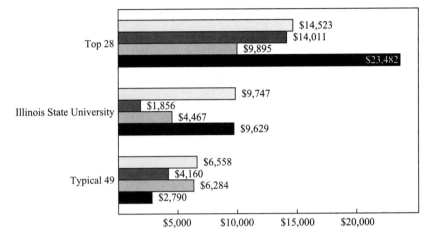

□ Tuition and Fees ■ Govt. Grants & Contracts ▨ State Gen. Fund ■ All Other

Source: IPEDS (http://nces.ed.gov/ipeds).

do more with less, figure 5-3 provides evidence in favor of this proposition. The salient question is whether this declining support is the major reason, or even the only reason, why tuition and fees have climbed so rapidly.

One can use IPEDS (the Integrated Postsecondary Education Data System of the U.S. Department of Education) to generate data that illuminate the situation for specific institutions.[4] Figure 5-4 shows us that the Top 28 institutions received far more general fund tax support per full-time equivalent (FTE) student* than either Illinois State University or the Typical 49. Given the distinctive missions and programmatic offerings of the Top 28, this hardly comes as a surprise, but it recalls the perhaps apocryphal remark of Ernest Hemingway in response to F. Scott Fitzgerald's observation that "the rich are different from you and me." Hemingway is said to have retorted, "Yes, they have more money."[5] So it is with the Top 28—they have far more money

---

*The FTE student count includes both resident and nonresident students and both undergraduate and graduate students.

to spend per student than the typical public college or university, and this is true of virtually every one of their major source of revenues.

FINANCIAL SUPPORT: GRANTS, CONTRACTS, AND GIFTS

Figure 5-4 also discloses that the average Top 28 member reaped more than triple the government grants and contracts revenue per FTE student than the average Typical 49 institution and about seven times as much as Illinois State. Further, the representative twenty-eight institutions collected substantially more revenue from other sources, such as investments. Indeed, this was the most fertile source of revenue for the elite institutions and reflects their flagship (and often land grant) status, which carries with it a variety of duties and opportunities. However, such revenues (which include private gifts) often are accompanied by earmarks that prevent discretionary use. Still, some dollars are fungible inside college and university budgets and can be moved across lines. This process of substitution enables institutions to redirect expenditures.

The message of figure 5-4 is straightforward—the elite public institutions have many more dollars per FTE student to spend than their less well-heeled public-institution brethren even without considering the revenues they collect from their students. Do they (or any public college or university) use their revenue streams to diminish their annual tuition and fee increases or even to lower tuition and fees? As we shall see, the answer to that question is "not very often." This has not gone unnoticed by either the public or elected officials.

FINANCIAL SUPPORT: ARE STATE GOVERNMENTS TO BLAME?

A recurring question is whether declining state general fund support can explain the full extent of the tuition and fee price explosion that has occurred in recent decades. The initial answer is "only some." Other factors such as increased institutional expenditures on administration, expensive noninstructional amenities such as exercise facilities and intercollegiate athletic teams, the relative inability of institutions to generate productivity increases, their own struggle for ratings, and the nature of federal loans programs potentially also are important. Weighing the relative importance of these factors is a task we pursue in chapter 7.

Robert Hiltonsmith, a senior policy analyst at Demos, a New York–based public policy organization, estimated in 2015 that 79 percent of tuition and fee increases at research institutions and 78 percent at master's and bachelor's degree institutions were due to "declining state support" of those institutions.[6] He did not, however, supply any data or analytics to support this contention, which did not disaggregate tuition and fee data and state funding data on an institution-by-institution basis. I do so in chapter 7, and my analysis results in lower estimates.

Using a more sophisticated methodology, economist Douglas Webber of Temple University concluded that a $100 decline in state funding led on average to a $257 increase in tuition and fees. His sample consisted of 479 four-year public institutions from 1987 through 2014. His estimate of the impact of state funding cuts upon tuition and fees increased to $314 for the years after 1999.[7]

The title of a 2017 Cato Institute study reveals its findings: "Not Just Treading Water: In Higher Education, Tuition Often Does More than Replace Lost Appropriations." Cato's Neal McCluskey concluded that only 57 percent of tuition and fee increases could be attributed to state appropriations cuts.[8]

The staff of the House Appropriations Committee in Virginia concluded that over a twenty-year period, reductions in state general fund tax support for Virginia's public institutions accounted for only about one-half of the size of the tuition and fee increases imposed by institutions during the same period.[9] Some institutions quibbled over the choice of time period, arguing that different time spans would have moderated the staff's conclusions.

We will have much more to say about the relationship between declining state funding and tuition and fee increases in chapter 7. Nonetheless, the flabby nature of the tuition/state funding relationship ought to temper the certainty with which some individuals assert that the clear reason why tuition and fees have increased so rapidly at public institutions is cuts in state funding.

A more productive approach to this question is to focus on individual institutions, which we will do in chapter 7. The situations and behaviors of individual institutions are highly diverse, and the tuition and fee behaviors of individual institutions in response to changes in state funding are anything but uniform. Averages that span all of public higher education provide useful information, but do not capture this diversity.

FINANCIAL SUPPORT: TUITION AND FEES

The significant gap that exists between the Top 28 and the Typical 49 institutions in terms of the levels of tuition and fees they collect per FTE student illuminates the difference in their available resources. Figure 5-4 illustrates that in 2013–14, the typical Top 28 institution collected almost $4,800 more in tuition and fee revenue per FTE student than Illinois State, and almost $8,000 more than members of the Typical 49. These revenues can usefully be divided into those derived from nonresident students and those coming from resident students. We will now examine each.

Financial Resources: Nonresident Enrollment

Out-of-state students who pay full published nonresident prices have become the equivalent of financial gold at public colleges and universities. Compared to in-state residents, nonresident students are considered fair game in terms of price increases, and virtually every institution behaves accordingly. They actively recruit more financially lucrative out-of-state students whom they can charge premium prices.

In fall 2016, 46 percent of undergraduates at both Georgia Tech and Purdue were out-of-state students. At the University of Michigan and Penn State, the comparable percentages were 49 percent and 47 percent, respectively.[10] These individuals uniformly paid much higher rates of tuition: in fall 2016 Michigan's nonresident tuition and fees premium over and above resident tuition and fees was the largest, at $31,008. All six University of California campuses in the Top 28 charged their out-of-state students $26,682 more than their in-state students.[11]

Table 5-1 reveals that the practice of assessing substantial out-of-state price differentials is a consistent strategy pursued by flagship state universities that enjoy substantial brand identification and magnetism. It can be very profitable: in 2016–17, the University of Alabama's Tuscaloosa campus raked in $311.2 million in incremental revenues from its out-of-state undergraduates over and above what it would have received had they been in-state. Thirteen institutions on the table 5-1 list earned more than $200 million in additional revenues during 2016–17 from the tuition and fee premiums they charged their out-of-state students, and only five garnered less than $50 million.

The three major determinants of the size of the incremental revenue an institution accrues from charging nonresident students higher prices are: (1) the total number of full-price out-of-state students it enrolls, (2) the size of the tuition and fee premium it charges them, and (3) the extent to which they discount their additional out-of-state revenues by granting scholarships and grants to out-of-state students. Some do not enroll as many nonresident students, but assess them very large tuition and fee premiums (examples: the Universities of North Carolina at Chapel Hill and Texas at Austin). The University of Alabama is well known for granting substantial scholarships to nonresident students it wishes to attract. Others successfully enroll both large proportions of out-of-state students and charge them high tuition and fee premiums (examples: the Universities of Alabama, Arizona, Colorado, Delaware, Iowa, Kansas, Kentucky, Michigan, Minnesota, Mississippi, Missouri, Montana, Oklahoma, Oregon, Purdue, Rhode Island, South Carolina, Virginia, West Virginia, Wisconsin, and Wyoming).[12]

The University of Michigan Ann Arbor indisputably ranked first in the table 5-1 sample as well as nationally in terms of the total incremental revenue it earned from charging higher prices to its out-of-state students. In 2016–17, I estimate that Maize and Blue administrators banked $433 million in additional revenues via this route. Likely, however, there were costs associated with generating these revenues (admissions expenses and scholarship aid, for example), and a precise accounting should take those costs into account. This qualification noted, Michigan nevertheless sits on top of a veritable revenue machine. It is not expending $433 million annually to attract these nonresident students.

The average flagship state university generated an estimated $145.42 million in incremental revenues from its nonresident tuition and fee premiums in 2016–17. Members of the Top 28 in the table 5-1 sample did a bit better, at an average of $160.8 million, and the Typical 49 trailed significantly at an average of $13.94 million (see table 5-2, which summarizes results for the forty-nine). *After the expense of generating these additional revenues is considered, these dollars constitute discretionary revenues that administrators can deploy for whatever other lawful purposes they decide and their governing boards approve.*

TABLE 5-1

The Total Revenue Premium Implied by Published Nonresident Tuition and Fees versus Resident Tuition and Fees for Undergraduate Students at Fifty Flagship Universities, 2016–17

Institution	Percent Nonresident Undergrads	Nonresident T&F	Resident T&F	Nonresident Price Premium	Approximate Undiscounted Incremental Institutional Annual Revenue (Millions)	Estimated Percentage of Resident T&F
U Alabama T	63%	$26,950	$10,470	$16,480	$311.20	165.20%
U Alaska F	11%	$21,584	$7,184	$14,400	$9.46	24.77%
U Arizona	45%	$36,017	$12,817	$23,200	$320.40	148.10%
U Arkansas	51%	$23,168	$8,820	$14,348	$151.80	109.32%
UC Berkeley	24%	$40,167	$13,485	$26,682	$176.21	62.48%
U Colorado	47%	$35,079	$11,531	$23,548	$289.42	181.10%
U Connecticut	34%	$35,858	$14,066	$21,792	$128.31	79.81%
U Delaware	62%	$32,250	$12,830	$19,420	$214.02	246.96%
U Florida	17%	$28,659	$6,381	$22,278	$120.14	71.51%
Georgia Tech	46%	$32,404	$12,212	$20,192	$130.18	140.85%
U Hawaii M	34%	$33,764	$11,732	$22,032	$86.84	96.74%
U Idaho	28%	$22,040	$7,232	$14,808	$36.89	79.63%
U Illinois UC	26%	$31,320	$15,698	$15,622	$124.12	34.97%
U Iowa	50%	$28,413	$8,325	$20,088	$221.50	241.30%
Kansas U	43%	$28,239	$11,455	$16,784	$125.61	110.53%
U Kentucky	39%	$26,156	$11,320	$14,836	$116.78	83.79%
Louisiana S U	19%	$27,491	$10,814	$16,677	$72.56	36.17%
U Maine	44%	$29,498	$10,628	$18,870	$69.34	139.50%
U Maryland CP	31%	$32,045	$10,181	$21,864	$182.20	96.48%
U Massachusetts	27%	$32,389	$15,256	$17,133	$97.37	41.54%
U Michigan	49%	$45,410	$14,402	$31,008	$407.79	206.86%
U Minnesota	36%	$23,806	$14,142	$9,664	$110.95	38.44%
U Mississippi	57%	$22,022	$7,754	$14,268	$137.15	243.92%

U Missouri	34%	$25,892	$9,518	$16,374	$119.24	88.62%
U Montana	36%	$23,669	$6,215	$17,454	$52.72	157.97%
U Nebraska	30%	$23,058	$8,537	$14,521	$82.15	72.90%
U Nevada R	30%	$21,052	$7,142	$13,910	$68.91	83.47%
U New Hamp	59%	$31,424	$17,624	$13,800	$95.30	112.68%
U New Mexico	17%	$21,929	$7,340	$14,589	$45.43	40.71%
UNC Chapel Hill	17%	$33,648	$8,566	$25,082	$72.38	59.97%
U North Dakota	64%	$19,290	$8,136	$11,154	$70.67	243.72%
Ohio S U	33%	$29,229	$10,037	$19,192	$324.59	94.18%
U Oklahoma	42%	$25,203	$10,881	$14,322	$119.27	95.31%
U Oregon	52%	$33,442	$10,762	$22,680	$205.28	228.30%
Penn S U	47%	$32,382	$17,900	$14,482	$250.15	71.75%
Purdue U	46%	$28,804	$10,002	$18,802	$250.12	160.13%
U Rhode Island	56%	$28,874	$12,884	$15,990	$121.75	157.95%
Rutgers U NB	18%	$30,023	$14,372	$15,651	$90.37	23.90%
U South Carolina	53%	$31,282	$11,854	$19,428	$244.30	184.82%
U South Dakota	39%	$11,688	$8,457	$3,231	$8.67	24.43%
Stony Brook U	26%	$26,239	$8,999	$17,240	$70.05	67.31%
U Tennessee	18%	$30,914	$12,724	$18,190	$65.73	31.38%
U Texas Austin	12%	$35,906	$10,110	$25,796	$112.81	34.97%
U Utah	31%	$27,039	$8,518	$18,521	$127.30	97.69%
U Vermont	79%	$40,364	$17,300	$23,064	$185.94	501.53%
U Virginia	34%	$45,058	$15,741	$29,317	$149.41	95.94%
U Washington	32%	$34,971	$10,753	$24,218	$218.53	105.99%
West Virginia U	55%	$22,488	$7,992	$14,496	$161.46	221.69%
U Wisconsin M	43%	$32,738	$10,488	$22,250	$270.02	160.04%
U Wyoming	49%	$16,215	$5,055	$11,160	$48.19	212.11%
Averages	38.7%	$29,151	$10,932	$18,218	$145.42	122.20%

Source: College Navigator, National Center for Education Statistics (http://nces.ed.gov/collegenavigator).

Note: FTE estimates are based upon IPEDS data for 2014–15 (https://nces.ed.gov/ipeds).

The interests of public universities and state governments may diverge where out-of-state students are concerned. Universities covet talented out-of-state students who pay premium prices and are not so concerned whether they remain inside the state to live and work once they have graduated. States like to import and retain this talent, but out-of-state students are less likely to stay inside the state after they graduate. Further, they take slots that could have been given to in-state students, who are more likely to stay in the state after graduating. Jeff Groen and Michelle White have done extensive modeling of these situations in their "In-State versus Out-of-State Students: The Divergence of Interest between Public Universities and State Governments."[13]

Other institutions, such as the University of Florida (17 percent undergraduate out-of-state students) and the University of North Carolina at Chapel Hill (17 percent undergraduate out-of-state students), confront formal political and legal constraints that limit the proportions of nonresident students they can admit. It should come as no surprise that advocating the enrollment of large numbers of out-of-state students is a losing campaign plank for a gubernatorial candidate in any state that boasts a strong, attractive flagship public university.

Whatever their individual circumstances, however, *table 5-1 reveals that twenty-three of the fifty flagship institutions could reduce to zero the tuition and fees paid by their resident undergraduate students with the premium revenues they earn from charging nonresident students high prices. The average flagship campus could cut in-state tuition and fees for undergraduates to zero and have money left over if it devoted all of its potential out-of-state tuition premium revenue to that purpose.*

This is not to argue that all nonresident premium revenues should be devoted to reducing resident student tuition and fees. Institutions have many obligations and needs. It is, however, appropriate to point out that most flagship institutions could, if they wished, find ways to reduce the prices they charge their resident students. It is an understatement to observe that at most of these institutions, reducing the prices paid by resident undergraduate students has not emerged as one of their highest priorities. The 2017 College Board *Trends in College Pricing* report informs us that the average tuition and fee charge at a four-year public institution rose from $1,910 in 1990–91 to $9,970 in 2017–18, an average annual growth rate of 6.31 percent.[14] This growth rate falls to 3.86 percent if one takes price inflation into account. Simultaneously, real median household income crept upward at an annual rate of only .39 percent.[15] *Simply put, public colleges and universities, led and perhaps even inspired by their flagship campuses, have made it increasingly tenuous for the broad range of their citizenry to be able to afford to attend them.*

Members of the Typical 49 usually do not enroll high percentages of out-of-state students and lack the branding power that would allow them to hike the prices they charge nonresidents. This is evident in table 5-2, where one can see (compared to the flagships) that their tuition and fee charges are lower, their nonresident tuition and fee premium per student is lower, and the total institutional premium revenue they earn from charging nonresident students higher prices is one-fourteenth the size of that earned by the flagships. In 2016–17, the average sticker tuition and fee price for a nonresident student to attend a flagship state university was 167 percent higher than the price quoted resident students, but only 117 percent higher at a Typical 49 institution. Simply put, flagship institutions (and especially the Top 28) have a greater ability to raise prices than the Typical 49.

Even so, were the typicals to decide to devote all their nonresident revenue premiums to diminishing resident tuition and fees, they could lower their average price to their resident students by almost 40 percent.

The fiscal lesson to be drawn from tables 5-1 and 5-2 is that nonresident students who pay full-price, nonresident tuition and fees are indeed financial gold on campuses across the nation. Thus, it cannot be completely surprising that between 2004 and 2014, the absolute proportion of out-of-state students rose by a momentous 36 percent at the University of Alabama at Tuscaloosa and more than 20 percent at the University of California, Berkeley, UCLA, and the universities of South Carolina, Missouri, Oregon, and Arkansas. Of the most prominent flagship state universities, the proportion of out-of-state students declined at only four—Florida, Georgia, Maryland, and Tennessee.[16]

To the uninitiated, it might seem as if the University of Alabama discovered a new, very persuasive religion approximately ten years ago.[17] In the space

TABLE 5-2

The Total Revenue Premium Implied by Published Nonresident Tuition and Fees versus Resident Tuition and Fees for Undergraduate Students at the Typical 49, 2016–17

Institution	Percent Nonresident Undergrads	Nonresident T&F	Resident T&F	Nonresident Price Premium	Approximate Undiscounted Incremental Institutional Annual Revenue (Millions)	Estimated Percentage of Resident T&F
Alabama A&M U	39%	$17,964	$9,456	$8,508	$6.68	61.16%
U Alaska Anchorage	7%	$21,774	$7,074	$14,700	$16.00	34.01%
Northern Arizona U	38%	$24,144	$10,764	$13,380	$134.74	94.06%
U Central Arkansas	14%	$14,447	$8,224	$6,223	$8.38	14.67%
Cal S U Chico	2%	$19,776	$7,044	$12,732	$4.19	3.96%
Adams S U	32%	$19,785	$9,009	$10,776	$6.94	67.75%
Central Conn S U	10%	$22,602	$10,936	$11,666	$11.13	88.12%
Delaware S U	68%	$16,138	$7,532	$8,606	$23.37	266.79%
Florida Gulf Coast U	19%	$25,214	$6,171	$19,043	$49.69	91.63%
Georgia C and S U	1%	$27,550	$9,202	$18,348	$1.11	2.17%
U Hawaii Hilo	25%	$20,580	$7,620	$12,960	$9.96	72.66%
Lewis-Clark S C	20%	$17,620	$6,120	$11,500	$9.03	74.60%
Western Illinois U	7%	$15,515	$11,245	$4,270	$2.55	3.21%
U Southern Indiana	15%	$17,177	$7,535	$9,642	$13.86	31.80%
U Northern Iowa	9%	$18,851	$8,309	$10,542	$9.59	13.95%
Pittsburg S U	40%	$17,662	$6,910	$10,752	$25.39	115.26%
Morehead S U	17%	$12,796	$8,530	$4,266	$7.07	16.25%
Nicholls S U	4%	$18,602	$7,661	$10,941	$2.34	7.10%
U Southern Maine	25%	$21,280	$8,920	$12,360	$19.12	104.97%
Morgan S U	40%	$17,504	$7,636	$9,868	$25.12	96.84%
Westfield S U	8%	$15,355	$9,275	$6,080	$2.74	6.48%
Grand Valley S U	8%	$16,392	$11,520	$4,872	$8.66	4.18%

Bemidji S U	13%	$8,393	$8,393	$0	$0.00	0.00%
Jackson S U	53%	$17,614	$7,261	$10,353	$41.11	180.66%
U Central Missouri	12%	$13,767	$7,322	$6,445	$7.57	14.82%
Montana S U Billings	9%	$18,093	$5,827	$12,266	$4.38	31.07%
Chadron S C	49%	$6,686	$6,656	$30	$0.34	5.80%
Nevada S C	0%	$16,244	$5,131	$11,113	$0.00	0.00%
Keene S C	64%	$21,997	$13,613	$8,384	$22.35	114.09%
Wm Paterson U NJ	2%	$20,466	$12,574	$7,892	$1.44	1.57%
East New Mexico S U	23%	$11,258	$5,510	$5,748	$6.07	62.81%
SUNY Potsdam	5%	$17,834	$7,984	$9,850	$1.68	6.68%
North Car Central U	21%	$18,509	$6,051	$12,458	$16.44	64.40%
Dickinson S U	38%	$8,917	$6,348	$2,569	$1.35	36.54%
Wright S U	4%	$17,350	$8,730	$8,620	$4.31	5.27%
U Central Oklahoma	10%	$16,459	$6,699	$9,760	$14.26	22.80%
Eastern Oregon U	36%	$18,804	$8,073	$10,731	$11.10	138.46%
Indiana U of PA	6%	$21,034	$11,368	$9,666	$6.23	5.77%
Rhode Island C	21%	$19,867	$8,206	$11,661	$18.12	50.38%
South Car S U	18%	$20,500	$10,420	$10,080	$4.59	27.95%
Northern S U	34%	$10,803	$7,887	$2,916	$3.05	41.40%
Tennessee S U	46%	$20,924	$7,568	$13,356	$43.09	183.31%
Sam Houston S U	3%	$21,756	$9,516	$12,240	$6.57	4.91%
Southern Utah U	23%	$19,810	$6,530	$13,280	$25.68	86.79%
Johnson S C	28%	$23,746	$11,290	$12,456	$4.74	62.20%
Radford U	8%	$21,716	$10,081	$11,635	$7.87	10.46%
Central Wash U	7%	$21,501	$7,653	$13,848	$10.78	16.61%
West Virginia U	29%	$15,572	$6,996	$8,576	$8.54	83.50%
U Wisc Platteville	22%	$15,454	$7,604	$7,850	$13.76	33.16%
Averages	**21.1%**	**$18,037**	**$8,326**	**$9,711**	**$13.94**	**52.30%**

Sources: Price data from "Tuition and Fees, 1998–99 through 2017–18," *Chronicle of Higher Education* (www.chronicle.com/interactives/tuition-and-fees?cid =wcontentgrid); enrollment data from College Navigator (https://nces.ed.gov/collegenavigator).

of approximately one decade, it doubled the percentage of nonresident students on its Tuscaloosa campus. My rough estimate of the total annual incremental revenue it realized from its out-of-state students in 2016–17 is $285 million,* though this does not consider any scholarship aid provided to these students. Thus, even though the proportion of its budget coming from the state of Alabama in the form of general appropriations fell by an absolute 9 percent over the past five years—not 9 percent of its appropriation, but a much larger 9 percent slice of its total budget—this has been a winning financial strategy. Its enrollment has increased significantly, as have the standardized test scores of its entering students. Other than a few articles in 2014 that noted that Alabamans had become a minority at one of their two flagship institutions, this admissions and financial reorientation does not appear to have made great waves. Indeed, Stephen Katsinas, who directs the university's Education Policy Institute, opined, "That this happened was no accident. It was the result of a deliberate plan and good leadership." This is even though the university, via its "UA Scholar Program," often wipes out up to two-thirds of the out-of-state tuition premium that highly talented nonresidents otherwise would pay.

Figuratively, there now is more than one Tide at the University of Alabama—the new one is the more than $285 million in annual incremental revenue that rolls into the university from nonresident students who pay price premiums. Out-of-state undergraduate students clearly have evolved into a substantial revenue source for the institution.

The reaction in many other states to such a development might not be so sanguine. In states that boast large numbers of highly qualified high school graduates—applicants who can present 4.0+ high school grade point averages and standardized test scores above the ninetieth percentile—flagship institutions take substantial flak from citizens when their out-of-state undergraduate percentages rise above 25 percent. As one parent forthrightly put it to a reporter from the *Washington Post*, "A state university's first priority should be to the residents of that state, period."[18]

---

*This estimate is the university's nonresident price premium per student ($16,480) times its number of undergraduate students (32,563) times the proportion of those students who are full-time (.843) times the proportion of those students who are nonresident (.63). Thus, the total annual revenue increment is $16,480 * 32,563 * .843 * .63 = $285,003,203.

Legislators hear this chin music and typically respond by uttering statements that warn campuses such as UCLA, the University of Colorado, the University of Michigan, and the College of William and Mary that legislative patience is wearing thin with respect to their large out-of-state student enrollments. Regardless, the fiscal models of these institutions now are so heavily dependent upon nonresident tuition revenues (which often dwarf state general fund contributions) that these institutions would be devastated if the nonresident revenue spigot were turned off to any considerable degree. Further, these institutions, most of which are members of the Top 28, are not tyros politically speaking and they work legislative halls assiduously. Some astutely employ the very legislators who could force them to reduce their out-of-state student rosters. Therefore, only a few states, such as North Carolina, place firm limits on the proportion of out-of-state students that are enforced.

Whatever the amount of the funds generated by means of nonresident tuition and fee premiums, these funds could be used to subsidize the educations of resident students. Institutions wield considerable discretion in this regard. No doubt nonresident students end up subsidizing resident students on virtually every campus to some extent. However, substantial portions of these semi-discretionary dollars are used for purposes other than reducing the tuition and fees paid by resident students. At the University of Virginia (UVA), for example, I estimate that UVA's nonresident tuition premium generated more than $141.3 million in 2016–17. Despite this revenue, the National Center for Education Statistics College Navigator reports that UVA's undergraduate tuition for Virginia residents in the same year was a lofty $16,412 (the fourth highest among flagship institutions in the country).[19] Further, UVA increased its published tuition and fee charges for Virginia residents by 8.0 percent, 11.3 percent, and 4.3 percent over the previous three years, and its average net price increased by 12.4 percent over the span of the two previous years for which College Navigator data are available.[20]

It seems very likely that some considerable portion of UVA's additional revenues from nonresident students (and those at many other Top 28 institutions) are being used for purposes such as maintaining its physical plant, paying its administrators, subsidizing faculty salaries and research, and the like. Undoubtedly there is complementarity between the quality of classroom and laboratory instruction and these other categories of expenditures. It would, however, be a Herculean task to demonstrate that the quality of the

UVA undergraduate experience for its resident students improved 12.4 percent over the same two years.

Nor is this a phenomenon confined to recent years. Between the 2001–02 and 2016–17 academic years, the *Chronicle of Higher Education* reports that UVA's published tuition and fees for Virginia residents rose at a compound annual rate of 9.1 percent annually, dwarfing the 2.0 percent compound annual growth rate of the Consumer Price Index between July 2001 and July 2016 and the 0.2 percent compound annual growth rate of real national median household income between 2001 and 2016 (real median household income actually declined by more than $1,600 in Virginia over the same period).[21]

Reality is that the University of Virginia scenario has been replicated to some extent at every Top 28 institution. The elite nearly always raise tuition and fees faster than the Consumer Price Index and much more rapidly than increases in median household income because they can do so without encountering major problems. They desire the additional revenue to spend on institutional priorities. They do not increase tuition and fees because there is a demonstrable connection between the increased expenditures and the quality of undergraduate instruction.*

While the data presented in tables 5-1 and 5-2 do not provide us with a definitive answer as to why in-state tuition and fees at four-year public institutions have been rising so rapidly, they do tell us that the increases have been significant. However, one could argue that these increases might have been even higher for some students were it not for the price discriminatory premiums these colleges and universities induced their out-of-state students to pay. Even so, at an institution such as the University of Arizona (UA), where the nonresident tuition and fee premiums generated an estimated additional $320.4 million in revenue, this bounty did not dissuade UA from increasing its resident tuition and fees by a compound rate of 5.0 percent over the previous five years.[22] *It seems apparent that nonresi-*

---

*It cannot be a surprise to anyone familiar with higher education that is often difficult to connect the dots between items such as additional funding for research institutes, or for reducing teaching loads, or for additional administrators, and the quality of undergraduate instruction. There may be some connection, but this connection has never been demonstrated in other than single instances. Indeed, one could levy a plausible argument that the net effect of some of these expenditures ultimately could be to reduce the quality of the undergraduate experience.

dent tuition and fee premiums fund many activities other than reducing the financial burden borne by resident students.

Extracting Funds from Upper-Income In-State Students

If institutions of higher education seek to reduce the effective net price paid by their lower-income students, one immediately available source of revenue to support that purpose is their own student bodies—namely, those students who come to them from upper-income households. Already, we saw in the previous chapter that in 2016–17, the ratios of the average net price paid by students coming from the highest income group to the average net price paid by students coming from the lowest income group ranged from a low of 1.47 at the University of Pittsburgh to a high of 7.69 at the University of Michigan. The Top 28 average was 3.10. Among the Typical 49, the ratios ranged from a low of only 1.15 at West Virginia State University to a high of 2.22 at California State University at Chico. The Typical 49 overall average was 1.64. The higher the ratio, the greater the extent to which the institution implemented internal price discrimination.

Let's use Ordinary State University (OSU, with apologies to Ohio State, Oklahoma State, and Oregon State) to clarify tuition and fee cost redistribution. Our OSU enrolls precisely 10,000 students, and as figure 5-5 reveals, those students spread themselves across the College Navigator's five household income classes in a fashion that approximates a normal distribution. OSU students pay average net prices by income group that roughly approximate the national averages for four-year public institutions in 2015–16.

However, the distribution of students across the five income groups in figure 5-5 does not represent the real world. Figure 5-6 provides the same analysis, but does so for the Top 28 institutions. They enroll considerably more upper-income students and proportionately fewer lower-income students than the model institution portrayed in figure 5-5. The average net prices paid by Top 28 students differ as well and their average 2015–16 values are utilized in figure 5-6. Note that the students from the highest household income class ($110,000+) provided 39.67 percent of the total net cost revenue at the Top 28 institutions, whereas it was only 21.0 percent at our model institution. Students from the lowest income households supplied only 10.86 percent of the total net cost revenues for the Top 28.

FIGURE 5-5

Percentage of Revenues (Based upon Net Price) Collected by a Model Institution from Five Household Income Classes, 2015–16

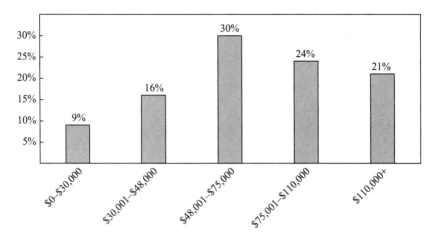

Source: College Navigator, National Center for Educational Statistics (http://nces.ed.gov/college navigator).

FIGURE 5-6

Percentage of Revenues (Based upon Net Price) Collected by the Average Top 28 Institution from Five Household Income Classes, 2015–16

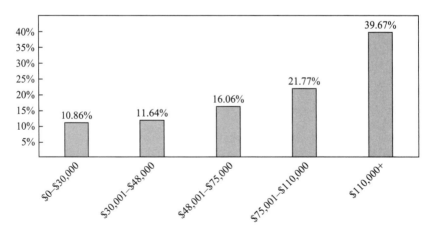

Sources: Tuition and fees: College Navigator, National Center for Educational Statistics (http://nces.ed.gov/collegenavigator). Income distribution data: IPEDS (https://nces.ed.gov /ipeds).

FIGURE 5-7

Percentage of Revenues (Based upon Net Price) Collected by the Average Typical 49 Institution from Five Household Income Classes, 2015–16

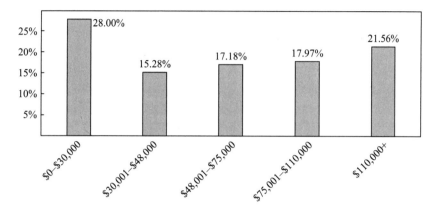

Sources: Tuition and fees: College Navigator, National Center for Educational Statistics (http://nces.ed.gov/collegenavigator). Income distribution data: IPEDS (https://nces.ed.gov/ipeds).

Next, consider the situation of the Typical 49 institutions, portrayed in figure 5-7. Significant differences emerge. The Typical 49 institution earned 28.00 percent of its total net cost revenues from students coming from the lowest household income class (these students nearly always are Pell Grant recipients). Only 21.56 percent of their total net revenues after considering financial aid were derived from the highest household income class.

The numbers used in these three models are estimates rather than precise measurements and therefore should not be taken to the bank. Nevertheless, they provide reasonable approximations of the net price discriminatory activities of the Top 28 and the typicals and the revenues attached to these net price differentials.

These graphs highlight how the revenues being collected from students coming from upper-income households potentially can be used to reduce the net prices paid by students coming from lower-income households. Or, of course, they can be used for other purposes. The relevant point is that institutions wield considerable discretion in terms of how they use these revenues.

Figures 5-5 through 5-7 also impart a story of the social stratification of public college and university student bodies. *Gradually, the student bodies of our flagship institutions, and particularly of the Top 28, have become domi-nated by students coming from upper-income households.*[23] A mixture of ex-pectations, perceived comfort, academic credentials, and financial means causes much larger proportions of students from lower-income households to attend Typical 49 institutions (or community colleges). Emphasis upon merit-based scholarship programs unrelated to financial need (such as those in Georgia and South Carolina) accelerate this trend.

A Look at Specific Institutions

The brand magnetism of the Top 28 institutions provides them with a much greater ability to transfer costs away from lower-income students toward upper-income students, if they wish to do so. Without exception, members of the Top 28 heavily redistribute costs away from students coming from lower-income households toward students coming from upper-income households—many of whom turn out to be nonresidents paying premium prices.

For each Top 28 institution, what is the size of these cost transfers that are based upon the household incomes of their students? One can approximate them by utilizing data provided by the National Center for Education Statistics (NCES) and the IPEDS system. Some of the cost transfers are quite large. Table 5-3 provides valuable information in this regard.

To approximate the dollar size of the redistribution, I analyzed the dif-ferences between the net prices paid by students from the five different income classes delineated by the NCES's College Navigator website. Thus, if students coming from households earning more than $110,000 annually paid a hypothetical net price of $20,000 per year at State U for their education, but the average net price was only $15,000, then a plausible measure of the possible reallocation of funds is the difference between the two, or $5,000. I assume that such reallocations are possible for students within the two highest annual income classes: $110,001+ and $75,000–110,000.* Funds for reallocation might also be generated within the middle-income class ($48,001–75,000); however, even though one can use IPEDS data to infer the

---

*The College Navigator income class data are for first-time students. I assume that the relative distribution of students across the College Navigator income classes remains the same as those students progress toward graduation. Intuitively, however, one might expect a larger proportion of students from lower-income classes to leave school prior to graduation. If so, then my estimates are conservative.

TABLE 5-3

Estimated Total Revenues Generated by
Differential Financial Aid Treatment of the Highest
Two Income Classes Based upon the Incomes of
Student Households for Twenty-Five of the Top 28
Institutions, 2016–17 (Millions of Dollars)

UC Berkeley	$56.2
UC Davis	$64.0
UC Irvine	$50.1
UCLA	$80.8
UC San Diego	$76.7
UC Santa Barbara	$68.9
Clemson U	$18.7
U Connecticut	$59.6
U Florida	$16.1
U Georgia	$14.2
Georgia Tech	$11.5
U Illinois CU	$138.9
U Maryland CP	$89.9
U Michigan	$88.5
U Minnesota TC	$119.6
UNC Chapel Hill	$76.7
Ohio S U	$85.4
Penn S U	$197.0
U Pittsburgh	$68.2
Purdue University	$117.5
U Texas Austin	$98.1
U Virginia	$84.4
U Washington	$139.0
College of W&M	$42.8
U Wisconsin	$124.0
Average	**$79.5**

Sources: College Navigator, National Center for Educational Statistics (http://nces.ed.gov/collegenavigator) and IPEDS (https://nces.ed.gov/ipeds).

approximate proportions of undergraduate students within this and other income classes, we do not know their precise distribution within the middle-income class. Hence, I do not make any estimate of reallocations of funds within the middle-income class.

Where the Top 28 are concerned, table 5-3 reveals that the average member collected $76,412,684 in revenue from students coming from the two upper-income classes that exceeded the average net price of attendance for the students at each institution.* This number was derived by multiplying the average difference between net prices times the estimated number of students in the income class in question.

Of the twenty-five members of the Top 28 institutions for which data were available, six generated more than $100 million annually over and above their average net cost per student, and these dollars were potentially available for reallocation to reduce the net price paid by students coming from lower-income households. Penn State generated the largest annual income-based reallocation revenue—slightly more than $197 million. We already have seen that Penn State also generated a hefty $250.1 million in annual revenue from the price premiums assessed out-of-state students.

Predictably, these numbers are much smaller when the focus is on Typical 49 institutions; the semi-discretionary revenues they generate from their differential, price discriminatory financial aid policies averages only $7.7 million per institution (see table 5-4). The Typical 49 enroll smaller student bodies, do not enjoy the same resources as the elite, and do not benefit from the same branding power as the elite. Michigan's Grand Valley State, with 22,209 undergraduate students, an attractive campus, and a wide range of academic programs, including engineering and other STEM-related majors plus a wide selection of programs in the health sciences, generated the largest amount of these semi-discretionary revenues ($32.1 million) in 2016–17.[24] Nevertheless, this amount is well less than one-half of the average for the elite institutions.

Many Typical 49 institutions enroll such large proportions of Pell Grant students that they have much less ability to price discriminate with the dispensation of their financial aid. Historically Black Colleges and Universities (HBCUs) exemplify this situation. At Alabama A&M, for example, 70 percent of all undergraduates and 74 percent of new freshmen are Pell Grant recipients.[25] There is precious little room for price discrimination here.

---

*Data were available for only 25 institutions among the Top 28.

TABLE 5-4

Estimated Total Revenues Generated by Differential Financial Aid Treatment Based upon the Incomes of Student Households for the Typical 49, 2016–17 (Millions of Dollars)

Alabama A&M U	$0.3
U Alaska Anchorage	$8.6
Northern Arizona U	$16.0
U Central Arkansas	$5.4
Cal S U Chico	$31.8
Adams S U	$1.2
Central Conn S U	$15.7
Delaware S U	$1.5
Florida Gulf Coast U	$10.6
Georgia Coll and S U	$4.7
U Hawaii Hilo	$2.1
Lewis-Clark S C	$1.1
Western Illinois U	$11.2
U Southern Indiana	$10.0
U Northern Iowa	$12.8
Pittsburg S U	$3.8
Morehead S U	$4.8
Nicholls S U	$4.9
U Southern Maine	$2.6
Morgan S U	$4.8
Westfield S U	$11.3
Grand Valley S U	$32.1
Bemidji S U	$5.9
Jackson S U	$1.0
U Central Missouri	$12.1
Montana S U Billings	$2.5
Chadron S C	$0.9
Nevada S C	$0.6
Keene S C	$2.6
Wm Paterson U NJ	$14.8
East New Mex S U	$1.2
SUNY Potsdam	$9.8
North Car Central U	$3.4
Dickinson S U	$0.2
Wright S U	$14.6
U Central Oklahoma	$11.5

(*continued*)

TABLE 5-4 (CONTINUED)

Eastern Oregon U	$0.8
Indiana U of PA	$23.3
Rhode Island C	$7.0
South Carolina S U	$0.8
Northern S U	$1.0
Tennessee S U	$0.5
Sam Houston S U	$6.8
Southern Utah U	$3.4
Johnson S C	$1.3
Radford U	$24.2
Central Wash U	$20.7
West Va S U	$1.1
U Wisc Platteville	$6.5
Average	**$7.7**

Sources: College Navigator, National Center for Education Statistics (http://nces.ed.gov/collegenavigator) and IPEDS (http://nces.ed.gov /ipeds).

PULLING TOGETHER THE REDISTRIBUTIVE REVENUES

Let's review the information that we have generated concerning price discrimination and the redistribution of costs among students. What I have estimated above are the potential or actual redistributive activities of institutions that are financed by students. First, I looked at the cost-shifting implied by the price premiums assessed out-of-state students; second, I examined the extent to which costs are shifted by means of using financial aid to adjust the net prices students pay. The sum of the two is a rough measure of the overall size of each institution's semi-discretionary redistributive activities that are financed by the students themselves. Table 5-5 provides summary data for both the elite and typical institutions.

The University of Michigan, with 28,983 undergraduate students, led the entire sample of institutions with a redistributive package that totaled more than $521 million in 2016–17. Viewed in a national context, Michigan is a high (published) tuition institution that offers significant financial aid to in-state students who go to Ann Arbor from lower-income households. A major source of revenue for its financial aid activities is the estimated $433.3 million revenue premium the institution earned from its more than 13,900 out-of-state undergraduate students.

Occupying roughly the same position was Penn State, a high-tuition institution that nonetheless enrolled 41,359 undergraduate students (approximately 47 percent of whom were nonresidents) in 2016–17. Penn State collected an estimated additional $476.5 million from its students in what I have termed discretionary revenues. At the other end of the elite spectrum, the University of Georgia collected only $67.5 million in discretionary revenues from its undergraduates, reflecting its home state's HOPE and Zell Miller merit scholarship programs and its relatively modest 12 percent nonresident enrollment. Nevertheless, this remains a huge sum when compared to Tennessee State University's puny $1.7 million in discretionary revenues, or Nevada State College's $2.2 million.

Table 5-6 places the total redistributive revenues of each institution in context by comparing them to the total dollar amount institutions would have collected from their in-state undergraduate students if those students lived on campus.* Consider the University of Washington (UW), which in 2016–17 collected an estimated $360.7 million in discretionary revenue from its undergraduate students, $221.7 million of which came from the premium it charged out-of-state students. In that year, UW enrolled 21,034 in-state undergraduate students. If it had wished to do so, it could have used the $221.7 million to reduce the tuition and fees of its in-state students by $10,064 each, or more than 93 percent of UW's in-state tuition and fee charge of $10,753 in that year.

The UW analysis is simplistic. It's not clear that it would be good social policy to offer close to zero tuition and fees to all Washington resident undergraduates, regardless of their financial need. Further, UW must retain funds to pay its electric bill, the salaries of its employees, and the like. Serving undergraduates is not UW's only reason for being.

Even so, the UW example demonstrates that when one takes a longer point of view, institutions usually have more degrees of freedom in their decision making than most wish to admit. Choice making is involved, and most elite public institutions have made choices that have not necessarily been to the benefit of their in-state undergraduate students. In UW's case, it chose

---

*The on- or off-campus residences of the undergraduate students described in tables 5-5 and 5-6 are unknown. A perusal of College Navigator data, however, reveals that there is little consistency in the estimated total cost of living on campus versus off campus. On some campuses, on-campus living is more expensive, but on others off-campus living is more expensive. Using on-campus cost estimates provides standardization.

TABLE 5-5

Discretionary Revenues Derived from Redistribution: 27 of the Top 28 and the Typical 49 (Millions of Dollars), 2016–17

Institution	Revenue from Nonres. Price Premium	Revenue from Price and Financial Aid Discrimination	Total Potential Revenues for Redistribution	Institution	Revenue from Nonres. Price Premium	Revenue from Price and Financial Aid Discrimination	Total Potential Revenues for Redistribution
UC Berkeley	$182.8	$56.2	$239.0	Alabama A&M U	$6.7	$0.3	$7.0
UC Davis	$136.6	$64.0	$200.6	U Alaska Anchorage	$16.0	$8.6	$24.6
UC Irvine	$184.6	$50.1	$234.7	Northern Arizona U	$134.7	$16.0	$150.7
UCLA	$182.8	$80.8	$263.6	U Central Arkansas	$8.4	$5.4	$13.8
UC San Diego	$193.6	$76.7	$270.3	Cal S U Chico	$4.2	$31.8	$36.0
UC Santa Barbara	$82.4	$68.9	$151.3	Adams S U	$7.0	$1.2	$8.2
Clemson U	$121.5	$18.7	$140.2	Central Conn S U	$11.1	$15.7	$26.8
U Connecticut	$128.3	$59.6	$187.9	Delaware S U	$23.4	$1.5	$24.9
U Florida	$109.0	$16.1	$125.1	Florida Gulf Coast U	$49.7	$10.6	$60.3
U Georgia	$53.3	$14.2	$67.5	Georgia Coll and S U	$1.1	$4.7	$5.8
Georgia Tech	$131.8	$11.5	$143.3	U Hawaii Hilo	$10.0	$2.1	$12.1
U Illinois UC	$141.5	$138.9	$280.4	Lewis-Clark S C	$9.0	$1.1	$10.1
U Maryland CP	$164.0	$89.9	$253.9	Western Illinois U	$2.6	$11.2	$13.8
U Michigan	$433.3	$88.5	$521.8	U Southern Indiana	$13.9	$10.0	$23.9
U Minnesota	$101.4	$119.6	$221.0	U Northern Iowa	$9.6	$12.8	$22.4
UNC Chapel Hill	$72.3	$76.7	$149.0	Pittsburg S U	$25.4	$3.8	$29.2
Ohio S U	$284.5	$85.4	$369.9	Morehead S U	$7.1	$4.8	$11.9
Penn S U	$279.5	$197.0	$476.5	Nicholls S U	$2.3	$4.9	$7.2
U Pittsburgh	$72.2	$68.2	$140.4	U Southern Maine	$19.1	$2.6	$21.7
Purdue U	$246.7	$117.5	$364.2	Morgan S U	$25.1	$4.8	$29.9
U Texas Austin	$103.9	$98.1	$202.0	Westfield S U	$2.7	$11.3	$14.0
College of W&M	$45.4	$42.8	$88.2	Grand Valley S U	$8.7	$32.1	$40.8

Institution			
U Virginia	$141.3	$84.4	$225.7
U Washington	$221.7	$139.0	$360.7
U Wisconsin	$244.7	$124.0	$368.7
Averages	**$160.8**	**$78.7**	**$239.5**

Institution			
Bemidji S U	$0.0	$5.9	$5.9
Jackson S U	$41.1	$1.0	$42.1
U Central Missouri	$7.6	$12.1	$19.7
Montana S U Billings	$4.4	$2.5	$6.9
Chadron S C	$0.3	$0.9	$1.2
Nevada S C	$0.0	$0.6	$0.6
Keene S C	$22.4	$2.6	$25.0
Wm Paterson U NJ	$1.4	$14.8	$16.2
East New Mex S U	$6.1	$1.2	$7.3
SUNY Potsdam	$1.7	$9.8	$11.5
North Car Central U	$16.4	$3.4	$19.8
Dickinson S U	$1.4	$0.2	$1.6
Wright S U	$4.3	$14.6	$18.9
U Central Oklahoma	$14.3	$11.5	$25.8
Eastern Oregon U	$11.1	$0.8	$11.9
Indiana U of PA	$6.2	$23.2	$29.4
Rhode Island C	$18.1	$7.0	$25.1
South Carolina S U	$4.6	$0.8	$5.4
Northern S U	$3.1	$1.0	$4.1
Tennessee S U	$43.1	$0.5	$43.6
Sam Houston S U	$6.6	$6.8	$13.4
Southern Utah U	$25.7	$3.4	$29.1
Johnson S C	$4.7	$1.3	$6.0
Radford U	$7.9	$24.2	$32.1
Central Wash U	$10.8	$20.7	$31.5
West Va S U	$8.6	$1.1	$9.7
U Wisc Platteville	$13.8	$6.5	$20.3
Averages	**$13.9**	**$7.7**	**$21.6**

Sources: College Navigator, National Center for Education Statistics (http://nces.ed.gov/collegenavigator) and IPEDS (http://nces.ed.gov/ipeds).

TABLE 5-6

Net Discretionary Revenues Compared to Net Price
Revenues at Selected Public Institutions, 2016–17

Resident Undergrad Institution	Discretionary Revenues as a Percentage of Net Price Revenues
UC Berkeley	64.2%
U Connecticut	87.6%
U Florida	35.5%
U Georgia	21.0%
U Maryland	96.5%
U Michigan	222.8%
Ohio S U	68.4%
Purdue U	202.2%
U Washington	184.1%
U Wisconsin	159.3%
Average	**107.7%**
Adams S U	36.9%
Cal S U Chico	33.0%
U Central Missouri	9.9%
Jackson S U	9.7%
Montana S U Billings	10.6%
SUNY Potsdam	3.3%
Radford U	7.4%
Southern Utah U	28.3%
Westfield S U	3.4%
Wright S U	2.4%
Average	**14.5%**

Sources: Tables 5-1 through 5-5 and the College Navigator, National Center for Educational Statistics (http://nces.ed.gov/collegenavigator).

to increase undergraduate tuition and fees for Washington residents by 185.9 percent between 2000–01 and 2016–17. This increase declined to 105.3 percent if we account for increases in the CPI.[26]

By contrast, SUNY Potsdam's discretionary tuition and fee revenues constituted only 3.3 percent of its net price collections from its in-state students. For California State University, Chico, 33.0 percent was the comparable percentage. Once again, the great diversity among four-year public institutions is evident.

One should not confuse the estimates contained in the tables above with the Tablets of Moses. These numbers represent approximations, not precision estimates. Even so, they provide us with a picture of the extent to which individual campuses price discriminate and thereby transfer costs from in-state students to out-of-state students and from students coming from lower-income households to students from upper-income households.

The numbers in the tables lead us to an obvious question: What do the institutions do with the redistributive dollars they generate? We've already seen that several institutions, including the University of Michigan, the College of William and Mary, and the University of North Carolina at Chapel Hill, made it a priority to reduce the cost of attendance of their lowest-income students. However, huge differences existed among institutions in terms of their treatment of lower-income students. Table 5-7 reports the absolute net prices paid in 2015–16 by Top 28 students who came from households where annual incomes ranged between $0 and $30,000.*

In the case of William and Mary, in 2016–17, the college enrolled approximately 700 undergraduates who were Pell Grant recipients (a calculation based upon its published 11 percent Pell Grant student recipient percentage). In that year, the college's published full cost for an on-campus, in-state undergraduate was $35,991. Assuming these students received the maximum $5,815 Pell Grant permitted in that academic year, this reduced each student's cost of attendance to $30,176. If the college assumed the total financial burden for reducing this cost to the $5,542 average net price paid by students situated in the $0–30,000 income class, then this would have cost the institution 700 * $24,634 = $17.24 million annually. Against this, my estimate is that the tuition and fee premium paid by out-of-state students at William and Mary generated $45.4 million in the same academic year.[27]

Thus, William and Mary, as is true for every other member of the Top 28 and nearly all other public colleges and universities in the country, generated what might be termed discretionary, investable funds by means of its pricing activities. These dollars were in excess of what was required to take care of the most obvious financial aid needs of its lower-income students.

---

*A cynic might observe that this a task more easily accomplished on these campuses because they enroll relatively small proportions of Pell Grant students.

TABLE 5-7

Net Prices Paid by Students Coming from
Households with Annual Incomes $0–30,000:
Twenty-Five of the Top 28 Institutions, 2016–17

UC Berkeley	$8,602
UC Davis	$10,316
UC Irvine	$8,546
UCLA	$8,233
UC San Diego	$8,692
UC Santa Barbara	$10,134
Clemson U	$12,679
U Connecticut	$11,196
U Florida	$6,542
U Georgia	$10,357
Georgia Tech	$6,856
U Illinois UC	$8,357
U Maryland CP	$9,084
U Michigan	$3,249
U Minnesota	$7,676
UNC Chapel Hill	$4,155
Ohio S U	$8,969
Penn S U	$21,514
U Pittsburgh	$21,247
Purdue U	$5,019
U Texas Austin	$11,333
U Virginia	$9,526
U Washington	$9,443
College of W&M	$5,542
U Wisconsin	$7,225
Average	**$9,380**

Source: College Navigator, National Center for Educational
Statistics (http://nces.ed.gov/collegenavigator).

What proportion of tuition and fee increases at four-year public colleges
and universities can be attributed to redistributive cost behavior? This a question that I will return to in greater detail in subsequent chapters, but for now
it is fair to observe that only about 40 percent of the additional revenue that
William and Mary raised with its out-of-state tuition premium in 2016–17
would have been necessary to pay for the entirety of the sum necessary to
reduce the average net cost of attendance from William and Mary's published

cost to the $4,459 level for its lowest income class of students. This estimate falls to about 20 percent if we include the semi-discretionary revenues William and Mary derives from its price discriminatory financial aid policies. These estimates assume that these students were receiving the maximum Pell Grant possible.

Each of the Top 28 institutions (and many public colleges or universities) raises substantially more dollars by means of their redistributive pricing behavior than they end up using directly to ameliorate the costs of education to its undergraduates. The redistributive funds generated by means of nonresident price premiums and differential net prices are utilized for many other legitimate institutional purposes, ranging from paying heating bills, to purchasing library materials, to increasing faculty salaries. There is nothing illegal or immoral about this behavior, and it is easy to argue that such an approach is praiseworthy given the circumstances and the alternatives.* Some institutional allocations, however, seem less directly connected to the essentials of providing a low-cost undergraduate education—for example, the University of Michigan's announcement of an $85 million plan to promote diversity, equity, and inclusion on its Ann Arbor campus, a worthy but expensive proposition for undergraduates.[28] In May 2018, University of Michigan economist Mark Perry listed ninety-three administrative positions with compensation totaling $11.08 million that were associated with this initiative.[29]

It is fair to observe that the institutional narratives that public colleges and universities dispense to the public via colorful brochures and alumni magazines tend to gloss over the redistributive impact of the pricing structures. Purdue University, one of the more innovative public research universities in the country, proudly and legitimately highlights its generally low cost to lower-income students (Purdue's in-state tuition and fees were third lowest in the Top 28). It prominently advertises its tuition freeze at 2012–13 levels, focuses on the ability of some students to complete their degree programs in three years, highlights the university's competency-based

---

*Articulate defenses of many aspects of current public college pricing behavior have been supplied by Robert B. Archibald and David H. Feldman, "The Anatomy of College Tuition" (Washington, D.C.: American Council on Education, 2012); Archibald and Feldman, "Federal Financial Aid Policy and College Behavior" (Washington, D.C.: American Council on Education, 2016); and Archibald and Feldman, *Why Does College Cost So Much?* (Oxford University Press, 2011).

awarding of academic credit, and notes its highly innovative income-share agreements.[30]

These are inventive accomplishments that are exemplary for other flagship institutions. Even so, Purdue does not choose to highlight that the net price paid by those among its students who come to the campus from the highest of College Navigator's income classes ($110,000+) is approximately five times higher than the average net price paid by its lowest-income students ($0–30,000).[31] Purdue is more transparent than most flagship state universities, yet the redistributive character of its tuition and fee charges and expenditures is lost in the shuffle. Purdue and most other institutions operate what some parents allege is the equivalent of a progressive income tax system. The purpose may be socially noble, but some parents resent the practice.

Given the significant decline in state general fund support for public higher education, some proportion of the redistributive pricing and financial aid behavior outlined in this chapter perhaps might be considered almost inevitable. Between the 1999–2000 and 2013–14 academic years, for example, real state funding per student (excluding loans) fell 31.89 percent at sixty-seven flagship state universities for which comparable data were available.

Between fiscal year 2012 and fiscal year 2017, however, real total state funding for all of public higher education increased 12.4 percent, even while head-count enrollment was declining. This means that real total state funding per student to support public higher education increased during this five-year period even while the tuition and fee increases being invoked were substantial, and the real net prices paid by students were increasing at all but a few public institutions (Purdue belongs to the few). A cynic might observe that nearly all public colleges and universities increase their tuition and fees charges year in and year out, regardless of their economic circumstances. It has become habitual.

The University of Alabama's flagship campus at Tuscaloosa once again provides an instructive example.[32] The university has become a "hot campus" that many students seek to attend, though it is not a member of the Top 28 and was ranked 110th among national universities in 2017 by *U.S. News and World Report*. The *New York Times* reported in November 2016 that Alabama had become the fastest-growing flagship state university in the country, at least partially because it employs thirty-six recruiters *outside* of the state of Alabama. It has taken advantage of its treasured sought-after status by levying well-above-average tuition and fee increases: 135 percent in real terms between 2001–02 and 2016–17 according to the *Chronicle of Higher Education.*

FINAL WORDS

Tuition and fee data and state support numbers can be parsed in many ways. At the end of the proverbial day, however, *it is difficult to avoid concluding that most flagship state universities have used their distinctive roles and positions to implement tuition and fee structures that generate net revenues far greater than what they utilize to meet the financial needs of their lower-income students. Similar pricing behavior is present at many Typical 49 institutions, though to a reduced degree.*

SIX

College Endowments and Tuition
Should There Be a Tighter Connection?

An endowment links past, current and future generations. It allows an institution to make commitments far into the future, knowing that resources to meet those commitments will continue to be available.

—American Council on Education, 2016

In the 2016 fiscal year, the value of the endowment at the University of Michigan was a tidy $9.743 billion. On the same date, the University of California system reported that its endowment was valued at $8.341 billion, but separately the University California, Berkeley, reported a $1.585 billion endowment. By all odds, these are large sums of money (see table 6-1 for these and other endowment values at the elite public institutions).[1]

Figure 6-1 reports the values of the endowments of twelve members of the Typical 49. If an institution is not included in the graph, that is because either it did not report its endowment data to the National Association of College and University Business Officers (NACUBO) or it had an endowment whose value was below the report's minimum cutoff, which was $714,000.[2] It will not escape the reader's notice that the members of the Typical 49 live in a different endowment world—one that is shaped by reduced opportunities for fundraising. The identities of these institutions' alumni, their institutional programmatic mixes (historically often focused on teacher education),

TABLE 6-1

2016 Fiscal Year Endowment Values for Top 28 Institutions, FY 2016 (Billions of Dollars)

U Texas System	$24.203[a]
Texas A&M	$10.529[a]
U Michigan	$9.743
U California System	$8.341[a]
U Virginia	$5.852
Ohio S U	$3.578
Penn S U	$3.602
U Pittsburgh	$3.524
U Minnesota	$3.280
U Washington	$2.968
UNC Chapel Hill	$2.889
U Wisconsin M	$2.419
U Illinois UC	$2.254
Purdue U	$2.290
Georgia Tech	$1.843
UCLA	$1.803
UC Berkeley	$1.585
U Florida	$1.461
Rutgers U	$1.083
U Georgia	$1.016
U Maryland CP	$0.969
Virginia Tech	$0.843
College of W&M	$0.804
Clemson U	$0.621
UC San Diego	$0.536
UC Irvine	$0.498
U Connecticut	$0.377
UC Davis	$0.325
UC Santa Barbara	$0.274

Source: National Association of College and University Business Officers (www.nacubo.org/-/media/Nacubo/Documents/Endow mentFiles/2017-Endowment-Market-Values.ashx?la=en&hash= E71088CDC05C76FCA30072DA109F91BBC10B0290).

[a] System-wide numbers that include more than a single campus.

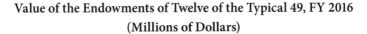

FIGURE 6-1

Value of the Endowments of Twelve of the Typical 49, FY 2016
(Millions of Dollars)

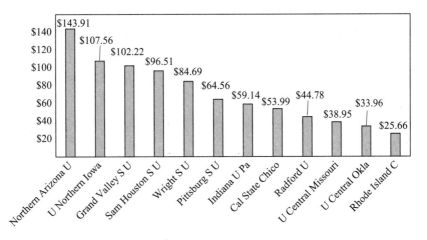

Source: National Association of College and University Business Officers (www.nacubo.org
/-/media/Nacubo/Documents/EndowmentFiles/2017-Endowment-Market-Values.ashx?la=
en&hash=E71088CDC05C76FCA30072DA109F91BBC10B0290).

and their locations often make it challenging for them to attract significant
private gifts.

Compare the University of Michigan's $9.74 billion endowment to the
largest endowment among the Typical 49 institutions—the $143.91 million of
Northern Arizona University. Michigan, with the largest reported endowment of any public university at the end of 2014, had an endowment that was
67 times larger than Northern Arizona's. Of course, large, long-established
institutions are likely to have large endowments.

Academic fundraising professionals often utilize some metric based upon
an institution's endowment per student as their measure of whether that institution has sufficient endowment resources. Figure 6-2 supplies endowment
data per undergraduate student for a selection of elite public and Typical 49
institutions. The disparity in endowment funds available to each set of institutions is obvious. The University of Virginia had $369,295 in endowment
assets per FTE undergraduate student, while California State University at
Chico had $3,401 per FTE undergraduate student.

FIGURE 6-2

Selected Endowments per FTE Student, FY 2016

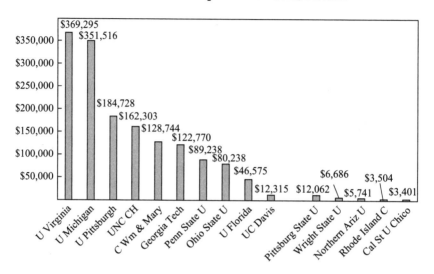

Sources: National Association of College and University Business Officers (www.nacubo.org
/-/media/Nacubo/Documents/EndowmentFiles/2017-Endowment-Market-Values.ashx?la
=en&hash=E71088CDC05C76FCA30072DA109F91BBC10B0290) and IPEDs (http://nces.ed
.gov/ipeds).

USE OF THE ENDOWMENTS

How should institutions use their endowments? While they might wish otherwise, the great majority of the funds in the endowments of the Top 28 are
earmarked for specific programs or tasks because this is what donors prefer.
Thus, at the University of North Carolina at Chapel Hill, more than 500 endowed professorships exist (for example, the Joseph P. Archie, Jr. Eminent
Professorship in Medicine).[3] The funds that support these professorships usually cannot be used for other purposes. This means that the amount of financial freedom the members of the Top 28 enjoy with their endowments can
be much smaller than some suppose.

Most institutions and their foundations have adopted spending rules that
specify how much of their endowment corpus they can spend each year. If
the University of Michigan (UM) were to spend 4.0 percent of the value of
its endowment each year to support its programs, then in its fiscal year 2016
this would have yielded almost $390 million to support UM programs. The

same spending rule, however, would have generated only a bit more than $1.0 million at Rhode Island College.

We already have seen that the University of Pittsburgh (Pitt) is a high-tuition, high-net-price, low-financial-aid institution. Pitt reported an endowment value of $3.524 billion at the end of fiscal year 2016. As one can see in figure 6-2, this corresponded to a bit more than $184,000 per full-time equivalent student.

Let's do a bit of counterfactual analysis with Pitt. Suppose it also utilizes a 4.0 percent spending rule with respect to its endowment, whereby each year it spends 4.0 percent of the endowment corpus. This would have generated more than $4,700 annually per student.

Next, assume that Pitt decided to use this $4,700 sum to reduce the average net price ($23,572) paid by its in-state undergraduate students in 2015–16. This would have sliced almost exactly 20 percent off that price. Or, if this benefit were restricted to in-state students with Pennsylvania residency, then it would have supplied each student with a more than $7,600 net price reduction—almost one-third of the average net price the National Center for Education Statistics College Navigator says they paid.

In the real world, life is more complicated. As just noted, very substantial proportions of most university endowments have strings attached and therefore cannot be utilized in the fashion just described. Further, financial life is full of uncertainty, and what goes up can also come down. Between May 2008 and March 2009, the Dow Jones Industrial Average lost approximately one-half its value.[4] Spending rules of the sort outlined here were suspended by many colleges and universities. More recently, Bloomberg reported that seven large college endowments declined in value between July 2015 and June 2016.[5] The seven unfortunates included some easily recognizable names—the universities of California, Colorado, North Carolina at Chapel Hill, Iowa, Washington, and Virginia, plus Ohio State. These losses occurred during a time period when the Dow Jones Industrial Average inched ahead by about 1 percent.

Nevertheless, if a flagship institution were to announce that henceforth its fundraising priority will be to raise funds that will allow it to decrease the net price paid by its students, especially those coming from lower-income households, then it would not take long for its undergraduate students to benefit. This also would send a powerful message about the institution's values and its commitment to providing access to talented students from all segments of society.

A single year's tuition and fee increase can easily cancel the beneficial effects of any fundraising that actually does focus on reducing student costs. Truly proficient fundraising for student financial aid is required when tuition and fees rise almost 3.5 times as fast as the Consumer Price Index—which is what has been true over the past decade.

It is true that university capital campaigns nearly always include an item that focuses on need-based financial aid; however, this is a goal that seldom is emphasized and usually accounts for only a small proportion of total fundraising activity. The glamor items—the ones that result in major donors' names being attached—usually involve buildings and facilities or the naming of entire academic colleges and schools. It isn't that fundraising that focuses on reducing the net price paid by students is ignored. Rather, it simply is not a point of emphasis.

ACCUMULATED CASH BALANCES

One should not overlook other existing available funds when thinking about tuition and fee pricing. The *Washington Post* reported in August 2016 that the University of Pittsburgh had accumulated reserve cash balances of approximately $2.3 billion.[6] Let's once again undertake what Germans label a *Gedankenexperiment*—a thought experiment. Suppose $100 million of those reserves were used to lower tuition and fees at Pitt. Evenly split over the university's 19,123 undergraduate students in fall 2016, this would have provided a one-year decrease in the institution's net price of approximately $5,200. If this benefit were restricted to in-state undergraduate students, then it would have generated a one-year decline in Pittsburgh's net price to in-state undergraduates of approximately $8,400 per student.

No doubt a set of obstacles (some attitudinal) exists that would make such a plan difficult, but fewer constraints usually exist with respect to the use of accumulated operational balances than is true for endowments. The salient point of this thought experiment, however, is straightforward. *Over time, universities (especially those that are members of the Top 28) have the ability to*

The endowment/tuition hypotheticals presented here have become more than rhetorical considerations. Portions of large college endowments now are taxable, and there is significant pressure upon institutions to adopt spending rules that will force them to utilize income from their endowment funds to reduce the prices paid by undergraduate students. Institutional pushback and shifting political winds may derail this movement.

alter their fundraising priorities, change their pricing structures, and make their campuses much more accessible to talented students from all rungs of society—if they decide to do so. What is not possible in the short run becomes plausible as time passes.

Several elite institutions currently offer what might be labeled lower-income-student-friendly pricing structures: the College of William and Mary, Purdue, Georgia Tech, and the universities of Illinois (Urbana-Champaign), Maryland, Michigan, Minnesota, and North Carolina (Chapel Hill). However, their commitments are limited. At none of these institutions does the percentage of Pell Grant recipients exceed 22 percent.[7]

On the other hand, each of the six campuses of the University of California that is a member of the Top 28 enrolled at least 30 percent Pell Grant recipients in their undergraduate student bodies in 2015–16, and one (the University of California, Irvine) reported that 45 percent of its undergraduates were Pell Grant recipients. This was true even though the average net prices paid by the lowest-income-bracket students on these campuses typically hovered close to the average of the elite institutions. This suggests that it is not simply net price, but also a state's demographics and accompanying institutional strategies that are critical to the success of institutions attracting students from lower-income households.[8]

Still, more of one good thing often means attaining less of another. It is difficult to avoid tradeoffs among an institution's net price, its Pell Grant percentage, the standardized test scores of its student body, and its retention and graduation rates. More Pell Grant students, for example, often translates into lower SAT scores and perhaps lowered rankings as well. These are not

> The benefits of the tax-free return on endowments accrue largely to institutions with sizeable endowments, which direct them toward programs they and their donors identify. This may or may not align with what public policy makers believe is important.[9]

easy choices for senior administrators, but such choices ultimately define what an institution stands for and the things it values.

Campus values in turn help determine the extent to which our society is opportunity oriented and thereby provides ladders of possibility for those with ability and energy. *It is difficult to construct an argument that the increasing economic stratification one observes in the student bodies of many American public colleges is consistent either with an opportunity-focused society, or with the rapidly changing demographics of the United States. With their strong concern for enhanced rankings and status, some public universities implicitly give short shrift to the idea that they have critical roles to play in assuring that the economic conditions of one's birth do not set in stone one's later life.*

FINANCIAL AID PROTOTYPES

The diversity of circumstances that characterize institutions reminds us that institutions can pursue many different strategies with respect to access and affordability. Presented here are three of the most obvious strategies.

Model 1: Institutions establish and subsequently maintain relatively low net prices for all students, thereby reducing the need for them to provide large amounts of need-based financial aid to lower-income students. Institutions lacking significant endowments and access to resources they can redistribute usually cannot afford this approach. Further, low net costs of attendance may make an institution more attractive to lower-income and Pell Grant students, but possibly less attractive to status-conscious, "price equals quality" students. Pell Grant and lower-income students not only will require more financial aid and place more demands upon on-campus resources, but also may bring with them less outstanding academic credentials (including lower standardized test scores) and a greater tendency to drop out of school. This may harm the institution's rankings and reputation and, in some states, even result in the institution losing general fund support. Most of the institutions in the Typical 49 pursue some variety of this general strategy, though there is considerable diversity in their specific approaches.

On occasion, institutions may gradually evolve away from this category into model two or three, below, by charging higher net prices and enrolling lower proportions of Pell Grant students. Miami University of Ohio, the twenty-sixth-most expensive public institution in the United States, was one of the earliest members of this evolutionary category.[10] This group now includes Colorado School of Mines, Missouri University of Science and Technology, SUNY Geneseo, Cal Poly, James Madison University, and the College of New Jersey. Quite a few other non-flagship public institutions aspire to this course of action, but for reasons that usually relate to their locations, finances, missions, programs, and reputations find it difficult to do so. It is challenging for non-flagship public institutions that are not located in large metropolitan areas to find distinctive institutional ground on which to stand so that they can charge much higher prices.

Model 2: Institutions develop a heavily price discriminatory net pricing structure whereby they charge much higher effective net prices to students coming from upper-income households than to those coming from lower-income households. This redistributionist strategy usually includes rather high across-the-board published prices that are discounted greatly to in-state students. Institutions traveling this path typically enroll large numbers of nonresident students who pay the full published out-of-state price in order to attend, thus generating revenues that can be used to drive down the net price paid by students whose roots are in lower-income households. Most flagship state universities pursue some variant of this strategy, with the Universities of Alabama, Colorado, Illinois, and Michigan providing the most obvious examples. Declining state funding for public colleges and universities has stimulated dozens, if not hundreds, of institutions to attempt to emulate this approach.

The University of Vermont (UVM), one of the ten most expensive public institution in the country and the third most expensive flagship institution, also falls into this category (in-state tuition and fees were $17,740 in 2017–18).[11] It quotes high prices to prospective students, but offers relatively generous financial aid. An attention-getting 79 percent of UVM undergraduates were nonresidents in 2016–17.

Model 3: Institutions deliberately limit the proportion of admitted students who might receive Pell Grants, thereby minimizing demands on resources required to provide such students financial aid. This "beauty contest" strategy usually enables institutions to fare well in most external ranking systems. Often, it is combined with a heavily price discriminatory net pricing structure and large nonresident student populations. This enables them not only to meet their more limited financial aid needs, but also to generate revenues that can be redistributed for use elsewhere in the institution. The College of William and Mary, the universities of Virginia, Michigan, and Wisconsin, plus Penn State, Pittsburgh, Georgia Tech, and Clemson walk this institutional path. In Penn State's case, only 12 percent of its undergraduates were Pell Grant recipients in 2016–17, but the institution drew almost 19,000 undergraduate students (47 percent) from outside of Pennsylvania.[12] These nonresident students pay premium prices and constitute a critical source of revenue for the university. Penn State's annual average $24,219 tuition and fee collection per student easily is the highest in the Top 28 and is 66.8 percent above the elite average.

THE ROLE OF BRAND MAGNETISM

The notion of institutional brand magnetism is a salient consideration in these discussions. The brand magnetism or lure of a college or university reflects a variety of factors, only one of which is the perceived quality of education at that institution. The institution's location and milieu, the local climate, the jobs obtained and incomes earned by its graduates, the admissions rate of its students into professional schools, its facilities, the reputation of its nonacademic programs including intercollegiate athletics, and even its possible reputation as a party school all come into play.

Outsider evaluators such as the *Princeton Review* assign scores of 0 to 100 to the "quality of life" on campuses. The highest 2016 score, a 99, was assigned to Virginia Tech. Penn State received a 96, which if the score has any validity, may explain some of its ability to prosper and attract students despite offering very high net prices. On the other hand, the University of Alabama, which has seen its enrollment skyrocket, was assigned a score of only 66. This should stimulate at least some doubts about the accuracy of the *Review*'s scoring system.[13]

Working under the aegis of the National Bureau of Economic Research, three University of Michigan faculty members found that campus amenities such as exercise facilities, climbing walls, successful athletic teams, and superb food do make a difference with students who attend institutions outside of the elite. Overall, many students value spending on amenities more than comparable spending on instruction.[14]

Ultimately, however, reality is that the package of attributes associated with a campus (price, location, activities, success of its graduates, etc.) jointly determine the price elasticity of demand for student attendance at the institution—literally, how responsive students and their families are to price increases.

Inelastic is the term economists use to describe the price sensitivity of most students who attend the elite publics. By definition, this means that a given percentage increase in the institution's price will evoke a smaller percentage decline in those who wish to attend. This describes the situation at the University of Michigan–Ann Arbor, which received 55,504 applications for its fall 2016 freshman class, but admitted only 29 percent of that number.[15] Michigan is indeed in the situation the senior university administrator described earlier: it possesses the enviable ability to raise its prices with virtual impunity because it enjoys an admissions pool composed of generous numbers of students and families who will pay almost whatever price is quoted to them in order to join the Maize and Blue.

One of the more perceptive observers of modern higher education is Georgia Tech's Rich DeMillo, who brought extensive private-industry experience to his academic posts. He currently directs Georgia Tech's Center for 21st Century Universities. DeMillo speaks of "the allure of the elite institution, regardless of cost or scholarship availability" and believes that the value proposition of the selective, elite institutions is quite strong.[16] They offer challenging programs that generate opportunities for employment at higher than average salaries. That is, the rate of return on student investment at the elite institutions often is quite favorable.

Our midrange public institution, Illinois State, has some price-making ability—as evidenced by stable enrollment and rising standardized tests scores even while it made significant increases in its net prices. Nevertheless, Illinois State must evaluate its market position carefully when it changes its prices. It is an institution of choice, but often a second choice when Top 28 institutions represent the competition.

The price elasticity of demand for higher education overall is "inelastic" (a 10 percent increase in price, for example, evokes a less than 10 percent decline in quantity demanded). However, the price elasticity of demand for attendance at a specific institution can be much more responsive ("elastic") because that institution faces immediate competition, especially as time passes. Students who receive financial aid have been found to have much more elastic demand curves. Elite institutions, on the other hand, typically face highly inelastic demand curves. Confounding such estimates, however, is the reality that many institutions can adjust the "quality variable." They have the ability to lower their admission standards to ensure they will not suffer any decline in their enrollment when they increase prices. Given a specific quality level of student applicant, however, many non-elite institutions find that their price increases evoke an elastic (negative) response as those students shift to other institutions.

Most of the institutions in the Typical 49 have little or no price-making ability. Realistically, their prices are determined in the long term by what their competition is charging. Institutions such as Bemidji State (MN), Nicholls State (LA), and Rhode Island College cannot get out of line price-wise with their competition without suffering enrollment consequences. Students and their families regard many Typical 49 institutions and similar public colleges and universities as viable substitutes for each other within their geographic spheres. In the language of marketing, they have commodity-like characteristics because many prospective students view them as substitutes for each other in much the same fashion as they see laptop computers or bananas. Price and convenience are more important than label. Thus, if one institution's costs are perceived to be out of line in terms of its value proposition, then students abandon it for its competitors.

One of the most important levers institutions can pull if the number of students willing to pay their prices begins to flag is student quality. Many institutions enjoy the option of lowering their admission standards in order to attract more students. Some within the Typical 49 have walked down this path, but at least a dozen institutions within this group already practice open admission. That is, they find a way to offer admission to virtually all applicants who possess a high school diploma or equivalent and do not present other complications. When the demand for space at these institutions begins to falter, they cannot adjust student quality downward. This usually places them in an enrollment squeeze, which soon leads to financial problems.

An increasing number of regional state colleges and universities now live in this world, or are headed toward it. They are experiencing declining numbers of applicants and suffer from an inability to adjust their student quality downward because they already offer admission to nearly everyone who applies and has a high school diploma. Naming these institutions would needlessly inflict injury on them; however, they do have common characteristics. As a group, they tend to be located in less dynamic, smaller towns in rural areas, or in small cities remote from population centers. Except in local circles, they are not known for any especially outstanding programs, and their brand magnetism is low. These endangered institutions also enroll large proportions of Pell Grant recipients, who simultaneously require more financial assistance and drop out more often than other students. Deteriorating general demographics also are part of this story. These institutions often are in states where high school graduating classes are declining in size and more often than not there is net domestic out-migration of citizens to other states. The state of Illinois provides a current example.

Pell Grant student retention and graduation rates are about 14 percent lower than for non–Pell Grant students, according to a 2015 Education Trust analysis. However, much of this differential appears to be a function of the institutions the Pell Grant students attend—colleges that have elevated dropout rates to begin with for virtually all classes of students. The gap closes to 5.7 percent inside the same institution. Lower percentages of Pell Grant students in student bodies are associated with higher Pell Grant graduation rates.[17]

Even so, most public institutions, including state colleges and universities, resemble lichen in the Artic. Once established, they never disappear. Instead, they activate regional political support to halt any moves toward closure. Nearly always, they underline the institutions' economic impact to their communities and highlight the number of people they employ via economic impact studies. Though mergers and reorientations of missions always are possible, seldom is the actual closure of a public institution in the cards.

Many of the Typical 49 state colleges and universities pose themselves as the "low-cost" alternative to larger flagship competitors. However, as we already have seen, their net prices often actually are higher than the flagship institutions, especially for students emanating from the lowest-income households. In Maryland, for example, the average net price paid in 2015–16 at the University of Maryland College Park by students coming from households with annual incomes $0 to $30,000 was only $7,645, while the comparable price at nearby Morgan State University (an HBCU) was $15,909. In Georgia, the average net price for students coming from the lowest income class was $9,168 at the University of Georgia and $6,293 at Georgia Tech, but $14,834 at Georgia College and State University. Posted tuition and fee charges often disclose remarkably little about actual costs of attendance.[18]

Lurking in the background as another substantive competitor for marginal institutions is Arizona State University's Global Freshman Academy, which has initiated a program whereby students located anywhere in the world can take the entire first year of college online and pay only $200 per credit hour. Further, they pay only if they pass the course. If a student completed ten three-hour courses via this route, then the cost to him or her would be only $6,000.[19]

THE UNIVERSITY OF VIRGINIA: A MINI-CASE STUDY

Virginia and three other states (Kentucky, Massachusetts, and Pennsylvania) officially style themselves as "commonwealths." This is an old English term that presumes that the government should act in support of the common public good. This notion recently was put to the test in Virginia. A sometimes animated discussion bubbled up in 2016 prompted by the pointed observations of the retiring rector (chair) of the University of Virginia's (UVA's) governing board. The rector, Helen Dragas,* noted that UVA had assembled a $2.3 billion discretionary treasure chest (which she provocatively labeled a "slush fund") that it proposed to dispense in support of a variety of projects designed to enhance activities that the university stated were aligned with its strategic plan and its "Affordable Excellence" initiative.[20]

The revelation of this fund, which at the time was larger the state's rainy day fund, prompted a legislative hearing to investigate the matter.[21] At the hearing, one legislator asked UVA officials why some of this reserve of funds had not been used to moderate or eliminate UVA's significant tuition and fee increases. These increases had averaged 9.15 percent annually for in-state students between 2001–02 and 2015–16.

The UVA student newspaper, the *Cavalier Daily*, queried why only 13 percent of UVA students were receiving Pell Grants, when the comparable percentages were 35 percent at the University of California, Berkeley and 22 percent at the University of North Carolina at Chapel Hill. Why shouldn't

---

*Dragas, twice an alumna of UVA (B.A., M.B.A.) and a very successful businesswoman, spearheaded a move in summer 2012 to fire Dr. Teresa Sullivan, who had been appointed president of UVA in 2010. President Sullivan, a well-published sociologist, came to UVA from the University of Michigan, where she was provost. The apparent grounds for terminating President Sullivan were that she was not preparing the university sufficiently for present and future academic and fiscal challenges. Ms. Dragas announced President Sullivan's termination and from all reports had a significant majority of board members behind this decision, however tenuously. A firestorm of protests from administrators, faculty, students, alumni, and others was sufficient to cause many board members to change their minds, and within a few weeks they revoked the termination. Popular opinion then turned visibly against Ms. Dragas. The UVA faculty senate urged her to resign from the board. She declined to do so and served out her term, including leading the board capably for several years as its rector. Originally appointed to the board by a governor who was a Democrat and subsequently reappointed by a governor who was a Republican, Ms. Dragas's tenure as rector was marked by her public concern that UVA was increasing tuition and fees too rapidly and that it was reducing the access to UVA of talented applicants from lower-income households.

President Sullivan's tenure was highlighted by a set of difficult events, including a story filled with falsehoods published in the November 19, 2014, issue of *Rolling Stone* magazine asserting that a rape culture existed on the UVA campus and that it was accompanied by administrative indifference. *Rolling Stone* subsequently retracted the story and later was found guilty of defaming a UVA dean. Other challenges during Dr. Sullivan's presidency included the 2016 "slush fund" allegation; assertions that the university did not defend academic freedom; bouts with armed, vociferous, violent demonstrators who converged on Charlottesville in 2017, ostensibly focused on a statue of Robert E. Lee; and the contention of some students that university founder Thomas Jefferson no longer should be quoted approvingly by UVA because he was a slaveholder. President Sullivan's eight-year tenure ended in summer 2018. Hers was anything but an easy presidency.

this percentage be higher at UVA, and why shouldn't UVA use some portion of the $2.3 billion fund to cause this to happen?[22] (This was a hot topic on other elite state university campuses as well. The *Detroit Free Press* headlined, "U-M Socks Away Millions in Endowment as Families Face Rising Tuition.")[23]

Virginia's state auditor opined that the university had not violated any laws in accumulating its discretionary investment fund, and the point was made that the accumulation of such funds was not unusual at large research universities with medical schools. In 2015, the University of Illinois held $2.4 billion in operating cash, while the University of Pittsburgh held the already noted $2.3 billion in analogous reserves.[24]

Nevertheless, the revelation of the fund's existence focused attention on the very purpose of the University of Virginia and similar institutions. For whose benefit should (do) UVA and other state universities operate?* If citizens and students wish to see moderation in in-state tuition and fees (at least for in-state students), should their desire trump the interests of faculty and administrators who may prefer increased investment in faculty research and other activities that often seem to focus intently on improving the institution's rankings and reputation?

It would be inaccurate to say that administrators and faculty at elite flagship institutions obsessively keep track of institutional rankings. It is fair to say, however, that they know what they are, often use them as measures of performance, and quote them to legislators. They understand that lofty rankings ultimately depend upon variables such as faculty salaries and research productivity rather than student affordability or measures of student learning.

---

*The Code of Virginia says almost nothing about the purpose(s) of Virginia's institutions of higher education. The constitution of the commonwealth says only, "The General Assembly may provide for the establishment, maintenance, and operation of any educational institutions which are desirable for the intellectual, cultural, and occupational development of the people of this Commonwealth" (http://law.lis.virginia.gov/constitution/article8/section9). The university's website states, "The central purpose of the University of Virginia is to enrich the mind by stimulating and sustaining a spirit of free inquiry directed to understanding the nature of the universe and the role of mankind in it" (http://records.ureg.virginia.edu /content.php?catoid=9&navoid=142). The ultimate authority at the university, however, nearly always is "Mr. Jefferson"—Thomas Jefferson, the founder of the university, who designed and developed a beautiful "academical village" on the edge of Charlottesville, Virginia, that remains today the university's signature architectural and spiritual center.

Should it be a matter of public concern that UVA's enrollment of Pell Grant recipients is among the lowest in the nation, and that the *New York Times* reported that only 15 percent of UVA undergraduates come from the entire bottom 60 percent of the income distribution?[25] What if broadening the access of students coming from households with lower incomes resulted in lower SAT and ACT scores and diminished institutional rankings? Or what if propelling faculty salaries upward drew dollars away from programs that would have reduced class sizes for undergraduates, or provided them with additional laboratory support? Further, if institutions such as UVA receive only 10 percent or less of their budgets from state governments, should they really be considered "state" universities and be subject to all the state's rules and regulations? Should they be allowed to privatize, partially or wholly?

These are questions that are central to the identity and purpose of most state universities today, not just UVA. They are difficult, complex issues to consider, and those who are thoughtful seldom respond quickly. Nor when they respond should they do so with absolute confidence.

However, these questions are being asked with increasing frequency. Some allege that public colleges and universities have evolved gradually into an environment in which they now are operated primarily for the benefit of administrators and faculty (with alumni and certain donors also carrying weight) rather than citizens, taxpayers, and students. Even robust supporters of public higher education (myself included) now question whether current modes of operation fit the times.

SEVEN

Declining State Support for Education and What It Means for America

Look around and tell me. Did declining state support force us to play Division I basketball? Did the legislature require us to build that nifty exercise facility you passed on your way in? Did budget cuts cause us to start our new doctoral programs?

—President of a non-flagship public university in the South who wishes to remain unnamed, 2016

L et's borrow a legal term and "stipulate" that real state financial support for higher education has declined on a per student basis. Between the 1999–2000 and 2014–15 academic years, the average total reduction in real state appropriations per full-time equivalent student at seventy flagship state universities was 31.95 percent. At thirty-six urban institutions (but not flagships), the decline was 33.97 percent. Meanwhile, forty-three typical institutions experienced a lower but still hefty 27.71 percent reduction.[1] Figure 7-1 summarizes the decline in state support that has occurred during this century.

Thus, there is little argument about whether state support for public higher education has declined on a price-adjusted, per FTE basis. It has. Instead, the central focus of this chapter is the extent to which the phenomenon has been a cause (or *the* cause) of rising tuition and fees. Some instinctively react to this investigation by uttering, "Of course so!" If they have a background in mathematics, they assign the equivalent of a Q.E.D. from a finished

FIGURE 7-1

**Real State Appropriations per Full-Time Equivalent (FTE) Student,
1999–2000 through 2014–15 (2016 Prices)**

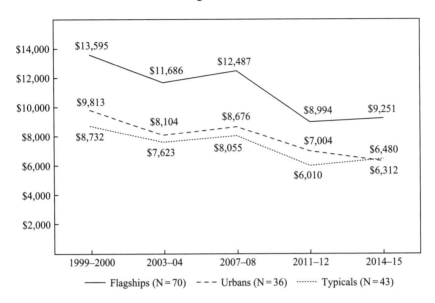

Sources: IPEDS (http://nces.ed.gov/ipeds) and Delta Cost Project (www.deltacostproject.org).

mathematical proof.* They believe it is readily obvious that declining state support has provoked high tuition and fee increases.

Even so, as we will now see, while diminished state support is an important cause of tuition and fee price inflation, it is only one of the causes. The individual circumstances of institutions matter a great deal. *Ultimately, whether one focuses on higher-education sectors or on individual institutions, the available evidence reveals that significant proportions (an easy majority) of all public colleges and universities have increased their tuition and fee charges more than was necessary to compensate them for the funds they lost because of state funding reductions.*

As we look at the evidence, we will see that there is great heterogeneity among institutions where funding is concerned. More than 10 percent of institutions suffered no financial cuts at all if one's measure is their real state

---

*Q.E.D. = *quod erat demonstrandum,* meaning "that has been demonstrated."

funding per full-time equivalent student. This fortuitous circumstance typically meant either that the institution was located in a state that benefitted from rising energy prices (Dickinson State University in North Dakota provides an example), or that it benefitted from special funding circumstances (for example, North Carolina Central University, a Historically Black institution).

Further, the greater the strength of an institution's brand and reputation, the greater was their ability to increase their tuition and fees. The political problem of the elite institutions, however, often is that governors and legislators understand that this is the case and therefore impose proportionately larger financial cuts upon them as a consequence.

SUMMARIZING THE AGGREGATE EVIDENCE

In chapter 5, I previewed one of the most comprehensive studies available on this issue, Douglas Webber's examination of 479 four-year public institutions and their tuition and fee reactions to changes in state appropriations between 1987 and 2014.[2] Webber appropriately focused on each institution's net tuition and fee revenue per full-time equivalent student and thus avoided the "sticker price" problem that has afflicted some other studies. He also addressed the possibility that institutions could combine a freeze in tuition and fees with a reduction in the grant-based financial aid received by their students, which would increase institutional net revenues per student and come at the expense of their students.

In Webber's words, "students are being asked to shoulder the burden of state disinvestment more now than ever before." He found a post-2000 "pass through rate" of 31.8 percent for reduction in state appropriations. That is, a $1,000 cut in state appropriations was responsible for a $318 increase in tuition and fees—actually a smaller amount than my analysis reveals. But tuition and fees have gone up far more than 31.8 percent (for example, more than 103 percent in inflation-adjusted terms at flagship institutions between 1999–2000 and 2014–15), a fact that Webber regards as persuasive evidence that institutions have been increasing tuition and fees for multiple reasons other than declining state appropriations.[3]

A recent Cato Institute study concluded that only 57 percent of annual per student increases in tuition and fees could be attributed to declining state financial support. In thirty-two states, real state appropriations decreased,

> **The staff of the House Appropriations Committee in Virginia** reported in January 2017 that Virginia's public institutions of higher education had raised their tuition and fees $2.00 for every $1.00 they lost in state appropriations between 1996 and 2015.[4]

but Cato found that real net tuition and fee revenue increased by a greater amount.[5]

Robert Hiltonsmith of Demos (a New York–based public policy organization), on the other hand, reported that "declining state support is responsible for 79 percent of increased tuition at research institutions and 78 percent at master's and bachelor's universities." He found that rising costs of instruction, driven by rising health insurance premiums, were responsible by themselves for about one-tenth of observed tuition and fee increases. The precise methodology Hiltonsmith utilized in his study is not clear.[6]

Studies focusing on the impact of state funding cuts on public institution tuition and fees face several common challenges. First, any national study with a large sample must rely on data coming from the U.S. Department of Education's Integrated Postsecondary Education Data System (IPEDS) or on the American Institutes for Research's Delta Cost Project, which in turn is substantially derived from IPEDS. IPEDS and Delta data sometimes are missing entirely for institutions, or are implausibly inaccurate (suggesting faulty inputting of the data), or are misleading because data from several institutions are aggregated under the label of one of them. The University of Texas at Austin provides an example of the latter: the observations for that institution represent all of the institutions in the University of Texas system. Jaquette and Parra, who have done the best work analyzing these deficiencies, conclude that Delta Cost Project data "should not be used to analyze public institutions."[7]

Few researchers take the advice of Jaquette and Parra, primarily because alternative comprehensive data sources are scarce. Instead, they eliminate faulty or suspect institutional observations (for example, those regarding the University of Texas) and keep their eyes out for nonsense data entries. This explains why the tables in this book often reflect institutional sample sizes smaller than the number of institutions in a category.

DISAGGREGATING THE EVIDENCE

Immense variability exists in the funding and expenditure situations of institutions of higher education, even inside the same system in the same state. Public colleges and universities are anything but common peas sitting in the same pod. Their individual financial situations often differ dramatically. Table 7-1 makes this clear by comparing samples of typical, urban,* and flagship institutions.

The first column reports the real percentage increase in the published in-state tuition and fees of the selected institutions. These are the tuition and fee numbers that draw the most attention, though most students do not pay them. *Net* tuition and fees, on the other hand, reflect the prices students pay after grants (but not loans) have been deducted.[†] Percentage changes in these figures are reported in the second column.

The third column lists the percentage change in each institution's state appropriation per FTE student. The fourth column tells us how much more (or less) revenue per FTE each institution had available at the end of the period compared to the beginning of the period—if we confine ourselves to net tuition revenue plus state appropriations. Hence, the data in the fourth column represent the sum of the real net tuition and fee revenues collected by each institution per FTE after locally funded grants have been deducted, plus each institution's real state appropriation per FTE. The data in the third

---

*Large urban areas usually report higher per capita and household incomes than rural areas. Prices of similar goods and services are higher in urban areas than in rural areas, and wage rates are higher as well. Rates of increase in the Consumer Price Index often are higher in urban than in rural areas. Plausibly, these variances result in different behavior.

†Local grant expenditures represent largely discretionary uses of funds. On some campuses, significant proportions of local grants are merit based and are dispensed to students coming from upper-income families. On other campuses, these funds focus upon students who are financially needy. The point is that most campuses (or their governing boards) exercise considerable discretion in how they utilize these funds and often in terms of the proportion of their internal funds they devote to this purpose.

Local campus grant expenditures represent a sword with multiple edges. Any local grant received by a student lowers the average net cost borne by all students. However, if it is a merit-based grant, it may do little to increase access to that institution because the recipient often would have attended college anyway. Need-based grants may increase access, but also cause standardized test scores to wane.

Locally funded grants are not trivial in amount. The Delta Cost Project reveals that the average flagship institution in my sample incurred more than $102 million in discretionary institutional grant expenditures in 2014–15.

TABLE 7-1

Changes in Published Tuition and Fees, Net T&F Revenue per FTE, and State Appropriations per FTE: Typical, Urban, and Flagship Institutions, 1999–2000 to 2014–15 (2016 Prices)

Institution	Percentage Change in Published Real Tuition and Fees	Percentage Change in Net Real Tuition and Fee Revenues per FTE	Percentage Change in Real State Appropriation per FTE	Net Change in Available T&F + State Appropriation Revenue per FTE
Typical Regional Institutions (N = 20)				
Alabama A&M U	169.33%	77.18%	-11.73%	$3,648
Northern Arizona U	210.80%	52.17%	-51.58%	-$2,950
U Central Arkansas	71.27%	124.21%	-21.69%	$1,349
Cal S U Chico	147.09%	70.80%	-40.84%	-$1,360
Central Connecticut S U	65.62%	26.12%	-3.43%	$908
Florida Gulf Coast U	109.93%	126.68%	-73.57%	-$11,149
U Hawaii Hilo	226.58%	118.24%	-11.00%	$3,654
Western Illinois U	107.86%	88.68%	-33.55%	$1,045
Jackson S U	72.86%	14.73%	-45.56%	-$5,248
E New Mexico S U	86.80%	107.06%	-23.26%	$720
Dickinson S U	84.98%	108.73%	123.68%	$10,341
Wright S U	48.83%	54.22%	-44.72%	-$1,504
U Central Oklahoma	111.05%	161.47%	-14.16%	$4,015
Indiana U of PA	51.57%	38.14%	-42.20%	-$266
Rhode Island College	64.12%	97.18%	-29.18%	$1,815
Sam Houston S U	155.08%	118.36%	-50.50%	$1,034
Southern Utah U	119.80%	263.58%	-19.78%	$6,985
Radford U	128.10%	86.24%	-13.12%	$2,123
Central Washington U	107.77%	73.77%	-52.10%	-$696
U Wisconsin Platteville	68.19%	50.52%	-63.19%	-$2,541

Urban Institutions (N = 20)

U Alabama Birmingham	181.66%	78.70%	−14.76%	−$317
U Arkansas Little Rock	137.62%	33.46%	−3.38%	$640
California S U Fresno	267.85%	81.33%	−48.00%	−$2,390
California S U Fullerton	248.50%	56.63%	−41.80%	−$388
U Colorado Denver	96.78%	86.15%	−94.38%	−$6,640
Florida International U	187.20%	74.76%	−35.37%	−$1,263
Georgia S U	262.34%	58.57%	−49.06%	−$4,524
Boise S U	194.07%	81.09%	−35.70%	$727
Towson U	93.81%	16.95%	−11.87%	$174
Montclair S U	190.51%	78.26%	−46.53%	$417
SUNY Albany	95.28%	15.96%	29.63%	$3,702
U Akron	144.64%	69.19%	−40.05%	$826
Portland S U	131.19%	46.23%	−53.80%	−$649
U Memphis	224.72%	81.75%	−35.27%	$1,266
U North Florida	183.11%	88.96%	−27.30%	−$606
U North Texas	265.25%	79.49%	−48.96%	−$181
George Mason U	181.88%	92.56%	−45.44%	$1,426
Old Dominion U	148.50%	44.33%	−24.62	−$82
Virginia Commonwealth U	252.48%	97.27%	−41.77	$620
U Wisconsin Milwaukee	155.84%	55.95%	−40.71	−$496

Flagship Institutions (N = 20)

U Alabama	135.57%	167.63%	−37.50%	$2,655
U Arizona	393.55%	105.85%	−50.34%	−$834
UCLA	261.26%	146.30%	−46.46%	−$987
U Florida	200.56%	143.19%	−22.25%	$788
U Georgia	264.22%	86.31%	−42.74%	−$4,655
Indiana U Bloomington	152.11%	72.97%	−45.03%	$2,163
U Kansas	323.15%	133.92%	17.96%	$8,641

(continued)

TABLE 7-1 (CONTINUED)

Institution	Percentage Change in Published Real Tuition and Fees	Percentage Change in Net Real Tuition and Fee Revenues per FTE	Percentage Change in Real State Appropriation per FTE	Net Change in Available T&F + State Appropriation Revenue per FTE
Flagship Institutions (N = 20)				
Kansas S U	255.43%	168.24%	–33.89%	$2,148
U Kentucky	208.77%	121.79%	–48.73%	–$3,013
LSU	209.73%	129.79%	–30.13%	$2,647
U Missouri Columbia	142.17%	45.77%	–51.38%	–$3,609
U Mississippi	137.03%	103.97%	27.03%	$7,032
U Montana	113.66%	45.73%	15.90%	$3,377
Stony Brook U	107.60%	30.21%	6.37%	$1,879
North Dakota S U	176.33%	92.75%	6.82%	$4,454
Clemson U	276.41%	169.27%	–66.06%	$50
U South Carolina	202.23%	105.31%	–72.29%	–$3,640
U Utah	190.04%	92.07%	–17.72%	$1,292
U Virginia	220.40%	110.49%	–47.48%	$3,654
Washington S U	216.99%	110.06%	–51.50%	–$1,585

Sources: *Chronicle of Higher Education* (www.chronicle.com/interactives/tuition-and-fees) for published tuition and fees; Delta Cost Project (www.deltacost project.org) for net tuition and fees, state support, and FTE.

column directly address the question of whether tuition and fee increases have equaled or exceeded cuts in state appropriations.*

The answer, as one can see in the third column, varies among the states and even among the colleges and universities inside a state. Heterogeneity rules the day. Thus, one can see that Northern Arizona University (NAU), a 30,000-student, non-flagship institution that is not located in an urban area, raised its published tuition and fees by 210.80 percent in real terms over this period, while its real state appropriation per FTE was cut roughly in half, by −51.58 percent. The fourth column records what difference these two counteracting influences made in the total revenue available to NAU on an FTE basis. In NAU's case, it ended the period in question $2,950 per FTE worse off than it began the period. (All these data are expressed in 2016 prices.)

Contrast NAU with Dickinson State University (North Dakota), which enjoyed a 123.68 percent increase in state funding per FTE at the same time its published real tuition and fee charges rose 84.98 percent and its net tuition and fee revenues per FTE rose 108.73 percent. Dickinson ended the period $10,341 per FTE better off in real terms than it was in 1999–2000. Indisputably, Dickinson emerged from this time sequence in much better financial shape than it had been fifteen years previous. Viewed from a big-picture perspective, it is difficult for one to argue that restraining the cost of undergraduate education was a high priority at Dickinson during this time.

Approximately 10 percent of flagship institutions happily experienced increases in their real state appropriation per FTE during the period 1999–2000 to 2014–15. One can see that North Dakota State University, a beneficiary of the shale oil boom in its home state, saw a 6.82 percent increase in its real appropriation per FTE, while the University of Montana, bedeviled by falling enrollments, did not see its state appropriation cut proportionately and ended the period with $3,377 more in real revenues per FTE than when the period began.

Table 7-1 also reveals, however, that the experiences of institutions inside the same state could be quite different. Witness the University of Kansas ending the period about $6,500 per FTE better off in real terms than its sister institution Kansas State. Or California State University at Fresno (Fresno

---

*Note, however, that the IPEDS/Delta Cost Project net tuition variable includes graduate students and out-of-state students.

State) ending the period $2,000 worse off in real terms than California State University at Fullerton.

Institutions such as Southern Utah University more than doubled in size between 1999–2000 and 2014–15. In Southern Utah's case, the Delta Cost Project reports that it did not discount nearly as great a proportion of its tuition and fee revenue as did most other institutions. This helps explain why it ended the period almost $7,000 per student better off in real terms than it was in 1999–2000.

In general, typical and flagship institutions increased their tuition and fees by amounts more than sufficient to cancel the cuts in state funding they endured. Urban institutions as a group ended up just about even.

Are the results reported in table 7-1 sensitive to sample size? No. Figure 7-2 reports results for seventy flagship institutions in terms of the real net revenue gain or loss per full-time equivalent student each institution experienced from 1999–2000 to 2014–15. All of the dots above the zero line represent institutions that ended this fifteen-year period with more real dollars per FTE, even after taking into account the grants their students received from them. There were forty-one gains and twenty-nine losses, with the average real net change in revenue per being $666 per FTE.

The lesson here is that it is almost a fool's errand to talk about changes in state funding across all of public higher education. It all depends upon the state and the institution. The University of Kansas, for example, ended this period $8,641 better off per student. The Kansas state legislature increased KU's real funding per FTE by 17.96 percent, and KU responded to this unusual generosity by increasing its published in-state tuition and fees by 323 percent. Cry not for the Jayhawks. But do shed a tear for the University of Minnesota (not listed in table 7-1), which ended the period $6,319 worse off per student.

What does an institution do when faced with reductions in state funding? In addition to increasing in-state tuition, many institutions during the first fifteen years of this century opted to change their admissions mix and admit more out-of-state students (to whom they charged premium prices). The University of Alabama (UA), for example, endured a 37.50 percent reduction in its real state appropriation per FTE, but adjusted its undergraduate admissions mix to such an extent that by fall 2016, the College Navigator reported that 68 percent of its undergraduates were nonresidents.[8]

FIGURE 7-2

Change in Real Net Revenues per Full-Time Equivalent Student: Seventy Flagship Public Universities, 1999–2000 to 2014–15

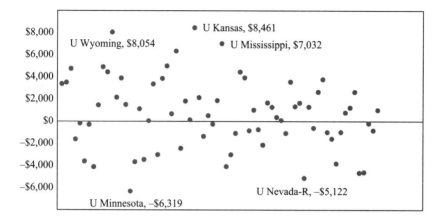

Sources: IPEDS and Delta Cost Project for financial data and number of FTEs; *Chronicle of Higher Education* for tuition and fees.

This helps explain why UA ended the period with net real revenues per FTE student that were $2,655 higher than in 1999–2000.

Some institutions introduced special tuition surcharges for segments of students (such as engineering majors at Purdue) to ward off some of the effects of state funding cuts. Most implemented more user fees for campus services that formerly were free. Room and board charges in campus residence halls increased about twice as fast as the Consumer Price Index for food.[9] Administrators often extracted higher central administrative charges from these and similar auxiliary enterprise funds.

These examples should convince readers that the specific financial circumstances of individual public colleges and universities in recent years have varied substantially. Hence, generalizations about tuition and fee behavior and the revenue situations of four-year public colleges and universities often miss the mark. Yes, the typical flagship state university ended the period a little bit better off. Even so, huge variations existed across flagship groupings such as the Big Ten and the SEC. This implies that rules and policies designed to address the phenomenon of rapidly rising tuition and fees may have sharply different impacts upon institutions, depending on their internal cost structures and market positions. Indeed, it may be difficult to devise any policy that would be capable of addressing the diversity of situations that exist on campuses.

SUMMING IT UP

Even those who place the blame for rapid tuition and fee increases upon stingy governors and state legislators agree that at least one-quarter or more of tuition and fee increases in this century at public four-year institutions have little or nothing to do with state funding cuts. Other reputable sources assert that the proportion of tuition and fee increases beyond state funding cuts may be one-half or more. The results I have presented above suggest that more than one-half of all four-year public institutions have raised their in-state tuition and fees by more than has been required to deal with state funding reductions.

The impact of state funding cuts on tuition and fees is not yet a settled issue, though all credible parties also agree that falling state appropriations have been a major reason why tuition and fee charges (even net tuition and fees) have risen so rapidly. But they are not the only reason. Other factors have been at work as well. We explore these possibilities in succeeding chapters.

EIGHT

William Bennett's Gauntlet

Is the Federal Government Part of the Problem?

There is an overwhelming danger, especially over time, that higher financial aid will lead to higher tuition.

—Andrew Gillen, "Introducing Bennett Hypothesis 2.0," 2012

or is it

The evidence for an unintended aid-tuition link at the nation's nonprofit universities is very weak.

—Robert B. Archibald and David H. Feldman, "Federal Financial Aid Policy and College Behavior," 2016

One of the most important and controversial hypotheses concerning the causes of tuition and fee price inflation was set down in 1987 in broad form by then United States Secretary of Education William Bennett. In a memorable essay published in the *New York Times* entitled "Our Greedy Colleges," Secretary Bennett opined that colleges were "at it again" with tuition and fee increases far in excess of the rise in the Consumer Price Index. He alleged that "increases in financial aid in recent years have enabled colleges and universities blithely to raise their tuitions, confident that Federal loan subsidies would help cushion that increase."[1]

Since then, the Bennett hypothesis has become fodder for almost radioactive debates about the purpose and impact of federal financial aid to college students. Instinctively, nearly all those who believe in the salutary effects of higher education are inclined to favor additional need-based federal financial aid to college students. After all, who doesn't *want* to help? Providing financial aid to those with great financial need strikes most individuals as just, especially in an economic world characterized by increasing inequality. However, a policy of generous student financial aid also can be promoted as an economically efficient policy that will spur economic growth. The argument posited is that this will enable society to avoid a variety of other costs down the road that accrue to a less educated populace.

Nevertheless, what if the actual tuition/financial aid dynamic differs from this ideal narrative? What if, as the *Wall Street Journal* put it, "Costs follow federal subsidies up, up and away"? Is it possible that federal financial aid is an enabling agent that ratifies collegiate tuition and fee increases?[2]

Those who answer true to the first question and yes to the second question assert that institutions know that the federal government will come to their rescue by semi-automatically allocating additional need-based financial aid when public institutions raise their prices. The result, they say, is a situation replete with a condition that economists label "moral hazard"—whereby decision makers take on more risks than they would ordinarily because they are aware that someone else (in this case, the federal government) will bear most of the costs associated with their risks.[3]

This is a point worthy of additional consideration. Moral hazard is commonplace in insured/insurer relationships. Those who are insured often behave differently after they are insured, even if they are unaware of doing so. Economist Sam Peltzman long ago demonstrated that the impact of federal automobile safety regulations approached zero because drivers adjusted their driving to take advantage of new safety features such as seat belts.[4] The same phenomenon could be at work for colleges and universities with respect to the federal financial aid that flows into their coffers via the students they enroll. If the "feds" are going to minimize the risks associated with any institution's tuition and fee increase, then why should that institution not move to increase tuition and fees by a generous amount?

The Bennett hypothesis extends beyond conventional federal student financial aid. Its most expansive versions include tax-favored college savings funds such as the Section 529 vehicles utilized by many parents and grandparents to support their children and grandchildren. The proposition in this instance is that colleges and universities are aware that many of their students come to campus with Section 529 savings accounts. They believe that these students are less responsive to tuition and fee increases and hence hike their prices more than they would otherwise.

THE CONSTANT COST ISSUE

Disputes over the Bennett hypothesis can devolve into arguments over statistical and econometric issues and how variables are defined. However, let's put these considerations aside and clarify what may be the major point of contention between the two camps. Suppose a new infusion of federal student financial aid enters the higher-education system. Should we expect this to influence an institution's tuition and fee charges? Think of the injection of student financial aid as an increase in the demand for a typical institution's academic offerings.

If institutions of higher education operate under conditions of constant average costs per unit, then they are capable of enrolling additional students without experiencing a rising average curve.* This is not the same as saying that there is no increase in costs when additional students appear because there will be some additional expense. Rather, it is that the average cost per student of educating additional students is relatively constant within plausible ranges of moderate expansion.

In a constant cost world, increased federal financial aid does not result in any increase in tuition and fees in higher education. Collectively, institutions are assumed to be able to handle incremental students in any given year without experiencing rising average costs per student. This is the implicit position that has been staked out by the American Council of Education (ACE), which energetically disputes that federal student financial aid has anything of substance to do with rising tuition and fees.[5] Respectable economists have published supportive monographs on the subject under the aegis of the ACE.[6] Not surprisingly, these individuals are sought-after speakers at higher-education association gatherings and meetings of boards of trustees when such groups perceive there is a need to deflect criticism concerning their tuition and fee increases.

---

*The marginal cost of enrolling an additional student may be higher (or lower) than the average cost per student, but enrolling more students allows institutions to spread their fixed costs over more student units. The net effect is a constant average cost curve.

Simply put, they argue that additional federal student financial aid has little or no impact upon their tuition and fees because they can handle the increased demand associated with the additional students supported by federal financial aid without driving up their average costs per unit. Thus, a constant cost world allows higher-education associations and many colleges and universities to beat the drums for additional federal student financial aid.

Those on the other side of the issue scoff at the notion of constant costs, believing that capacity constraints exist even in the short run in the form of limited faculty, classrooms, laboratories, and programs. Further, it is possible that institutional and disciplinary accreditation requirements can impose increasing marginal costs, even in the short run. Also, the construction of new, up-to-date physical capacity usually cannot be accomplished without incurring higher per unit costs because of accelerating technology, environmental, and accessibility requirements. Plus, many popular, high-student-demand majors (nursing, engineering) are more expensive to mount than other majors, which pushes unit costs upward.*

Consequently, the critics of the constant cost hypothesis believe that the supply curve for individual institutions of higher education should reflect increasing marginal costs per student, and that this soon overwhelms the spreading of fixed costs effect that accompanies additional enrollment. Hence, they expect increasing average unit costs. In the jargon of economics, this implies an upward sloping institutional supply curve, moving from left to right.† Finally, this means that enhanced federal financial aid might well lead to higher tuition and fee charges that are passed on to students.

---

*There are significant counterexamples, including large section and massive open online courses that enroll thousands of students. Further, in the short run, there may be empty seats in some classrooms, and (other things such as quality held constant) it is possible to expand enrollment without incurring significant additional costs. Cost functions in such circumstances often are discontinuous and jump upward only when incremental groups of students are added rather than when a single student is added.

†Those who advocate the constant cost view of the higher-education world finesse a portion of these objections by noting that the classic economic cost curve describes how unit costs vary as units of *identical* output increase. If the units of output are not identical, then what is billed as a cost curve is not a cost curve at all because the units along the horizontal axis differ. Applied to institutions of higher education, this suggests that the character of institutional output changes as institutions grow. Hence, they opine that those who posit increasing marginal and average costs are comparing apples and oranges as output expands. By definition, this is true. However, if applied generally, it would invalidate a significant proportion of economic cost studies because the output mix of nearly every multiproduct firm (and universities are

SUMMARIZING THE EVIDENCE

The salient issue is whether the typical public institution of higher education can "tax" the federal government's flow of student financial aid into that institution and draw off funds to use for purposes that do not involve directly reducing the cost of education to their students. If they can, then this provides them with an incentive to increase tuition and fees, because the federal government is going to subsidize a considerable portion of the increased tuition and fees (as well as room and board) that students pay.

In general, the older and less rigorous the evidence, the more likely it is to conclude that federal financial aid has had little or no impact upon college tuition and fees. By itself, this is not a condemnation because Occam's Razor reminds us that the simplest explanation with the fewest assumptions that explains a phenomenon is the preferred explanation. *Nevertheless, more recent studies typically have found that public institutions are able to "capture" some portion of increased federal student financial aid and use it for other purposes.*

Empirical evidence relating to the link between federal student financial aid and tuition and fees is complicated, controversial, and contradictory. The complications are primarily definitional and statistical. For example, when one talks about "federal financial aid," does the term include both loans and Pell Grants, or only one of them? Some empirical studies look at both, but others only at one or the other.

The controversies reflect a fundamental reality: the financial stakes are huge and carry with them political ramifications. In 2015–16, Stafford subsidized loans to undergraduates exceeded $22.95 billion, while Stafford unsubsidized loans topped $50.71 billion.[7] Further, if a link exists between federal student financial aid and rapid tuition and fee increases, then this carries implications for how higher education should be funded and operated. If loans and Pell Grants enable public colleges and universities to increase their tuition and fees charges even more rapidly, then perhaps these programs should be reformed or curtailed. The mere mention of this possibility stimulates heated political discussions.

---

multiproduct firms) changes as they grow. This view of the world would invalidate some of the most important cost studies ever completed in economics. The relevant consideration is how much the mixture of an institution's output changes as it grows.

The contradictory nature of the available statistical evidence should give pause to anyone who is inclined to strong conclusions. While more sophisticated recent studies typically have provided support for the Bennett hypothesis, the complicated nature of the statistical problems militates against concluding that this issue is settled.

Libby Nelson's 2015 nontechnical summary of the many studies that have examined the link between federal student financial aid and tuition and fees is an excellent place for a non-economist, non-econometrician to start.[8] Those in the "it isn't true" camp concerning a possible financial aid/tuition link assert that: (1) the overall impact of federal financial aid on tuition and fees may be greater than zero, but is not large; (2) it is not in the best economic interests of the typical public institution to attempt to diminish ("tax") its own financial assistance to students by substituting federal financial aid dollars in their place; (3) what sometimes is labeled the Bennett effect is confined to for-profit institutions and to colleges and universities that enroll large proportions of lower-income students; and (4) one should examine net prices rather than published sticker prices to obtain an accurate idea of the impact of enhanced federal student financial aid on tuition and fees.

Fundamental to these conclusions is an assumption that also turns out to be a conclusion: that most public colleges and universities operate in a world characterized substantially by constant costs. This means that any increased demand for higher education by students stimulated by additional federal financial aid will not by itself increase unit prices.

On the other side of the coin, a variety of recent econometric studies have generated support for the Bennett hypothesis. One of the most detailed and rigorous (generated in 2015 by economists from the Federal Reserve Bank of New York) concluded: "We find a pass-through effect on tuition of changes in subsidized loan maximums of about 60 cents on the dollar, and smaller but positive effects for unsubsidized federal loans. The subsidized loan effect is most pronounced for more expensive degrees, those offered by private institutions, and for two-year or vocational programs."[9]

It is the "pass-through" estimate of 60 percent on subsidized Stafford loans that has drawn the most attention. It means that institutions in effect are able to tax federal student financial aid flowing via them to their students at a 60 percent rate. The prime means of doing so are to diminish their own institutional provision of financial aid to the same students or simply to increase tuition and fees more rapidly.

The authors of the New York Fed study (Lucca, Nadauld, and Shen) discovered less dramatic relationships for other kinds of federal student financial aid: "Increases in unsubsidized loan and Pell Grant per-student maximums are associated with sticker price increases of fifteen cents on the dollar and forty cents on the dollar, respectively." Even these lower effective percentages of taxation are destructive to those who do not accept the Bennett hypothesis, but not nearly as injurious as the 60 percent pass-through statistic, which has been widely cited.

The New York Fed study has sustained criticism on several counts. The authors chose to focus on published sticker prices rather than the net prices that students actually pay. In my sample of flagship public institutions, the simple correlation coefficient between sticker tuition prices and net prices was only .567, though it was .629 for my sample of urban public institutions and .662 for my sample of Typical 49 public institutions. Plausibly, the New York Fed results might have differed in amount or kind had the researchers focused on net prices. One must allow for the possibility that institutions increasing their sticker prices simultaneously were increasing their own institutionally based financial aid by an equivalent amount. In fact, some of this has occurred in recent years. However, as we already have seen in chapters 2 and 3, those increases have been insufficient to offset a sharp increase in the real net price of attendance at a four-year public institution.

More recently, Gordon and Hedland (2016) relied upon a sophisticated structural economic model to ferret out the separate effects of four things on college and university tuition and fees: (1) federal student financial aid changes; (2) generally declining state financial support; (3) rising college graduate wage premiums; and (4) Baumol's cost disease (which we will discuss in chapter 9).[10] These economists examined both the independent and public sectors of higher education between 1987 and 2010 and focused on net prices. While the assumptions that underpin their analysis are strong, they boldly concluded: "These results accord strongly with the Bennett Hypothesis, which asserts that colleges respond to expansions of financial aid by increasing tuition." Specifically, they argue that increased student borrowing is responsible for more than one-half of observed increases in tuition and fees, while more than 20 percent of observed increases in tuition and fees can be attributed to more generous grant aid.

Among their other conclusions: (1) tuition increases that result from additional federal student financial aid overcome any positive enrollment effect that the financial aid generated; (2) independent institutions often use the funds they capture to increase the quality of their student bodies; (3) Baumol's cost disease cannot explain very much of tuition and fee behavior; and (4) holding other things constant, an injection of new federal student financial aid causes the federal loan default rate to spike upward.

A side issue in this study (and many others) is whether increased federal student financial aid *causes* higher tuition and fees, or instead simply *enables* tuition and fee increases. Most economists (and even Secretary Bennett) favor the latter language—that federal financial policies have enabled institutions to raise their prices, rather than caused them to do so. Gordon and Hedland, however, adopt the language of causation, and this has subjected them to criticism.

Taken without qualification, Gordon and Hedland's conclusions constitute incendiary material in the debate over the Bennett hypothesis and higher-education policy. However, the pair hastened to note, "We suspect that our model exaggerates the explanatory power of the demand-side theories."[11] Even so, their findings broadly support the New York Fed study and directly

Simultaneity bias exists when two variables simultaneously affect each other and each is both a cause and an effect of the other. This situation presents peculiar statistical problems to those attempting to put numbers on the relationships. We know, for example, that federal financial aid formulas incorporate a particular institution's tuition and fee charges. Hence, it is clear that some degree of causation runs from tuition and fees to federal financial aid. The key dispute relates to whether a reverse causal relationship also holds true, whereby federal financial aid encourages institutions to increase their tuition and fees. Relatively sophisticated econometric techniques are required to deal with this possibility, and many studies and reports that assert there is no connection between federal student financial aid and tuition and fees have not controlled for simultaneity bias. On the other hand, the New York Federal Reserve Bank study does so.

contradict the anti–Bennett hypothesis narrative that most public universities, higher-education associations such as the American Council on Education, and some previous researchers have developed.

OTHER STUDIES

We owe the first substantive study of the financial aid/tuition issue to the economists Michael McPherson and Morton Schapiro, both of whom went on to become successful college presidents (McPherson at Macalester College and Schapiro at Williams College and Northwestern University).[12] In 1991, this duo found no connection between financial aid and tuition at independent institutions, but estimated that public institutions raised their tuition by about 50 cents on each additional dollar of federal student financial aid.

A 2001 study generated by the National Center for Education Statistics found no statistical relationship between financial aid and tuition, while a 2007 study by Singell and Stone concluded that the most selective independent institutions did raise tuition and fees in response to increased Pell Grant aid, though public institutions did not.[13] A 2004 study authored by Rizzo and Ehrenberg failed to find any relationship between financial aid and tuition.[14]

Archibald and Feldman's 2011 book, *Why Does College Cost So Much?*, utilized an econometric technique known as the Granger Causality Test to focus on the impact of rising Pell Grant aid and tuition and fees.[15] They found no relationship between increases in Pell Grant aid and tuition and fees at public colleges and universities and actually reported an inverse relationship at independent institutions.

Do colleges and universities really have the power to set their own prices? In twenty-two of the fifty states in 2012, each institution's board had this authority. In only two of fifty cases did legislatures retain that authority. Virtually every institution, however, had the ability to use resources to make grants that impacted the net price its students paid. Thus, public institutions really do exercise considerable independence in determining the prices their students pay.[16]

A 2014 study by Cellini and Goldin concentrated on for-profit institutions in Florida, Michigan, and Wisconsin and found that they taxed away nearly all of the increased financial aid their students were receiving by means of tuition and fee increases.[17] Subsequently, Turner's 2014 study found that colleges and universities in general are able to tax away for their own uses some of the Pell Grant dollars their students were receiving, but only at a much less impressive level: 12 percent.[18]

Apart from these studies, the state of Georgia's HOPE scholarship program, which was introduced in chapter 2, provides an interesting but different kind of test of the Bennett hypothesis because it involves state rather than federal financing of student grant aid. In 2015–16, 36 percent of undergraduate students in the Georgia university system received either a HOPE scholarship or a Zell Miller scholarship, an even more rigorous merit-based aid program. HOPE and Zell Miller scholarship grants covered 84 percent of tuition and fees of individual recipients at public colleges and universities of Georgia.[19]

A series of studies have concluded that the HOPE program has accelerated tuition and fee increases and the cost of attendance for Georgians who go to the state's universities.[20] That is, Georgia's public institutions (primarily the University of Georgia and Georgia Tech) succeeded in capturing a significant proportion of the HOPE and Zell Miller financial subsidies supporting their students.

By 2003, less than 1 percent of all college financial aid provided by the state of Georgia was distributed on the basis of need only rather than merit.[21] In 2012, the *Wall Street Journal*, relying upon zip codes, concluded that students coming from neighborhoods with median incomes greater than $50,000 were about three times more likely to win a HOPE or Zell Miller merit-based scholarship than students from less affluent areas.[22] White students, who constituted 54 percent of public college enrollments, received 64 percent of HOPE scholarship awards and 68 percent of Zell Miller awards.[23] Thus, these scholarship programs, while worthy, redistribute income away from lower-income students and toward higher-income students. Jonathan Cohen is one of several who have made this argument in the popular press.[24]

HOPE scholarship recipients must be residents of Georgia and most commonly have earned a 3.0 grade point average in high school while satisfying a rigorous curriculum. They must continue to earn the 3.0 grade point average in college.

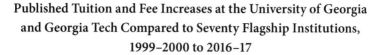

FIGURE 8-1

Published Tuition and Fee Increases at the University of Georgia
and Georgia Tech Compared to Seventy Flagship Institutions,
1999–2000 to 2016–17

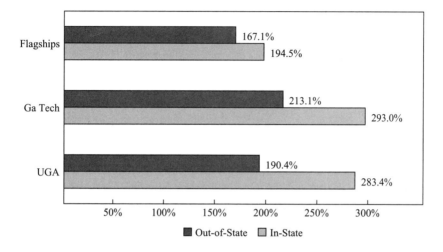

Source: *Chronicle of Higher Education* (www.chronicle.com/interactives/tuition-and-fees).

Figure 8-1 reveals that published, sticker-price tuition and fees at Georgia and Georgia Tech, for both in-state and out-of-state students, increased much more rapidly than they did in the seventy-institution sample of flagships we have examined previously. Indeed, it isn't close. Between the 1999–2000 and 2014–15 academic years, real in-state tuition and fees increased 66 percent more rapidly at Georgia Tech and 59 percent more rapidly at Georgia than the average at seventy flagship institutions. Only limited net price data are available, but they tell a similar story. Between 2013–14 and 2015–16, the average net price paid by students nationally rose 5.80 percent, but 12.56 percent at the University of Georgia and 9.46 percent at Georgia Tech.[25]

By themselves, these numbers are not decisive evidence of the Bennett effect at work because many other causal factors could have been involved. Nevertheless, in simple fashion, figure 8-1 provides visual support for the scenario painted by supporters of the Bennett hypothesis. *Though almost surely it did not intend to do so, the state of Georgia may well have set into motion a dynamic in which its HOPE scholarship program increased the cost of attendance at George public institutions for non-HOPE students and at the same time forced the state to provide increasingly large amounts of money to fund the program.* This is consistent with the increasing-per-unit-cost view discussed above, with Long's 2004 work, and with Condon, Prince, and Stuckhart's 2011 study of the impact of the HOPE scholarship program on published tuition and fee charges at Georgia's public institutions.[26]

Note once again, however, that figure 8-1 reports sticker prices at Georgia and Georgia Tech rather than net prices, which did not begin to be reported regularly by the National Center for Education Statistics until the 2012–13 academic year.

Georgia's HOPE and Zell Miller merit-based academic scholarships reflect a visible national trend toward increased state funding of merit-based scholarships.[27] Between fiscal year 1999–2000 and fiscal year 2017–18, the funding provided by states for merit-based scholarship programs increased by an average of 12 percent annually, while need-based awards increased only 4 percent annually. Critics charge (with some validity) that this practice has contributed to further stratification of public-university student bodies based upon income and social class. A group of prominent economists led by Raj Chetty and John Friedman examined the enrollments of 381 selective public universities and found that they had reduced their share of low-income student enrollees by 4.6 percent between 1999 and 2013. They concluded that "income segregation across colleges is comparable to segregation across Census tracts in the average American city."[28] Their findings are consistent with the *New York Times* income distribution data presented in chapter 2. Rising net prices at public colleges and universities are the engine propelling these developments.

ANDREW GILLEN'S BENNETT 2.0

Andrew Gillen is an economist affiliated with the Center for College Affordability and Productivity, which has been a persistent critic of the status quo in higher education. He has proposed three major refinements to the basic Bennett hypothesis.[29] First, he argues cogently that financial aid directed at students from lower-income backgrounds is much less likely to lead to higher tuition and fees than if the same dollars were directed at students coming from upper-income households.* Lower-income students exhibit more

---

*This is a straightforward price elasticity of demand argument.

elastic (price-sensitive) demands for higher education. Hence, to avoid having institutions capture federal student financial aid, the federal government should ensure that it is directed at the most needy students.

Second, he also believes that raising tuition and fees is only one of several possible actions that institutions might undertake in response to increased federal student financial aid. Other plausible institutional actions include becoming more selective in admissions or increasing the size of their admissions pool. Adding amenities that are attractive to students is another possible course of action. Each of these is a ratings-oriented activity designed to improve an institution's relative position on the higher-education prestige ladder. The relevant point, however, is that institutions might be capturing substantial portions of federal student financial aid, but one would not necessarily see it in their published tuition and fee charges.

Third, he invokes Bowen's Rule, which we will examine in detail in chapter 10. It predicts that colleges and universities are organizations led by bureaucrats who will raise all the money they can and spend everything they raise. The more money and the bigger the institution, the better for such university bureaucrats. In this view, federal student financial aid is but one more substantial source of revenue that contributes to higher costs and higher tuition and fees.

Taken as a whole, Gillen's Bennett 2.0 hypothesis narrows the scope of the original hypothesis by focusing upon its differential impact upon low-income versus high-income students, but broadens it by recognizing that federal student financial aid revenues captured by institutions can be used for a multitude of purposes in addition to making college attendance less expensive.

SUMMARY OBSERVATIONS

Arguments over the Bennett hypothesis have not yet been settled. However, recent studies clearly have placed the critics of Bennett on the defensive. The Obama administration essentially accepted elements of the Bennett hypothesis in 2016 when it attempted to tie a portion of the federal student financial aid received by colleges and universities to their ability to control their prices.[30] Similarly, bipartisan attempts to force colleges and universities to bear a portion of the cost of student loan defaults might be seen as an implicit adoption of the Bennett hypothesis.

Those who have promoted the "no effect" narrative (primarily the higher-education establishment) often have been reduced to making methodological criticisms of the new studies rather than being able to rely upon sophisticated recent statistical studies of their own. *While hardly unanimous, a bipartisan consensus seems to have emerged that the Bennett hypothesis holds some validity.*[31]

In addition, the eyeball test has not been kind to the narrative that declares there is no link between student financial aid and institutional tuition and fee increases. Relatively uncomplicated scenarios such as the Georgia HOPE scholarship program suggest that there appears to be a link and that the impact of financial aid on tuition and fees is empirically significant. Collateral to this, elementary economic analysis also suggests that the existence of a link is plausible and should not be summarily rejected. The upshot is that proponents of the Bennett hypothesis no longer can be dismissed as ideologues. The wind is blowing at their backs, though not yet at gale speeds.

The salient considerations, however, relate to which policies we should pursue if the Bennett hypothesis holds some substantial degree of water. Eliminating federal student financial aid would be disastrous because millions of students absolutely depend upon it, and it has become a vital rung on the ladder of mobility and opportunity. In any case, it would take years for the federal government to ease back on its commitments in this arena even if it were determined to do so.

One interesting alternative is to have governmental units provide students with financial vouchers that they could use at the institution of their choice rather than having the states fund the institutions directly.* This would break the funding link between institutions and the state and force institutions to compete to attract students. It is a proposal that evokes memories of the G.I. Bill after World War II, and proponents contend it would discipline public institutions of higher education. In 2005, the state of Colorado implemented a version of a higher-education voucher program, but it does not appear to have made much difference either in student or institutional behavior.[32]

If federal financial aid (including loans) were restricted to students coming from lower-and middle-income households, then the available evidence

---

*This is one of Archibald and Feldman's suggestions (Robert B. Archibald and David H. Feldman, *Why Does College Cost So Much?* [Oxford University Press, 2011]).

suggests that the size of any Bennett effect would diminish appreciably. Also, if institutions had to bear some portion of losses realized by the federal government when former students default on their loans, it might stimulate colleges and universities to exercise greater prudence in arranging loan packages for their students. In turn, so the argument goes, this might cause the institutions to moderate their tuition and fee increases because they would no longer be able to benefit from such a healthy flow of federal student financial aid.

The ultimate solution, however, is to find ways to control the upward spiral of institutional costs that has gripped American higher education for many decades. Most of the adverse consequences of the Bennett hypothesis are a result of the inability or unwillingness of colleges and universities to control their own costs. I will have more to say about this phenomenon in succeeding chapters. However, if the Bennett effect is empirically valid, then this means that institutions consistently drain off the additional revenues provided to them by federal student financial aid and use the revenues for purposes other than reducing the net price that students pay. The persistent increases in the real net prices students pay to attend state colleges and universities provide first-order evidence of this phenomenon.

Controlling costs at colleges and universities is, as a topic, not easy to broach for several reasons, one of which is that the cost inflation we have observed in higher education has many sources and roots. In fact, it is the consequence of the operation of multiple forces, and only the uninitiated would regard it as anything other than a complicated problem.

Another challenge is that formal rules dictating cost controls smack of oleaginous federal price controls accompanied by voluminous dictums from on high. Such an approach to life eventually proved to be one of the reasons for the demise of the former Soviet Union.* This is hardly a scenario we should seek to imitate because it is generally viewed as a recipe for decline.

Cost and price controls are very difficult to implement in any situation, much less the distinctive, complicated wilderness of higher education, whose peculiar dynamics are so difficult to master. Whom should we trust to

---

*When in 2003 Congressman Howard P. "Buck" McKeon proposed to assign financial penalties to institutions that increased their cost of attendance by more than two times the rate of inflation for two years in a row, he was met with a storm of protest. Stephen Burd, "High Stakes on Tuition," *Chronicle of Higher Education*, May 2, 2003.

decide whether the purchase of a new computer server at Regional State U., or an airplane ticket for a faculty member from Flagship U. to attend a conference in Berlin, are worthwhile expenditures? Who is appropriately situated to decide how many students and what quality of student institutions will (should) admit? This is a vital concern since quantity and quality adjustments are among the first reactions of decision makers to price controls and rules.

Nonetheless, it is within the special province of boards of trustees to monitor costs, control tuition increases, and insist that institutions be increasingly attentive to productivity-increasing and cost-reducing approaches to the academic enterprise. Very few boards actively evaluate their presidents on the basis of such criteria; boards are much more attentive to traditional dashboard variables such as enrollment, fundraising, research dollars, graduation rates, ratings, and the like. Certainly, these traditional performance variables are relevant, but excellent performance in those areas actually may be achieved on the financial backs of the students and their families, who pay higher net prices. *It should make a difference how an institution achieves what commonly is perceived as "success." Boards (and ultimately legislators and governors) should be more sensitive to the means by which goals such as national rankings are achieved, and, for example, pay more attention to how lower-income students are affected by policies than most appear to be.*[33]

Collaterally, persistent cost-inflationary behavior by institutions is one of the reasons why "zero tuition" proposals are unlikely to work as hoped. Over time, zero tuition will not succeed without some form of fiscal control that discourages or prevents institutions from increasing prices or adding to their cost structure. After all, if the "feds" are going to pay the bill, or students can be made to pay higher prices, why should institutions not increase costs? Additionally, why shouldn't states diminish their tax support for their public colleges and universities if the feds are going to ride to their rescue by eliminating tuition and fees? The moral hazard problem I identified earlier applies not only to the Bennett hypothesis, but also to the increasingly common proposals for zero tuition and fees.

NINE

Baumol, Bowen, and the Overworked String Quartet Simile

Most contemporary critics of higher education fail to credit the power of the cost disease argument in explaining the long evolution of higher education costs. The artisan nature of higher education explains much of this past experience.

> —Robert B. Archibald and David H. Feldman, *The Anatomy of College Tuition*, 2012

No place is more conservative in its management practices than a college or university campus.

> —Brian Mitchell, "Higher Education: The Stubbornly High Cost of Doing Business," 2016

In 1966, William J. Baumol and William G. Bowen published *Performing Arts: The Economic Dilemma*, which perhaps unexpectedly turned out to be one of the more influential economics books written during the second half of the twentieth century.[1] Baumol and Bowen's penetrating but easily understood analysis not only changed our understanding of the seemingly perpetual financial problems of the fine and performing arts, but also proved to be applicable to a variety of other situations, including higher education.

Baumol* and Bowen† developed a simile involving symphony orchestras that has been cited repeatedly. The pair noted that the same number of musicians today is required to play a Beethoven string quartet as held true in the early 1800s. Similarly, they observed that any specific composition, for example Beethoven's famous String Quartet no. 14 in C-Sharp Minor (1826), habitually is performed today at the same tempo as it would have been almost two hundred years ago.

If the magnitude and speed of output are the focus of our attention, then there has been no improvement whatsoever in the productivity of a typical string quartet over the intervening centuries. The members "produce" the same music at the same speed as they did when Beethoven was in his prime. Nevertheless, over time, their wages have increased even while most other costs associated with their performance (heat, light, transportation, rights to music, etc.) also have ratcheted upward. These rising costs have forced string quartets and orchestras to raise their prices.

Why do the wages of the musical performers continue to rise even though their measured productivity is constant? Higher compensation is required to entice the musicians and those around them to forgo alternative employment opportunities. Like all other workers, they have opportunity costs: alternative activities they must forgo when they choose to become musicians. Instead, they could become high school music teachers, accountants, or even Uber drivers. The possibilities are endless.

Meanwhile, the members of the string quartet also must contend with rising prices of the things they purchase daily—food, shelter, etc. If their wages do not rise to help them deal with gradually inflating prices, then many

---

*William J. Baumol (1922–2017) was professor of economics emeritus at Princeton University. He wrote eighty books and several hundred refereed journal articles. While not a recipient of the Nobel Prize in Economics, he easily qualifies as one of the most distinguished and important economists of the last fifty years. His seminal work spans many areas of economics, including labor economics and entrepreneurship.

†William G. Bowen (1933–2016), also a professor of economics at Princeton University, served as president of the Mellon Foundation. He was the author of influential books on higher education, including The Shape of the River: Long-Term Consequences of Considering Race in College and University Admissions (coauthored with Derek Bok), Equity and Excellence in American Higher Education (with Eugene M. Tobin and Martin A. Kurzweil), and Crossing the Finish Line: Completing College at America's Public Universities (with Matthew M. Chingos and Michael S. McPherson).

will find continuing to play in the string quartet an untenable economic proposition and will depart for other pursuits.

The symphony orchestra simile has proven to be very appealing to many who seek to explain why public college and university tuition and fees have increased despite minimal increases in measured productivity in higher education. They perceive that the activities of institutions of higher education bear some resemblance to Baumol and Bowen's string quartets in at least two ways. First, the measured productivity of institutions has remained relatively constant in recent decades if one's metric is credit hours generated per faculty member, or the number of courses taught per faculty member.

Second, colleges and universities typically utilize large numbers of highly educated faculty and professionals, most of whom command premium salaries. Exemplary are the information-technology and data-management specialists, whose numbers have burgeoned on most campuses. In December 2016, www.datajobs.com advertised "big data" jobs that ranged from $85,000 to $170,000, with managers earning up to $240,000 annually. Compare these salaries to the $43,000 median annual salary of a full-time American worker in the third quarter of 2016.

As a group, faculty typically account for 25 to 35 percent of the total expenditures of a public college or university; personnel expenditures of all kinds eat up two-thirds or more of most institutional budgets. Salaries and associated fringe benefits (which usually add 30 percent or more to salaries) are the highly visible two-ton gorilla in the room insofar as higher-education costs are concerned because of the labor-intensive nature of modern colleges and universities. Thus, expensive labor inputs require higher prices, or at least so the argument goes.

Archibald and Feldman, who credit the string-quartet argument, write that "most contemporary critics of higher education fail to credit the power of the cost disease argument in explaining the long evolution of higher education costs. The artisan nature of higher education explains much of this experience." Arguing that the price increases observed in higher education are "not even particularly unusual," the duo sees higher education as a highly visible yet unremarkable example of a labor-intensive industry whose characteristics are closer to the string quartet than to those we observe in steel mills, shoe factories, restaurants, and farms.[2]

Finally, the inputs utilized by these expensive individuals (laboratories, technology, etc.) also can be quite pricey. True, the prices of some heavily used items in higher education, such as personal computers, have plunged, but the same cannot be said for scientific and technology equipment and commodities in general. As we already have seen, the Higher Education Price Index (HEPI) has increased more rapidly than the Consumer Price Index (CPI).

One can argue that the expenditures made by colleges and universities on expensive personnel, technology, equipment, and the like have been necessary to maintain or increase quality. There is some validity to this argument. We would prefer not to teach or do research in the sciences today with the equipment in Marie Curie's late nineteenth-century laboratory. The new personnel and equipment are expensive, no doubt.

However, advances in technology also have made it less expensive to teach and do research in many disciplines. One faculty member can be effective in teaching hundreds of students,* and all faculty have become addicted to having digitized access to journals and research materials that previously they only dreamed about. Hence, the extent to which quality maintenance and enhancement are responsible for the price increases we have observed is an arguable proposition, particularly in view of the indifferent performance of today's undergraduates on many standardized examinations that attempt to measure their learning.

SOME PRODUCTIVITY EVIDENCE

Whether or not institutions of higher education have had to pay prices for people and things that have been increasing more rapidly than prices in general, it is fair to observe that the campus processes that jointly generate baccalaureate degree recipients have been resistant to most attempts to make them more productive. However, I use the term *productivity* here in the fashion it would be employed if we were discussing the production of items such as corn or automobiles. This is conventional textbook economics usage and

---

*For fifteen years I taught managerial economics annually to undergraduate classes that numbered up to 500 students. The students were located in many different spots around the world, but were complemented by a control group of students doing it "the regular way" in front of me. At the end of every semester, I undertook a statistical analysis of student performance. There was no statistically significant difference in the performances of students based upon location or method of receiving the course once one controlled for SAT scores, age, math background, etc. I do not contend that all disciplines can be transmitted effectively in this fashion, but many can.

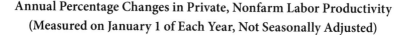

FIGURE 9-1

FIGURE 9-1

Annual Percentage Changes in Private, Nonfarm Labor Productivity
(Measured on January 1 of Each Year, Not Seasonally Adjusted)

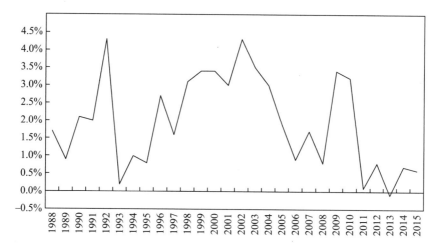

Source: Federal Reserve Economic Data (FRED), MPU4910063 (https://fred.stlouisfed.org).

as such directly relates inputs to output. If 1,000 workers endowed with a given set of machines and equipment currently can produce 10,000 automobiles in one week, but subsequently find a way to increase their output to 11,000 automobiles with the same inputs, then this is considered an increase in productivity.

The Bureau of Labor Statistics (BLS) is one of several federal agencies that publish productivity statistics. The BLS tracks output per labor hour, which is the most commonly cited measure of economic productivity. Figure 9-1 illustrates the annual average percentage changes in the labor productivity of private, nonfarm, business-sector employees between 1988 and 2015. These changes ranged from a low of −.1 percent to a high of 4.3 percent. The central point, however, is that the changes nearly always have been positive, reflecting workers who on average were increasingly productive.

Nothing like the concept of output per labor hour exists today in higher education because the inputs and outputs of higher education are so variegated. What is it that professors actually do? As Bowen himself observed, the productivity of professors and others connected to higher education is multidimensional.

The disconnect between the public and faculty over faculty duties and responsibilities is aptly captured by an old bromide that circulates among college presidents. The story may be apocryphal—but perhaps not. A state legislator asks a faculty member how much he teaches, and the faculty member replies, "I have a nine-hour load." The legislator responds respectfully, "I'm impressed. That's a good day's work." The faculty member, of course, was referring to his weekly teaching responsibilities, not his daily work. It will suffice to note that many members of the public do not understand what faculty members do, and vice versa.

Nevertheless, many institutions and boards collect data such as credit hours generated per faculty member as one means of assessing faculty involvement and productivity. The duties of most faculty members extend far beyond their presence in classrooms and laboratories and include their research and scholarly productivity, institutional service, and public service. We would not want to measure the productivity of Nobel Prize–winning professors based on the number of credit hours they generated in the previous year. It is not possible to encapsulate everything that faculty members do into a single number.[3] In any case, credit-hour numbers are not generally available or comparable on an institution-by-institution basis.

Insofar as public college and university faculty are concerned, the dynamic of gradually increasing measured productivity that we observed in figure 9-1 largely has been absent. Figure 9-2 discloses faculty/student ratios (the reciprocal of student/faculty ratios) for a variety of classifications of faculty that were reported by the flagship, urban, and typical institution groups introduced earlier. Over the twelve-year period represented in figure 9-2, the ratio of total faculty members per 100 full-time equivalent (FTE) students crept upward slightly—less than 1 percent. This means that the typical faculty member was handling slightly fewer students at the end of the period as compared to its beginning. A fair assessment is that this measure of faculty productivity has been constant over time.

FIGURE 9-2

The Number of Faculty and Graduate Assistants per 100 FTEs at 131 Public Colleges and Universities, 1999–2000 and 2010–11

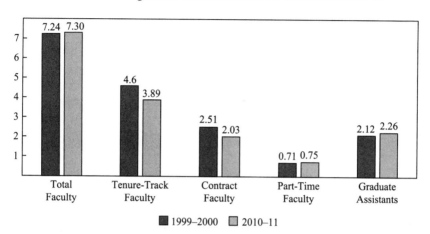

Source: Integrated Postsecondary Education Data System (http://nces.ed.gov/ipeds).

A study of teaching loads in the University of North Carolina system, while critical of the absolute number of courses being taught by faculty each semester, did not find any trend toward lighter teaching loads.[4] Also, a 2009 study of teaching responsibilities of sociologists between 2001 and 2007 found that faculty taught an average of 6.33 courses annually in 2007 as opposed to only 5.72 in 2001.[5]

On occasion, a former college president will opine that faculty should have been teaching more classes with more students in them to begin with, and therefore studies focused on changes are not instructive.[6] A problem in evaluating this and similar assertions is that we do not have any reliable recent data that speak to faculty teaching loads on a national basis. The most recent credible data were collected by the National Center for Education Statistics in 2003. At that time, 36.1 percent of full-time faculty were teaching six or fewer hours per week, and 47.6 percent were meeting fewer than fifty students per week. These numbers differed substantially among institutional types. At public research institutions, 57.3 percent of full-time faculty taught six or fewer hours per week, and 63.0 percent taught fewer than fifty students weekly. On the other hand, at comprehensive institutions (like the Typical 49), the percentages were 20.4 percent and 34.7 percent, respectively.[7]

It is fair to say that individuals unfamiliar with the academic enterprise likely would not regard as oppressive any of the teaching loads just mentioned. Nevertheless, we lack recent data that would allow us to see how circumstances may have changed in the intervening years.

Whatever the teaching duties of faculty, figure 9-2 underlines that there has been a change in the mixture of faculty at public colleges and universities. The relative presence of tenure-track or tenured faculty members on these campuses has dramatically declined—from 4.597 per 100 FTEs to only 3.890, representing a 15.4 percent decrease. In their stead, the institutions hired more part-time faculty and graduate assistants.

The changes illustrated in figure 9-2 come as no surprise to anyone close to public higher education. Increased use of part-time and adjunct faculty members has become commonplace, and on most public university campuses today there are more part-time faculty members than full-time. Flagship state universities are no exception.*

This behavior, however, leads us to an interesting and important modification of the Baumol/Bowen postulate. When existing faculty and professional employees become more expensive, institutions frequently seek to substitute less expensive contract and part-time employees for them.† Figure 9-2 catches this phenomenon. Provosts and deans do not live in a world of fixed proportions, except when prescriptive accrediting bodies force them to employ a given proportion of credentialed faculty per student.

A moral to this story is that most colleges and universities do not sit idly by when confronted with the "expensive personnel" situation. Like corporate executives and city managers, they substitute less expensive inputs for more expensive ones. This implies using relatively more contract, adjunct, and part-time faculty and relatively less tenured and tenure-line faculty. This vitiates the allegorical power of the string quartet.

A variety of studies reveal that the typical faculty member now devotes an increasing share of her time to research, public service, and other non-instructional activities, though this trend has slowed since 2000.[8] Reflective

---

*On some campuses, faculty unionization has mitigated this trend somewhat. However, even faculty unions have turned out to be relatively impotent to reverse this substitution phenomenon, which is driven by administrators who desire to spend available funds on a variety of tasks (especially research) rather than on full-time tenured or tenure-line faculty positions.

†An economist would aver that the demand curve has the expected negative slope.

of this trend, a recent study conducted by Peter Hinrichs of the Cleveland Federal Reserve Bank found that expenditures on research at public institutions of higher education expanded four times more rapidly than expenditures on instruction between 1987 and 2013. Public-service expenditures expanded two and a half times as rapidly as those on instruction.[9]

Reality is that the typical tenured or tenure-line faculty member is devoting more time to research and public service, as mentioned above, which suggests that this individual likely is teaching fewer classes that enroll fewer students than was true in the 1980s. This deduction does not follow automatically from the data, but the data point in this direction. The same faculty member cannot be in two places at once.

Today, the simile of the string quartet is associated primarily with Baumol and sometimes is labeled "Baumol's curse" or "Baumol's cost disease." Some regard the cost disease as a malady of great importance. Bowen, on the other hand, has achieved his own fame on a variety of fronts, including affirmative action, the matching of students with institutions, and the analysis of the dynamics surrounding degree completion.

Given their view of the inner workings of the higher-education enterprise, Archibald and Feldman no doubt would find the "no increase in measured productivity" result less than surprising. In their view, if one is determined to maintain educational quality, then it may be as difficult a task to spur measured faculty productivity as it is to increase the productivity of our now proverbial string quartet. Of course, the same might said of the work of barbers, dentists, or numerous other labor-intensive service-oriented occupations.[10]

Those who place credence in Baumol's cost disease devote considerable time to demonstrating that it (or something like it) is present in many other service-oriented occupations, such as health care provision and social services, both of which traditionally have required the use of highly educated, highly paid professional workers and whose measured labor productivity has not changed very much in recent decades. Nevertheless, they also cite markets for barbers and hair stylists, where workers typically do not boast high levels of formal education, but operate in labor-intensive situations with fixed proportions. Barbers, for example, dispense haircuts on a one-to-one basis, and there appears to be little prospect that this will change.

One might still include lawyers on this list, even though the digitization of legal records and the development of legal software with artificial intelligence have begun to enable legal firms and their clients to substitute machines for people and to employ less expensive individuals (paralegals and the like) to do tasks that previously were accomplished only by members of the bar. In fact, the incomes of attorneys continue to vault upwards; the legal services prices in the Consumer Price Index for All Urban Consumers (CPI-U) increased more than twice as fast as the overall CPI-U between January 2000 and January 2016.[11]

Proponents of Baumol's cost disease also often contend that the quality of the outputs of many of these labor-intensive workers has increased over time, which therefore provides a justification for their rising wages and incomes. This argument holds some water, but only in selected cases. In favor of it, few of us, when ill, would trade today's doctors, medical technology, and medical knowledge for those of a hundred years previous. On the other hand, it is not clear that work products in labor-intensive occupations such as law, social work, and hair styling have improved noticeably in recent decades.

As applied to higher education, the rising-quality hypothesis asserts that the knowledge imparted in classrooms, student experiences in laboratories, access to technology and amenities, and the like are superior to those we observed fifty or one hundred years ago. Accordingly, this is one reason why increases in real tuition and fee charges are merited: today's higher-education product and the college experience simply are superior to those enjoyed by our fathers and mothers and warrant higher prices.

The notion that today's higher-education product excels that generated years in the past is a contentious proposition, to say the least. Many voices argue otherwise, and relatively recent studies, such as the one by Richard Arum and Josipa Roksa, paint a bleak view of what college students today actually are learning.[12]

Arum and Roksa followed 2,300 college students at twenty-four institutions representing the breadth of American higher education to determine if college made a difference in the students' ability to think critically, undertake complex reasoning, and write cogently. They found that 45 percent of the students in their sample showed no improvement in these skills and understandings during their first two years of college, and approximately one-third showed no difference after four years. Disturbingly, they found that 37 percent of students in the sample were spending less than five hours per week preparing for their classes. Fully one-half of the students reported that in their previous semester, they did not have a single class that required twenty or more pages of writing. Nevertheless, the mean grade point average of the 2,300 sampled students was 3.2.

Interestingly, Arum and Roksa's conclusions did not vary significantly across types of institutions, though some institutions clearly were more effective in enhancing student performance than others. Elite colleges and universities were no more successful than their run-of-the mill compatriot institutions in instilling improvement, though their better prepared students usually performed better than less well prepared students. Specific local practices and an institution's overall educational culture appeared to be important determinants, and great variability in results sometimes appeared inside the same institution.

One might be inclined to set Arum and Roksa aside were it not the case that a variety of other studies point us toward similar conclusions. Even though we cannot measure all aspects of learning, one can assess higher-order critical thinking and reasoning skills. When we do so by means of tools such as the well-regarded Collegiate Learning Assessment Plus (CLAP), which challenges students to demonstrate skills rather than to recall information, the results often are discouraging. In its results for 2015–16, although seniors out-performed freshmen, the CLAP found that only 57 percent of college seniors were "proficient" or better in the basic skills being assessed. At 5 percent of the institutions, freshmen outperformed seniors, though at 8 percent of the institutions, performance improved by more than one standard deviation between students' freshman and senior years. Institutions without heavy commitments to graduate education exhibited the highest student value-added between students' freshman and senior years.[13]

In both 1991 and 2003, the National Assessment of Adult Literacy (NAAL) found that most college graduates fell below what was termed "proficiency" in verbal and quantitative literacy. Indeed, between 1992 and 2003, the average score earned by a college graduate fell noticeably in the NAAL's "prose" and "document"* categories and remained constant in its "quantitative" category.[14]

---

*The NAAL explains its "document" literacy category this way: "The knowledge and skills needed to perform document tasks (i.e., to search, comprehend, and use non-continuous texts in various formats). Examples include job applications, payroll forms, transportation schedules, maps, tables, and drug or food labels." National Center for Education Statistics, "National Assessment of Adult Literacy (NAAL): Three Types of Literacy" (https://nces.ed .gov/naal/literacytypes.asp).

Of course, not all groups of students, or all institutions, were affected in the same way. Ethnic background, family circumstances, and institutional type made a difference. Further, additional social engagement by students did not improve their performances, and Greek social organization affiliations exercised a negative influence. On the other hand, students who studied alone, read more, and wrote more often registered better performances.*

There is no need to flog the higher-education-quality argument to death or to unnecessarily simplify what is a complex phenomenon. Measuring the outputs of higher education is challenging, and in any case we should not hold colleges and universities responsible for all of society's educational ills. However, we can reasonably conclude that it is difficult to make the case that either today's undergraduate instructional products or today's baccalaureate degree recipients, taken as groups, are superior to those observed decades previous. Perhaps they are, but the jury clearly is deliberating. Consequently, assertions of improved quality as a condition that justifies increases in tuition and fees that are multiple times higher than increases in the Consumer Price Index are just that: assertions. One needs to look elsewhere for arguments in defense of the escalation in tuition and fees.

IS BAUMOL'S COST DISEASE STRONG OR WEAK IN HIGHER EDUCATION?

The nub of the problem is that higher education has been running in place for many years in terms of labor productivity. As figure 9-1 revealed, measured labor productivity has been increasing in the remainder of the economy (though not as fast as many would prefer). This has supported some wage increases, reduced some prices, and enhanced our standard of living. Unfortunately, measured labor productivity in higher education has idled. Even though public colleges and universities typically have failed to generate measured instructional productivity gains, they nevertheless have increased

---

*An indirect and imperfect measure of the quality of higher education is the rates of return students earn on their financial investments in higher education. Problems include the fact that rates typically are computed for students who complete their degrees, but not for those who drop out; the rates often fail to include student borrowing; and the rates vary dramatically across majors and institutions. Hence, rate of return information is not as valuable as it first might seem.

their prices markedly—by many multiples of the rise in the Consumer Price Index. Baumol's cost disease is the most commonly cited rationale for this phenomenon. Hence, it is well worth our time giving Baumol's cost disease a closer inspection. I will preview the discussion by opining that in my view, Baumol's cost disease does apply to higher education, but not nearly to the degree that some contend. Consider the following:

Fixed vs. Variable Proportions

Baumol and Bowen's string quartet contains the traditional four members—two violin players, a cellist, and a viola player. Seldom if ever does this membership change. The data presented in figure 9-2. however, demonstrate that administrators have been reducing the proportion of tenure-track faculty they employ. Figure 9-2 additionally reveals that administrators have been reallocating funds away from instructional activities inside their institutions. This trend is especially apparent at flagship universities. The reality is that administrators routinely substitute one faculty input for another to meet instructional needs and satisfy institutional budgets. This means that (to borrow a legal term), the string quartet example is not "on all fours" with the reality of higher education. Their situations differ. Institutions, unlike performing arts organizations, have considerable freedom (if they wish to exercise it) to change which faculty appear in classrooms and laboratories and how often they do so. For example, even research institutions have the freedom to decide to employ contract faculty whose sole responsibility is skillfully teaching and advising students (and some do). Or they can hire more part-time faculty or utilize graduate assistants. The point is, public colleges and universities are not stuck with the faculty and staff equivalent of two violin players, a cellist, and a viola player.

Use of Technology in Instruction

The use of technology has its limits in higher education and should not be regarded as the solution to all productivity challenges of institutions. Even so, viable alternatives exist to the traditional "sage on the stage" model of instruction whereby a faculty member faithfully stands in front of a group of student and lectures them. "Flipped" classrooms, for example, involve students studying course material outside of class by means of conventional readings, prerecorded video lectures, and research assignments. When students come to class, faculty members involve them in learning activities that frequently utilize technology. Thus, economics students may be presented with a series of choice-making situations and then respond with their choices or answers. The answers of the class are dissected and analyzed along with illustrative videos (perhaps taken from a popular movie or television show) or analysis of real-world situations borrowed from sources such as the *New York Times* or the *Wall Street Journal*. There is little opportunity for students to go to sleep in such an environment. Not only do students typically learn more, but also a single faculty member usually can handle more students in a flipped classroom situation. Bowen himself was one of the authors of a very influential, controlled study of technology-enabled interactive instructional systems in 2012 in which students using hybrid interactive technology achieved "at least equivalent educational outcomes," thus opening the possibility for "saving significant resources which then could be redeployed more productively."[15]

One should not discount the use of massive open online courses (MOOCs) that enroll tens of thousands of students in a single course. While MOOCs do not suit the learning styles and needs of many students, they nonetheless present opportunities for impressive economies of scale that should not be ignored. Particularly noteworthy prototypes include completely online degree programs such as Georgia Tech's online master's program in computer science. Tech has partnered with Udacity and AT&T to offer an online, fully accredited, and demonstrably successful master's program at a small fraction of the cost that a student would pay to do the same program on Tech's Atlanta campus. As of spring 2016, Tech had enrolled more than 3,000 students in the program, which a student could complete with a tuition of expenditure of less than $7,000.[16] Numerous other institutions now offer complete degree programs online. Once again, these programs are not for everyone. Younger, less mature students do not fare as well in MOOCs, and not all academic material can usefully be presented in the form of a MOOC, not the least because some disciplinary accreditation bodies frown on the use of MOOCs to satisfy some core requirements.

In general, the use of technology often (though not always) can enhance learning, which presumably is the pot of gold at the end of the rainbow. Ironically, learning technologies frequently offer faculty and students greater opportunities to individualize both instruction and assessment of learning than the conventional lecture approach. No longer is it one-size-fits-all for students, who can use what works best for them.

A characteristically optimistic view of how technology will transform higher education is offered by the blog *The Conversation*, which often focuses on higher education: "Enormous amounts of information are now available online for free, ready for watching, listening or reading at any time, by anyone who's connected. For more than a decade, private companies, non-profits and universities alike have been experimenting with online courses, often offered for free or at low cost to large numbers of students around the world. Research has shown that it's as effective for students to use a combination of online courses and traditional in-classroom instruction as it is to just have classes in person."[17] Few would argue with the proposition that the promise and potential of technology in higher education are immense. Not yet demonstrated fully is how widely applicable technology is to the diverse teaching-learning processes in higher education and which technological approaches can be cost effective.

Replicability and Repurposing

In Beethoven's day, a string concert was performed, and that was it. No means of recording those performances existed. Today, however, a performance by a string quartet or a professorial lecture can be recorded and reused almost infinitely and supplied to new audiences at very low marginal cost.

Our best professorial efforts can be recorded, refined, and reused at a fraction of their original unit costs. Like a treasured, inspiring TED Talk, a superb presentation on genetics or a thought-provoking exploration by a master teacher of the intellectual roots of the United States Bill of Rights can be captured and made available to future students at the time and place of their choosing. The potential economies of scale are immense and can be used to drive down instructional costs. At the same time, the ability of students to access knowledge when it is most convenient for them is an intellectual freedom about which one could only dream even fifty years ago.*

Baumol and Bowen focused their attention on original performances rather than subsequent recorded renditions. One can argue that there is some utility attached to being present at a live performance, but this argument carries less weight in non-contested situations such as classrooms and

---

*Of course, the music of the string quartet itself now can be recorded and consumed in the same fashion. The string quartet narrative is not as limiting as it first might seem.

laboratories as opposed to competitive events. Musical performances, perhaps by the Rolling Stones or the Chicago Symphony Orchestra, lie somewhere in between. The atmosphere at such events sometimes can be compelling but in other cases can be unsatisfactory.

Assessment and Communication

As is true for instruction, the use of technology provides faculty members with multiple new ways to assess and keep track of the progress of their students as well as to communicate with them about the course, recent developments or examples, and their performance. Of course, there can be too much of any good thing, including e-mails and digital exercises. Nevertheless, Georgia State University's (GSU's) innovations in these areas merit special kudos. GSU, a 32,000-student urban institution with a very diverse student body, is in Atlanta. The university prides itself on keeping track of its undergraduates—not only their grades on examinations, but also whether they are attending class, eating meals, going to events, using tutors, etc. The university uses "big data" analysis to identify students who might be going off track by, for example, failing to register for a course required for graduation. Its alert system "pings" students so identified and invites them for voluntary face-to-face meetings to see if a problem exists and a solution can be devised. GSU also makes heavy use of peer advisors and supplemental instruction sessions that resemble tutoring. These approaches, which some might argue already exist at many smaller institutions, have spiked GSU's performance upward: its six-year graduation rate has climbed 22 percent over the past decade. The lesson, however, is that Georgia State has become more productive as an institution by becoming activist in its approach to the teaching-learning process. It can handle more students better.[18]

Higher-Education Calendars

Most public college and university campuses operate well below their productive capacities. Summer sessions at most institutions enroll a fraction of the number of students attending during the regular fall and spring semesters. Most campuses are unused for instructional purposes on Saturdays, and many professors reject the notion that they should teach on a Friday or at 8:00 a.m. (For that matter, many students feel the same; for them, Thursday night gradually has become the new Friday night and signals the beginning of their social weekend. A Friday class at 8:00 a.m. is not part of their plan.)

Technology has the ability to extend academic calendars into the fallow grounds of summers, weekends, and vacations and to utilize academic resources more fully. Stated differently, technology can reduce the impact of Baumol's cost disease.

FINAL OBSERVATIONS

A portion—but only a portion—of higher education's productivity malaise can be attributed to some version of Baumol's cost disease. Higher education is constrained in a variety of ways, especially including by its own traditions and by inertia-generating faculty handbooks that discourage innovation and alternative approaches. Faculty figuratively may vote for the modern equivalent of Karl Marx in the next election, yet remain rather cautious with respect to their own work. While many might vouch otherwise, more than a few fear change. Some revel in their ability to resist the blandishments of administrators, legislators, and members of the public who would prefer to see the academic enterprise embark in new directions.

In the realm of higher education, much of the rigidity associated with the Baumol-Bowen string quartet simile exists in professorial and administrative minds rather than being dictated by conditions on the ground in classrooms and laboratories. The players on the college and university stage can be changed, as can the ways in which they work separately and together.

I know. I was a *résistant* for many years until it dawned on me that I might be able to teach economics both more effectively and to more students using alternative approaches. Yes, Baumol's cost disease exists, but it is not nearly as confining as its proponents argue.

The string quartet narrative has become a convenient skirt for academics to hide behind. It permits them to say, "Ah, there really is nothing to be done." Not so.

Realistically, there may be fewer degrees of decisional freedom available to decision makers at small, elite public institutions such as the College of William and Mary or St. Mary's College (Maryland) than at the University of Massachusetts at Boston, Hunter College, Miami-Dade College, the University of North Texas, Portland State University, or San Diego State

University. However, by far the greatest proportion of American college students today are educated at these latter institutions (all of which enroll Pell Grant students in proportions equal to or above the 38 percent national average and in multiples larger than William and Mary's 11 percent). Likely, it will be in these precincts where the greatest strides are made to demonstrate that the string quartet simile is not as binding as some would have us believe.

TEN

Bowen's Rule

Faculty Activity, Administrative Bloat, Amenities, and Mission and Curriculum Creep

No government agency forced universities to add armies of sustainability coordinators, diversity specialists, communications officers and assistant deans of everything.

> —Richard Vedder, economist at Ohio University, in the *Wall Street Journal*, October 8, 2013

or is it

The distracting but ultimately unconvincing claim that a ballooning of the number of administrators in college—so-called administrative bloat—is what lies beyond the rapid growth in public college tuition.

> —William G. Bowen and Michael S. McPherson, *Lesson Plan: An Agenda for Change in American Higher Education*, 2016

One of the most interesting hypotheses concerning tuition and fee inflation also has been contributed by a Bowen, but in this case, it is "the other Bowen," Howard R. Bowen, rather than William G. Bowen. Howard R. Bowen was a college president (Grinnell College, the University of Iowa, and Claremont Graduate University). He will forever be known for five propositions that collectively have become known as "Bowen's Law":

- The dominant goals of institutions are excellence, prestige, and influence.

- There is virtually no limit to the amount of money that an institution could spend for seemingly fruitful educational ends.
- Each institution raises all the money it can.
- The institution spends all it raises.
- The cumulative effect of the preceding four laws is toward ever-increasing expenditure.[1]

Those familiar with higher education no doubt can recognize aspects of this behavior—institutional pursuit of rankings, the waging of seemingly perpetual capital campaigns, construction of new facilities, new study and research centers, upgraded campus food, climbing walls, lazy rivers, expanded student services and entertainment, extra layers of administration—all of which eventually are paid for partially or wholly by students or those who fund students.

In this view of the world, college boards and administrators raise tuition and fees not because they have no realistic alternatives, but instead because they want the additional revenue that will enable them to spend more on the things they value at their institutions. The more they spend, the happier they are. The more they spend, the more likely they are to attain more prestige and influence in the distinctive world of higher education. And, not coincidentally, the more they spend, likely the higher will be their own salaries.

The essential question of fact here is not whether some of this behavior occurs; only those with deliberately covered eyes could deny that to some extent these things are true. Rather, the salient consideration is how widespread such behavior is in higher education. That is, what evidence do we have that most institutions behave in this fashion when they can do so?

THE SEMINAL MARTIN-HILL STUDY

Easily the most rigorous study of the incidence and importance of Bowen's Law is a 2012 study performed by two economists, Martin and Hill.[2] The pair examined 137 Carnegie I and II public research universities over the period 1987 through 2010 by analyzing the National Center for Educational Statistics IPEDS data set. They controlled for price changes and, where appropriate, weighted numbers by enrollment so they could look at real per-student expenditures.

Among other things, Martin and Hill found that student/faculty ratios declined modestly over the period, the use of part-time faculty increased, staff salaries increased faster than professorial salaries, the number of administrators increased faster than the size of student bodies, fringe-benefit costs rose rapidly, and the real, after-inflation operating revenues per student increased 2.4 percent annually at the typical institution.*

Ultimately, these researchers concluded that the Howard Bowen view of the higher-education world was twice as important quantitatively as the William Baumol view. That is, Bowen's hypothesis that institutions themselves were substantially responsible for tuition and fee price inflation triumphed over Baumol's cost disease in their econometric formulations. In the language of well-known economist Ron Ehrenberg of Cornell, colleges have become cookie monsters who "seek out all the resources that they can get their hands on and then devour them."[3]

Figure 10-1 shows these proclivities in action. It is apparent that instruction became relatively less important as an expenditure class over the period from 2000–01 to 2014–15. The 2.3 percent decline at flagship institutions translates to an average reduction of about $45 million per institution.

None of this comes as a surprise to public-choice aficionados, who would be surprised if they did not discover "rent-seeking"† behavior in public organizations.[4] They would anticipate finding many individual actors in public colleges and universities who attempt to obtain special privileges and protections that will favor them over outsiders. Faculty tenure is an oft-cited example of successful rent-seeking behavior, but one also might include a variety of shared governance procedures that insulate faculty and staff from some of the decisions that characterize profit-driven enterprises.

One of the important predictions of rent-extracting models is that such behavior results in a significant waste of resources. This occurs because the rent seekers successfully impose an inefficient allocation of resources, often discourage adjustments, frequently establish low or zero prices for the internal resources they wish to command, and ignore economic signals. Thus, in

---

*Martin and Hill focused on sticker price tuition and fees rather than net prices, which requires us to insert a note of caution. While most of the duo's conclusions do not depend in any way on the distinction between sticker prices and net prices, some conceivably could.

†An economic agent earns a rent when it receives a payment in excess of its opportunity cost— the value of its best foregone alternative. Rent seekers attempt to arrange such circumstances.

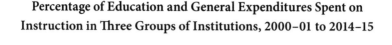

FIGURE 10-1

Percentage of Education and General Expenditures Spent on Instruction in Three Groups of Institutions, 2000–01 to 2014–15

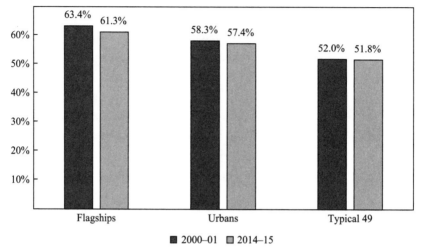

Source: Delta Cost Project (www.deltacostproject.org).

times of financial cutbacks, a tenured faculty member who teaches, say, the Italian language and culture to a very small number of students may retain his job, while an untenured faculty member who teaches computer science to rooms bursting with students may lose her job because of the way the rules have been written in a faculty handbook or union contract. Mine is not to impose a value judgment here about the wisdom of such decisions, but rather to note that this is the type of circumstance that would generate the results found by Martin and Hill.

It is easier to accept the notion of faculty, administrators, and staff seeking and obtaining special privileges and protections in their bureaucratic institutions than it is to explain why the student consumers of higher education largely have accepted this behavior. Martin and Hill, along with Andrew Gillen, have suggested several possible reasons. First, they note that a college education is an "experience good."[5] This means that typical consumers cannot really determine the quality of such a good or service until they purchase and consume it. That is, they must register, pay the price, and go to class before they really can begin to formulate an opinion about the worth of their college experience. Unfortunately, they soon find that the market for reliable information about colleges and universities is imperfect and some end up being influenced substantially by rumor and reputation rather than hard numbers that demonstrate learning and earning. The advent of internet sites such as the College Navigator of the National Center for Education Statistics has been helpful, but substantial proportions of students and families don't know it exists.

Even when students have acquired higher-education experience specific to an institution, there may be switching costs that discourage them from moving from one major to another, or from one institution to another. They may not be able to transfer all their credits and may have to pay a variety of fees if they move among disciplines and institutions.

Institutions, their administrators, and their faculty may conclude that their interests diverge from those of students. This reflects what economists label a principal-agent problem.[6] Citizens, legislators, students, and their parents plausibly have different goals and values than administrators and faculty, and typically lack effective ways to bend administrators and faculty to their will. Both institutional and individual administrative/faculty prosperity may be tied to their salaries and accoutrements, which in turn influence reputations and rankings. Institutions may be able to improve their standing in the public imagination if they allocate their resources and make expenditures in ways that impose financial costs on students, most of whom are ill-informed and slow to react to institutional decisions. The argument may be levied that these administrative/faculty behaviors improve educational quality, but as we have seen, this is a difficult argument to sustain.

Higher education is a quintessential "trust market" situation in which consumers often have little choice but to trust the seller of a good or service because they simply do not have sufficient expertise to make astute decisions on their own.[7] This is not necessarily pejorative; most of us trust our physicians to tell us if we need a prescription just as we trust a computer software company to tell us if our PC has been infected with a virus.

Likewise, in higher education students instinctively trust professors to devise appropriate curricula, and for administrators not to force them to pay for people or services they do not need. This situation typifies a principal-agent problem because the individuals making the decisions (faculty and administrators) may not have the best interests of students at heart. Faculty, for example, may favor higher faculty salaries and lower teaching loads—for which students must pay—even if there is no demonstrated connection between those things and educational quality at the margin. Administrators, alumni, and friends may advocate high fees to support their institution's intercollegiate athletic teams even though student attendance at athletic contests may be minimal.

How does the principal convince the agent to do what the principal desires? This is a recurring problem in economics, since many principal-agent situations exist. The standard answer is to make it worth the while of the agent to behave as the principal desires. For many years, for example, it was thought that incentivizing managers with stock equity would provide them with significant reason to behave in the best interest of stockholders in general. Results here have been mixed, however. On the other hand, accumulated evidence is more favorable for profit-sharing plans for employees even though such arrangements may encourage free-riding behavior.

In the case of college and university presidents, most are evaluated based on traditional metrics such as enrollment, fundraising, new programs developed and buildings constructed, research funding, academic rankings, and the like. What if they also were evaluated based on their ability to control costs and minimize the cost of achieving a given level of educational quality? That is, what if it were made worthwhile to senior administrators to think in terms of the best financial interests of their students? There is abundant evidence that compensation affects performance. Perhaps administrative performance needs to be redefined.

It isn't only presidents and administrators who are part of the principal-agent challenge. Members of public college and university boards gradually but habitually tend to evolve into strong advocates for the institution on whose board they serve. Board members usually value most of the things that presidents and administrators treasure, including institutional growth, higher academic rankings, and, lest we forget, successful intercollegiate athletic teams. Institutional success so measured makes their board service seem more pleasurable and worthwhile.

There is nothing necessarily wrong-headed about institutional growth, rankings triumphs, or winning athletic teams, yet attaining such goals can be quite expensive and perhaps not in the best interests of many students and their families. Witness the mandatory $1,961 per full-time undergraduate student fee for intercollegiate athletics that the 2017 Division I Football Championship Subdivision champion (and second in 2018) James Madison University imposed upon its in-state undergraduates in 2016–17, or the $3,813 in fees that the College of William and Mary required its in-state undergraduates to pay for campus student-union facilities and intercollegiate athletics.[8] Some agile mental tap dancing is required to justify such fees if they result in student debt.

The presence of these and similar fees at public institutions around the country provokes an important question. What if members of public college boards perceived that their prime responsibility was to act in terms of the best interests of the citizens of their state and the students at their institutions rather than semi-automatically endorsing the Bowen's rule agenda of their institution's administration? Would the result be increased access to public institutions and reduced levels of student debt? Probably so.

Accrediting bodies (both regional and disciplinary) have roles to play in the principal-agent drama. Rather than almost uniformly imposing cost-increasing rules and regulations, or insisting that institutions spend more money on whatever the accreditors perceive to be virtuous, what if they also rewarded fiscal prudence, access, and affordability? For example, should the percentage of an institution's undergraduate student body that consists of Pell Grant recipients be an accrediting standard? If not, why not?

George Stigler, a famed University of Chicago economist and Nobel Prize winner, hypothesized that regulatory agencies eventually become dominated by the very firms and industries they are supposed to be regulating. A version of this hypothesis may have relevance in higher education, where governing board members and state higher-education bodies often become partisan supporters of institutions and their presidents. This stance is to the detriment of students.[9]

FIGURE 10-2

FIGURE 10-2

Number of Full-Time Employees per 100 Full-Time Equivalent Students at Seventy-Four Non-flagship, Nonurban Public Institutions, 1999–2000 to 2010–11

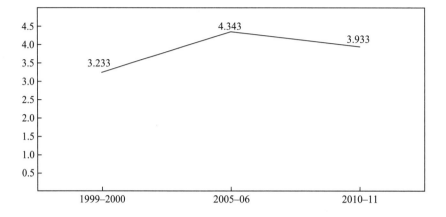

Sources: Integrated Postsecondary Education Data System (http://nces.ed.gov/ipeds) and the Delta Cost Project (www.deltacostproject.org).

DECOMPOSING BOWEN'S RULE

Bowen's rule carries with it implications for many different aspects of university behavior, several of which are measurable. Martin and Hill measured such behaviors for research institutions. Let's look at some of the evidence with different samples of institutions and for specific variables. The patterns disclosed apply to virtually every type of institution, but it is instructive to view the evidence in the context of institutional types.

Full-Time Employees per Student

Bowen's rule asserts that if institutions can raise additional funds, they will do so and then expeditiously find ways to spend that money. Non-elite institutions do not have the same ability to raise funds as flagship institutions, but they nonetheless provide evidence in support of Bowen's notion. One can see in figure 10-2 that the number of full-time employees per 100 students increased at non-flagship institutions between 1999–2000 and 2010–11, albeit (as was true for the employment of full-time faculty) the ratio peaked in 2005–06.

FIGURE 10-3

Number of Administrative Staff per Tenured Faculty Member at Fifty-Four Urban Public Institutions, 1986–87 to 2010–11

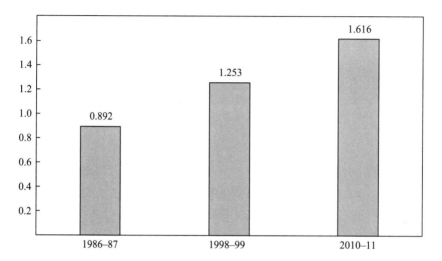

Sources: IPEDS (https://nces.ed.gov/ipeds/) and the Delta Cost Project (www.deltacostproject .com).

Staff per Student or Faculty Member

Bowen's rule suggests that a conventional means by which colleges and universities expand their expenditures is to hire additional administrative staff. This is a conventional faculty and occasional citizen complaint. Desrochers and Hurlburt, who spent considerable time analyzing Delta Cost Study data to ascertain collegiate spending patterns, found that the model held true for public and independent institutions of all types between 1990 and 2012— but much more so for "other professional staff" than for administrators in general.[10] These "other" administrators are middle- and lower-level employees who occupy sundry positions, including burgeoning information technology posts and student services positions. Desrochers and Hurlburt hypothesize that this growth reflects the preference of students for more services as well as an accompanying desire among faculty to be relieved of administrative responsibilities, including advising.

Figure 10-3, which focuses on fifty-four large urban institutions, provides some specific evidence in support of this hypothesis. Simply put, there has been a growth in the number of administrative staff per tenured faculty member over the past twenty-five years. Similar, though less dramatic, patterns are present at the typical and flagship institutions.

However, figure 10-3 is not quite as persuasive as it first seems because the denominator in the ratio—the number of tenured faculty members—has not grown as fast as the number of faculty overall. Tenured or tenure-line faculty members now comprise fewer than 40 percent of all appointed faculty in public colleges and universities in the United States and only about one-half of the full-time equivalent faculty in those institutions. When all faculty are considered, the dramatic increase illustrated in figure 10-3 is approximately cut in half.

Nevertheless, these data remain supportive of the findings of Martin and Hill. As Martin has put it, "While the rest of the economy was shrinking overhead, higher education was investing heavily in more overhead."[11]

Fringe-Benefit Price Inflation

Public college and university salary increases sometimes are constrained by state legislatures. An alternate (and usually nontaxable) way for institutions to compensate their employees is to increase the value of their fringe-benefit packages. In some cases, legislators play a vital role in this scenario because they approve enhanced fringe benefits whose payout lies far in the future. Hence, they can approve a compensation increase that they do not have to pay for during the current legislative session. Retirement programs fall into this category.

Supportive evidence in favor of the Martin and Hill finding that fringe-benefit increases energize tuition and fee increases may be found in the fringe-benefits price index within the overall Higher Education Price Index (HEPI). As figure 10-4 discloses, between the 2005–06 and 2014–15 academic years, the HEPI fringe-benefit index increased at the annual rate of 4.01 percent, substantially faster than the overall HEPI (2.61 percent) and the Consumer Price Index for All Urban Consumers (2.03 percent). The essential point is that enhanced fringe benefits represent a cost that exerts upward pressure on tuition and fees.

Amenities Competition

There is, as we have seen, credible empirical evidence that large proportions of undergraduate students not only prefer institutions that offer them upgraded amenities (buildings, food, activities, etc.), but also are willing to pay

FIGURE 10-4

Fringe-Benefit Cost Increases versus the HEPI and CPI-U, 2006–15

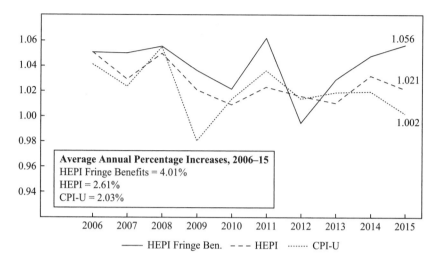

Sources: For HEPI variables: Commonfund, Higher Education Price Index (www.commonfund .org/commonfund-institute/higher-education-price-index-hepi); for July-over-July CPI-U changes: Bureau of Labor Statistics (www.bls.gov).

for those amenities. Institutions small and large, elite and not so elite, have responded by making some amenities virtually standard (for example, spiffy exercise and workout facilities) and adding others that differentiate their campuses. Innovative offerings include (from a wide variety of sources):

- a personal dairy bar (South Dakota State University)
- a lazy river, a beach club, and an upscale pool with a "high-powered vortex" (University of Missouri, Columbia)
- an adventure outfitter (Western Washington University)
- an on-campus ski resort (Michigan Technological University)
- eating lobster every day (Virginia Tech)
- 130 different meal entrees daily (Kennesaw State University)
- a campus recreation center with an eighteen-foot diving well, bubble benches, and lazy river (University of Iowa)
- a thirty-foot rock-climbing wall (California State University, Fullerton)

- a shuttle bus that runs students to and from businesses and bars until 3:00 a.m. (University of Maryland College Park)

- the Game Lab, for students interested in the design and engineering of computer games (UCLA)

- the "Sky High" trampoline center (University of California, Santa Cruz)

- two full-time nutritionists to work with students (University of Nebraska Lincoln)

- luxury "condo" dorms (if the measure is any comparison with the standard of fifty years ago, then virtually every campus falls into this category)

Room and board charges at four-year public institutions rose 89.1 percent between the 2001–02 and 2016–17 academic years, according to the College Board. The food price index in the Consumer Price Index rose only 41.8 percent during the same period.[12] Even though room and board charges loom large in the financial calculations of undergraduate students, there has been hardly a peep heard from the nation's major higher-education organizations on this topic. We would like for the nation's undergraduates to eat well when they are on campus, but perhaps not this well.

More examples would be easy to provide, but they are unnecessary because it is difficult to avoid concluding that many public institutions of higher education have become contestants in the equivalent of an amenities arms race. Enhanced amenities enable institutions to raise their tuition and fees. Higher tuition and fees in turn enable them to offer more amenities and attract more students. Causality runs in both directions in a self-reinforcing circle, about which I have written in the *New York Times*.[13]

The amenities competition results in higher tuition and fee increases than one would have seen otherwise. But this competition also subtly introduces differentiation among institutions that might be likened to an informal caste system. Which students can pay the new, elevated prices? Those fortunate enough to come from upper-income families. Students from lower-middle-class households begin to disappear, as do Pell Grant students—unless their campus takes specific financial aid action to counter this trend. Only a few well-endowed institutions find themselves able to provide such financial assistance.

Many elite public institutions finesse the problem by not admitting more than a certain percentage of lower-income students so that they do not overtax their financial aid resources. Thus, in 2015–16, for *U.S. News and World Report*'s Elite 28 public institutions, Pell Grant percentages ranged from a low of 11 percent at the College of William and Mary to a high of 45 percent at the University of California, Irvine. The Elite 28 average was 23 percent, and the national average in the same year was 36 percent.[14]

Students sort themselves out accordingly, with students from lower-income families opting to attend less expensive institutions, especially community colleges. The surge in enrollment at for-profit institutions that occurred after the turn of the century was at least partially due to the ability of those institutions to find ways to supply financial aid (especially loans) to lower-income students. Even so, many students who opt for lower-cost alternatives find themselves unable to pay for their educations and consequently drop out, or begin to attend part-time. The eventual impact is clear: students from upper-income families are eight times more likely to earn a bachelor's degrees by the time they're twenty-four than those from lower-income families.

Note that all of this has been occurring at a time when many states and public institutions have been moving away from need-based financial aid and toward financial aid based upon test scores and high school performance. Georgia's HOPE and Zell Miller scholarships evince this trend.

The relevant point is that the amenities competition has real-world consequences that affect and structure both the institutions that engage in the competition and society at large. It is not a harmless competition without importance. This is a reason why some argue that public higher education has become a vehicle that increases economic inequality rather than occupying its historic role as a broadly accessible ladder of opportunity that leads to greater equality in economic outcomes.

There is one aspect of the amenities competition that deserves special mention. The Urban Dictionary informs us that an "edifice complex" is "a serious budget-busting illness that typically manifests itself on modern college and university campuses."[15] Like cities and counties that exult in building large, highly subsidized, unprofitable stadiums, many public colleges and universities act as if their academic virtue is defined by the number of square feet they deploy on campus, or the grandeur of their buildings. Never mind what is going on inside those buildings, or if major elements of the taxpaying population are unable to pay the prices that would allow them to access these buildings.

I will not subject you to another listing of grand campus facilities. Readers can see for themselves the extent to which both the size and the quality of public college and university facilities have increased steadily over time on most campuses. Yes, it is true that institutions with large endowments and generous donors often pay for these grand buildings with private gifts. *Lost in the edifice shuffle, however, are two fundamental questions. First, what evidence is there that these magnificent facilities promote learning or increase graduation rates? That is, do they really make a difference? Second, why could not some of the dollars used for these glorious buildings have been used to decrease the institution's tuition and fees?* I addressed this question conceptually in chapter 6 by looking at the hypothetical use of institutional endowment funds and accumulated financial balances to defray undergraduate tuition and fee increases. These are legitimate questions.

Mission and Curriculum Creep

Institutions change, and often we are better for it. Oregon State University, a flagship research institution that is part of the PAC-12 Conference, had humble beginnings in 1856 as Corvallis Academy. It was operated first by Freemasons and subsequently by the Methodist Episcopal Church (South), whose own interesting roots lay in the Southern Confederacy.[16] The University of Central Florida, which enrolled more than 63,000 students in 2016–17 and now boasts the largest enrollment of undergraduate students of any public university in the country, was founded in 1963 as Florida Technological University primarily to serve Cape Canaveral.[17] Over the past two hundred years, many dozens of state normal schools evolved to become state teachers' colleges, later state colleges, and subsequently state universities.

The evolution of public colleges and universities has been a continuous process over time and doubtless will continue, partially because ambitious administrators, faculty, alumni, and business supporters wish it to be so. However, this does not imply that the evolutionary process has been, or will be, either economically efficient or a good idea from the standpoint of students and taxpayers.

The problem is that institutional ambition and mission expansion are cost drivers. Graduate programs are expensive, as are the engineering and health sciences offerings that many campuses wish to develop or expand because they are job-market winners. Faculty teaching loads tend to decline as missions expand, sometimes because of prodding from disciplinary accrediting agencies. Institutional catalogs get thicker as departments add specialized courses, practicums, and laboratories. None of these things ordinarily occur without an influx of additional administrative staff or, what is almost the same thing, reducing the teaching loads of faculty so they can tend to the administrative details of such programs.

In the public sector, mission creep and curricular expansion have been virulent at former teachers' colleges, many of which now offer broad ranges of graduate programs, including doctorates. When these institutions are in metropolitan areas, their mission and programmatic evolution often makes a great deal of sense because it is responsive to local job-market and cultural needs. However, the same arguments cannot be made when the institutions are situated in remote rural regions.

In either the metropolitan or the rural cases, mission and curricular inflation often reflects a desire on the part of administrators and faculty to move up a few notches in the perceived academic hierarchy—to become a doctoral institution, or a research institution, or a STEM institution. Faculty members who were trained to be researchers in graduate school frequently place great value on their being able to teach graduate students the finer points of their disciplines, even more so if it enables them to teach, research, and publish in the areas covered by their own doctoral dissertations.

It isn't that such activities are devoid of value. Instead, the lesson is that they are expensive and may generate graduates whose education and skills are not in great demand in job markets. In the field of English, for example, less than one-half of all Ph.D. graduates over the past thirty-five years have obtained a tenure-track university position. Nonetheless, approximately 140 doctoral programs in English exist, and most persist in focusing on the preparation of their graduates for positions that do not exist.[18] Change comes slowly.

The ladders of opportunity that the former teachers' colleges provide their students, their reputations for teaching excellence, and (in many cases) their cost competitiveness mean that they are important cogs in the public higher-education enterprise. This said, they also have contributed to public college cost inflation.

SUMMING IT UP

The groundbreaking work of Martin and Hill defines the state of the art with regard to estimating the size of the Baumol and Bowen effects. Their contribution is consistent with other data describing public higher education, some of which has been presented in this chapter. Martin and Hill found that the Bowen effect is about twice as important as Baumol's cost disease in terms of their effects on tuition and fees, and that together the two hypotheses can explain approximately two-thirds of the increases we have observed in public-institution tuition and fees over the past quarter century.

One of the most important implications of Martin and Hill's contribution is that declining state appropriations have been much less important in explaining tuition and fee increases than the institutions themselves have insisted. This finding is consistent with the evidence presented in chapters 7 and 8 and directly implies that institutions have been raising tuition and fees for many reasons in addition to declining state appropriations. That this evidence contradicts the consistent narrative of most public colleges and universities that "the state is to blame" cannot be denied.

By the same token, one also cannot deny that real state financial support per student for public higher education not only has been trending downward in most states, but also that this funding has been highly erratic and frankly undependable. This fact confers some legitimacy to the tendency of institutions to raise tuition and fees even in years when state funding is constant or increasing. In effect, institutions could be considered to be putting money in the bank to prepare themselves for unpredictable lean years. This, however, is a charitable interpretation of public college and university tuition behavior.

ELEVEN

Parsing the Evidence and Evaluating Solutions to the College Cost Crisis

A series of surveys . . . show[s] **widespread skepticism about how colleges and universities are run, how much they cost, and whether or not they're worth the money.**
—Jon Marcus, *Hechinger Report*, 2016

et's sketch the challenge. The American Council on Education (ACE), a respected but mainstream national advocate for higher education, represents 1,800 college and university presidents at every type of accredited institution. What is the ACE all about? The "About" page on its website states that it is an advocate that "is consistently at the center of federal policy debates in areas critical to higher education," and that it is the most frequently cited source when national media address higher-education issues.[1]

The ACE web page highlights its well-known leadership-training and renewal programs and its advocacy concerning budgets, and offers information on the Higher Education Act, labor and employment, law and the courts, veterans, leadership diversity, faculty issues, gender equity, and institutional effectiveness. These are important topics. If one clicks on the site's "Institutional Effectiveness" icon, one sees material on graduation rates and a commendable need to understand financial data. However, the affordability of higher education and students' access to colleges and universities are not topics included on this list.

In April 2018, one needed to dig deep into the ACE website to find material relating to the affordability crisis that confronts middle- and lower-income American families and students who wish to access public higher education. Several clicks within the "Institutional Effectiveness" page brings one to a list of "Other Campus Issues," which included topics such as technology and intercollegiate athletics.

Let me be clear. The ACE is a vital organization and serves many laudatory purposes. Even so, it downplays cost and affordability issues except when it has commissioned now-outdated studies that in essence have given institutions a free pass by saying either that there's no problem, or that it's not their fault anyway if there is a problem.

The Association of Governing Boards (AGB) receives higher grades. Under the "Research and Reports" link on its website, there is a "Finance and Business Model" category that contains a 2011 publication entitled "Tuition and Financial Aid: Nine Points for Boards to Consider in Keeping College Affordable," and a 2015 white paper labeled "Financial Aid and Enrollment: Questions for Boards to Consider." The AGB's *Trusteeship* magazine provides useful information to board members on a wide range of relevant topics and periodically addresses affordability and access. Hence, we must credit the AGB for paying attention to affordability and access even though its web page suggests these are not front-burner topics for the organization.[2]

It isn't that the ACE and similar organizations have no concern for rising college costs; they do. Rather, the problem is that their concerns in this arena seldom are high-priority items. The ACE's website in particular demonstrates this. When the subject of rising college costs arises, mainstream national higher-education organizations such as the ACE typically expend more effort attempting to justify the current regime of tuition and fees rather than recognizing the problems that exist and thinking about solutions to those problems.

Why so? To begin, nearly every mainstream national higher-education organization has bought into Baumol's cost disease argument and the accompanying simile that likens the labor-intensive work of higher education to that of a string quartet. Collaterally, they adopt the position that increased federal financial aid has had minimal impact on public college tuition and fees. And they tend to downplay or ignore recent research that suggests that public-sector tuition and fee increases have exceeded levels necessary to compensate institutions for reductions in their state funding.

With respect to the impact of federal financial aid on tuition and fees, on three occasions (2013, 2015, and 2016), the ACE issued news releases that advised readers that federal student aid increases do not drive tuition increases. The ACE further has endorsed and published summaries of the work of Robert B. Archibald and David H. Feldman.[3] As we have seen, these individuals argue that years of rapidly rising public college tuition and fees are not the fault of the institutions imposing those increases, but instead are an unfortunate byproduct of economic forces substantially beyond their control and of miserly state governments. Collateral to this, ACE also supported a study that contradicted recent research indicating that the Bennett effect (federal student aid driving college prices upward) was either small or zero.[4] More recent research disputes all of these offerings.

Mainstream higher-education organizations actively propagate such views, which are oft-repeated in higher-education circles, because they largely excuse institutions from significant blame for most of the affordability and student debt problems that clearly do exist. After all, if there really are powerful forces outside the control of public institutions that bear responsibility for the increases in tuition and fees that have far exceeded increases in variables such as the Consumer Price Index and median household income, then colleges and universities are innocent, and the finger of blame should be pointed elsewhere.

In this view, the major culprits behind rapidly rising tuition and fees are the following three long-term economic trends:

- Colleges and universities, like a variety of other service providers ranging from physicians and nurses to barbers and physical therapists, operate in worlds that are labor intensive. Unavoidably, institutions must pay premium wage rates to attract and retain the highly educated personnel they regard as central to the quality of their labor-intensive efforts.

- Consistent with the simile of the string quartet, institutions lack the ability to increase their own productivity as fast as firms that operate in many other segments of the economy.

- Real state financial support per student has declined in a large majority of states over the past quarter century, but especially during the Great Recession of 2008–10. Institutions have responded by raising tuition and fees to make up for the reduction in state support.

It will suffice to observe that the accumulated empirical evidence presented in this book is only partially supportive of these views.

WHAT DOES THE EVIDENCE TELL US?

Tuition and fee price inflation is a complicated issue, and therefore so also is the empirical evidence that focuses on its proximate causes. Further, a fair reading of the evidence tells us that it is not one-sided. Hence, one cannot assert with confidence that "the issue now is settled." Not so. Nonetheless, I will offer several generalizations about the evidence with confidence:

- *The more recent the evidence, the more likely it is to assert that there are many causes in addition to declining state appropriations that are responsible for rapidly rising tuition and fees.* Recent empirical studies have not been kind to those who argue that diminished state appropriations for public higher education are the major, or perhaps even sole cause of rapidly rising tuition and fees.

- *The more rigorous the statistical evidence, the more likely it is to point to additional causes of tuition and fee price inflation besides declining state appropriations.* These other reasons include federal financial aid policies, administrative bloat, fringe-benefit increases, expensive amenities enjoyed by both students and faculty, and competition for rankings.

- *Analyses of tuition and fee price inflation that focus on the entire sector of public higher education disguise important individual institutional circumstances.* Between 1999–2000 and 2016–17, and after adjusting for price inflation, a firm majority of four-year public institutions of higher education in the United States increased their tuition and fee charges more than any decline they experienced in their state appropriation per full-time equivalent student. State Higher Education Executive Officers Association data reveal that between 1999–2000 and 2016–17, after adjusting for price inflation and full-time equivalent enrollment, state general fund tax support for public higher education rose 17.7 percent. However, during this period, their net tuition revenue per full-time equivalent student, also adjusted for price inflation, rose 71.6 percent.[5] Whether one examines overall public sector data or disaggregates the data on an institution-by-institution basis, the disconnect between tuition and fees (even after institutional grants are deducted) becomes impossible to ignore.

- *Bowen's rule, which inter alia hypothesizes that institutions raise all the money they can and then spend all that money, almost regardless of their circumstances, appears to have considerable explanatory power.* Accumulated empirical evidence provides substantially more support for Bowen's rule than it does for Baumol's cost disease.

- *Baumol's cost disease has some relevance; however, its applicability to twenty-first-century higher education is not precise because institutions do not live in the frozen world of fixed proportions suggested by the popularized simile of the string quartet.* Both then and now, a string quartet includes two violinists, one viola player, and one cello performer. The intimation is that colleges and universities similarly operate in such a world of fixed proportions and invariant technologies. However, this is not true. Institutions can and do vary the sizes of classes, the identity of instructors, and instructional modalities. More important, they can substitute less expensive inputs for more expensive ones.

- *Nearly all institutions have the option to use technology to tailor learning experiences and strategies to individual learners. These experiences can be not only encouragingly effective, but also cost efficient (though not for all students, or in all disciplines, or at all levels).* Amazon's newish "Machine Learning" platform allows both faculty and students to evaluate and rate learning tools and approaches in terms of their effectiveness—a desirable step in the direction of producing incremental learning at reduced cost.[6] Georgia State University's use of technology to follow student progress provides an out-of-the-classroom example.[7]

- *Technology also can capture, record, and repeat professorial efforts and learning episodes. Put simply, these opportunities did not exist in the era of Beethoven.* Hence, the pessimistic, confining predictions that accompanied the string quartet are off the mark if our focus is upon the ways a massive majority of American undergraduates is educated today. The heavily structured world of a four-person string quartet playing a rather rigid, forty-minute version of a Beethoven opus is not an apt descriptor of the current choices available to higher-education administrators and faculty.

- *Alternative paths to higher-education credentials—for example, those that lead to badges and certifications rather than degrees—hold some promise as a way to diminish affordability pressures.* However, these microcredentials typically are very specific to particular jobs and thus could lead to disappointment if labor-market preferences change. Further, while a certification that leads to a computer programming job may be less expensive than earning a baccalaureate degree, it is not necessarily less expensive on a course-by-course basis.

- *Many institutions siphon off significant portions of federal financial aid that they use for other purposes. Many of the dollars in public college budgets are fungible and can be moved from one spot to another. Hence, when the federal government infuses additional financial aid, many institutions tend to reduce their own institutionally based financial aid.* A credible 2015 study by economists at the New York Federal Reserve Bank estimated that many institutions effectively redirect as much as 60 percent of the federal financial aid they receive.[8] An earlier, related study published by the National Bureau of Economic Research in 2013 concluded that some institutions "game" the federal financial aid system by increasing tuition and fees to receive (via their students) additional federal financial aid. Qualifications attach to each of these studies. The siphoning effect in the National Bureau study was much larger at independent institutions than at public ones.[9] Also, the Federal Reserve Bank study focused upon sticker-price tuition and fees rather than net tuition and fees after financial grants to students had been deducted.

  In tandem, these two studies plus others strongly suggest that there is reality attached to the once-heretical hypothesis concerning the impact of federal financial aid originally offered by Secretary of Education William Bennett a quarter century ago. That this evidence has been disconcerting to many is putting the matter mildly, because the results suggest that one of the pillars of our national approach to making college affordable may be shaky and even counterproductive. Even so, this revelation should not have come as a surprise, because under reasonable assumptions, basic supply and demand analysis predicts that the provision of additional federal financial aid will push tuition and fees upward.

- *Public institutions of higher education gradually have added administrative complexity. Many kinds of administrative staff positions have grown in number more rapidly than either faculty positions or student bodies.* There are counterexamples (an illustration being the decline of traditional secretarial positions because faculty and administrators now utilize technology instead of secretaries), but the overall trend is unmistakable. Institutions often choose to blame increasing state and federal regulations for administrative proliferation, and there is general agreement that they have been a contributing factor. Nevertheless, governmental regulations usually are not responsible for the forays of institutions into areas such as globalization, corporate liaisons, community service, wellness, diversity awareness and training, intramural athletic competition, intercollegiate athletics, campus entertainment, and the like. It is not that these initiatives lack virtue; rather, they represent gradual, discretionary extensions of the resources of colleges and universities into spaces they did not occupy to the same extent fifty years previous. Institutions have utilized their independence and discretion to choose new paths, which have turned out to be expensive. In many instances, students end up paying for the new directions.

- *Elite public institutions have established brands that enable them to impose tuition and fee increases to provide them with additional revenue, whether or not they actually need such revenue to make up for cuts in public funding.* They need worry little about student rejection because they enjoy a surfeit of applications over student slots they make available. Relieved of having to worry about student numbers, they imitate Bowen's rule by taxing their students to raise additional funds and then never failing to find ways to spend those dollars on projects deemed meritorious.

- *Most elite public institutions engage in significant price discrimination such that students pursuing identical courses of study often end up paying dramatically different effective net prices.* There are two common threads to this price discrimination. One is that students coming from higher-income families pay higher net prices than those coming from lower-income families. The other is that nonresident students pay far more than resident students. One can erect plausible arguments for both of these pricing strategies; however, they tend to exert upward pressure on tuition and fees. Place yourself in the position of a senior administrator at the University of Michigan Ann Arbor, which in 2016–17 charged out-of-state undergraduate students $45,410 in tuition and fees.[10] If nonresident students were competing to pay such prices, how could Michigan's administrators resist?

The University of Maryland, College Park, chose to clothe its proposal to initiate special tuition and fee surcharges in fall 2016 for those pursuing degrees in business, engineering, and computer science as "Affordable Flagship Excellence, Access, and State Economic Growth." The press release stated, "Most of the pricing differential will be invested to enhance the academic quality and competitiveness of these three programs vis-à-vis their counterparts at other flagships with which we compete for students, faculty, and research dollars."[11] To one extent or another, nearly every flagship institution has relied upon similar verbiage to justify imposing higher costs on its students.

- *With respect to price discrimination based upon income, however, there is substantial variation among institutions.* Penn State is a high-cost but relatively low-financial-aid institution with respect to Pennsylvania residents. Its average net price in 2015–16 was $25,055 for in-state students, which fell only to $20,873 for students coming from families with annual incomes between $0 and $30,000. At the University of North Carolina at Chapel Hill, on the other hand, the average net price for North Carolinians was a much reduced $10,077, while lower-income students paid an average net price of only $3,889.[12]

- *Institutions vary dramatically in their reliance upon out-of-state students.* In 2016–17, only 6 percent of Texas A&M undergraduates were nonresidents, while at the University of Alabama 68 percent were. Or consider that in 2016–17, the University of Minnesota charged its out-of-state undergraduate students tuition and fees that were only 1.68 times its price for in-state students, whereas the same ratio at the University of Florida was a hefty 4.49.[13]

- *These examples demonstrate that many different pricing and student financial aid models exist in American public higher education.* Not all institutions walk the same path. Indeed, the degree of variability among institutions and state systems in terms of their pricing and financial aid policies is huge. Therefore, it is deceptive and self-serving for institutions to assert that their current pricing and financial aid approaches constitute the only way to do things, or that they are caught by their circumstances and really do not have any degrees of freedom to change their tuition and financial aid policies.

- *As time passes, the pricing of undergraduate education becomes more a matter of what administrators and boards decide they wish to do rather than constituting an inevitable and unavoidable choice.* In reality, over time, there are many ways to bake and price the higher-education cake. This general dictum applies as well to endowment funds and institutional use of sometimes remarkably large fund reserves.

- *Institutions drive up costs by competing based on the amenities they offer—though perhaps for understandable reasons.* Except in the cases of a very few elite institutions, the available evidence indicates that many students are attracted by additional amenities. The upshot is that spending on amenities as opposed to instruction has increased over time. Upscale residence-hall rooms and upgraded campus food are but one part of the amenities competition, but they provide instructive examples.

- *Meanwhile, college catalogs continually grow fatter, and degree programs multiply.* By no means is the expansion of knowledge a negative development. Instead, the relevant question is what portions of that knowledge colleges and universities should seek to present to their undergraduates and at what cost. The University of North Carolina system reported that 221 of the approximately 1,000 bachelor's degree programs offered by its public institutions had graduated twenty or fewer individuals over the previous two years. To its credit, it then moved to discontinue or consolidate 56 of these programs.[14]

    Is it critical that every institution offer baccalaureate degrees in areas such as music therapy, French, or biomedical engineering? Is it wise public policy to allow more than one-half of all four-year public institutions to offer a doctoral degree in something? The broad sweep of the law of diminishing returns applies to incremental courses added to catalogs and majors. If twenty courses already exist that could be taken by an undergraduate economics major at the University of Oregon, then what is the probability that the addition of a twenty-first course will add benefits to the student's education that will exceed its costs, either to that individual student or to the university?

- *In general, the number of usable square feet owned or controlled by public colleges and universities has increased over time, even while the intensity of use of that space has declined. The result has been upward pressure on costs, some of which ultimately are borne by students.* A July 2016 study of eighty-two four-year public institutions by Ad Astra Systems found that the typical classroom was in use during only 50 percent of standard classroom hours each week, and only 57 percent of seats in those classrooms were being used when the rooms were scheduled.[15] A study conducted by the University of North Carolina system of its use of space during its 2010 fiscal year revealed that the average public-university classroom in North Carolina was used only 43.7 percent of the time (8:00 a.m. through 9:00 p.m.) during a standard school week.[16] Thus, more than one-half the time, classrooms in the system stood empty. Nevertheless, this did not diminish the requests of the same institutions for additional classroom space.

Anyone familiar with higher education knows that 8:00 a.m. classes and Saturday classes have become much less common, and some students (and their faculty) confine their official activities to Tuesdays and Thursdays. A major exception to this trend is evening classes, which have become more common as undergraduate student bodies have aged and a greater proportion of students are employed and attend part-time.

Space is a vital input to the process of higher education. Even so, some variant of the "edifice complex" mentioned in chapter 10 appears to hold many administrators, faculty, and board members in its thrall. Logic tells us that someone must pay for and maintain any new space that is constructed or acquired, and in many cases that someone turns out to be the student body. Already in 2009, the average public college or university spent an estimated $1,303 per full-time equivalent student on maintaining and operating their facilities.[17]

MODEST SOLUTIONS

Unfortunately, the adjective *modest* must be fully operational in this section because it is not clear that many viable, politically acceptable solutions exist to combat the cost inflation we observe in public higher education. The primary reason for this pessimistic inference is clear: nearly any action taken by a well-intentioned governing board, or even by a legislative body, potentially can be frustrated or even reversed by institutions and their supporters over time. Implementing substantive change in higher education too often turns out to be an exercise equivalent to an attempt to land a solid punch on a 1,000-pound cube of Jell-O. The slab of gelatin moves, twists, jiggles, and quivers in response to the punch, but then reverts to its original shape. Often, it is the same in higher education. I'll have more to say about this in a moment.

It is fair to observe that the current way of doing things in public higher education increasingly has denied access to some students and inflicted high levels of debt on others. Nevertheless, only intermittently has this circumstance resulted in organized opposition and strongly voiced complaints. There are several reasons for this. First, we know that undergraduate students come and go. They and their families usually focus intently on college costs for a period of one to six years. After this, their attention dissipates. There is no permanent constituency of interested parties or victims analogous to those that exist for well-organized groups such as technology firms in Silicon Valley, the steel industry, or federal workers. Hence, it is difficult to organize student or parent pressure groups that might address tuition and fee issues because of the episodic attention spans of those immediately affected.

Second, higher-education finance is an arcane subject that most people do not understand. The economics of a university are unlike those of an automobile manufacturer, dry cleaner, or grocery store. One can start with a perennial puzzler—what do universities do (or produce), and how can we measure whatever it is that they are doing or producing? Good luck to anyone who attempts to explain the rationale for a six-hour weekly teaching load to a taxicab driver or policeman, or to promote notions such as tenure and shared governance to construction workers or Uber drivers. Consider also the profusion of deceptively "independent" foundations, auxiliary enterprises, research institutes, and interest groups such as alumni associations that characterize public institutions today, but seldom are replicated in other sectors of the economy. The economics of a modern university are understandable, but it takes a good deal of time to master their peculiarities.

Third, higher education is rife with third-party payment arrangements whereby the individuals who pay the bills frequently are not the individuals who consume the service. Thus, agencies such as the federal government pay, but students consume. Practically, this means that students (and their institutions) emerge less concerned about a variety of costs than they would be if they had to pay the costs themselves. This is an understandable and economically rational reaction. If the federal government (or a foundation) is going to pick up a cost, then why lose sleep over that cost?

Fourth, as we have seen, higher education is a trust market, in which the customers (student and parents) rely upon the counsel of those they respect to advise them what they ought to do. Analogously, in the realm of medicine, when a physician tells us that we need a certain prescription, most of us choose to purchase that prescription. Accordingly, when students are told by counselors, friends, parents, and employers that they need to become educated, or that they should purchase a particularly expensive textbook package, or that they should pay for amenities at their college or university, they usually follow that advice until experience informs them otherwise. The overall trust-market effect is to make students and their parents less sensitive to price increases because they are reliant upon the views of others (who usually do not pay for the consequences of their advice).

Fifth, as the previous example reveals, higher education also is an experience market. Most students must attend an institution, sit in classes, and try out the institution's placement office before they can conclude whether these are things that actually do (or do not) work for them. Then they must decide whether such things are worth the price they are asked to pay. Simply put, it takes students (and parents) a while to catch on to the value of what they are receiving in return for the money they spend on higher education. By the time they do catch on, years may have passed. Further, there can be substantial switching costs attached to changing majors, moving to a different housing arrangement, transferring institutions, or even dropping out.

Sixth, most institutions of higher education, and especially the elite ones, possess brand magnetism that produces lifelong loyalists who support the programs, athletic teams, activities, and appropriations of their cherished institution. Witness the "War Eagle" cry of an Auburn University supporter, the tribal devotion of a Michigan Wolverine (the blue baseball cap with the maize M on it is one of the most recognized symbols in the United States), or the almost spiritual intensity of a Montana Grizzly. Further, on occasion, these loyalties extend to subdivisions of institutions—for example, the strong, lifetime Greek social organization affiliations of students at many Historically Black Colleges and Universities, or to engineers at Georgia Tech.

Many graduates of public colleges and university and their followers (who may never have attended so much as a single class) are inclined to believe that their chosen institution can do little wrong. Hence, why should anyone seriously question whether a Clemson University degree is worth its cost, or if a tuition increase at *The* Ohio State University is appropriate?

It will not escape the reader that many of these institutional loyalties are nurtured and extended by means of nonacademic activities, especially intercollegiate athletic programs. Who among us doubts that football is an identifying feature of The Ohio State University, or basketball at Gonzaga University? One flagship state university president to whom I have talked averred to me that his board and legislators always were "easier to convince" when his institution's football team was ranked in the top ten nationally.

Seventh, there is the matter of regulatory capture, which is related to each of the factors just noted. Those who are supposed to regulate higher education (members of governing boards and those working at state agencies) gradually become institutional advocates absent major scandals. Over time, regulatory and governance bodies become staffed by alumni of the very institutions they are supposed to regulate and monitor. In other jurisdictions, these circumstances might be deemed a conflict of interest. In higher education, however, such "conflicts" usually are deemed a desirable qualification.

The remainder of this chapter is devoted to my presentation of an agenda of "modest" solutions to the challenges described throughout this book.

Restructure Governing Board Membership and Duties

In most instances, members of public-institution governing boards are appointed by state governors. In some cases, they are elected or appointed by a variety of constituencies. Whichever the mode, the tendency is for new board members to be individuals who either have been generous academic or political donors, or have an axe to grind. Their knowledge of complex modern public universities may be small even though they spent four or more years on campus.

Long story short, these individuals need education and training before they should be allowed to serve. The training should be mandated by legislation and include not only factual information (much of which has been presented in previous chapters), but also balanced discussions by multiple individuals of major issues and challenges in public higher education. Even major donors should have to complete these exercises.

Some states have created blue-ribbon boards of citizens who recommend the names of qualified prospective board members to governors. This does not always result in vastly improved board memberships, and may suffer from an inability to identify minority candidates, but usually is helpful.

The major thing that must be accomplished, however, is for governors and legislatures to make it clear to board members that they represent the public (citizens, taxpayers, and students), not the institution upon whose board they sit, or the charismatic administrators who lead that institution. This reorientation of culture and duties could be accomplished by governing boards themselves and result in their adopting such a guiding statement after careful consideration and public debate. More likely, however, this will require legislative action.

Alas, governors and legislators may voice support for the "you're representing the public" ideal, but practical political realities will cause them to find ways for such proposals to disappear or die. Current ways of conducting governing board appointments and business did not arise by accident; they reflect decades, even centuries, of political give and take. Well-established, well-funded constituencies prefer the current milieu and will fight to keep it. Nevertheless, changing the composition of boards and their purpose for being is easily one of the most important steps that could be taken to reduce public college cost inflation.

Enhance Transparency

By all odds, this is the least controversial solution I proffer to deal with rapidly rising college costs. It is quite simple: we need to find ways to make students and their families better informed about college choices. Classic economic models assume that information is valuable. The better informed an individual is, the more likely it is that her decisions will help her achieve her specific goals. This also applies to decision making by students and their families.

Nevertheless, a recurrent problem in higher education is that market information is asymmetric: one party (the college or university) knows more than the other party (the student). Many prospective students and their households are miserably informed about the institutions they may seek to attend. Among the things they do not understand are the true cost of attending the institution, the reputation of specific academic programs, and the

Anthony Carnevale, who directs Georgetown University's well-regarded Center on Education and the Workforce, has been a strong advocate for providing additional information to prospective students and parents so that they can make better decisions. A recent example of this philosophy in action is "Good Jobs That Pay without a BA: A State by State Analysis."[18]

job prospects of graduates. One way to deal with this challenge is to require institutions to fully disclose vital information pertaining to them.

Accurate price and cost information is fundamental to intelligent student and family decision making. This information must include both published sticker prices and net prices across family income levels, and it should clearly communicate both the nature and likely consequences of student debt. Similarly valuable are data that inform prospective students and their families of student persistence rates, graduation rates, employment rates, and alumni incomes, ideally broken down by academic majors. Also useful are data that describe campus living arrangements, student and alumni demographics, and student activities.

Frequently ignored, but essential, are data that pinpoint how specific institutions spend their money. Complete line-item budgets should be posted on institutional websites so that any student or citizen can see what institutions value and support. *Actual* expenditures of funds similarly should appear on the website in a timely fashion. Thus, if Old Dominion University is spending $38 million annually on intercollegiate athletics, subsidizing research activities, or increasing administrative salaries, then it ought to be possible for an ordinary citizen or student to see that this is true.[19]

Related to this, some flagship state universities maintain fifty or more independent foundations related to their activities. The affairs of these bodies largely are protected from public scrutiny; this has enabled many institutions to hide some of their most important and expensive actions. The budgets of these bodies (and those for all auxiliary activities such as intercollegiate athletics, residence halls, and hospitals) relate to the public purposes of the universities, and therefore their budgets also should be posted on each institution's website. At least biannual disclosure of their expenditures should appear on the website as well. If, for example, foundation funds are being used to augment the salaries of individuals such as the president and the football coach, then this should be public knowledge and subject to freedom of information requests.

Some states permit public college and university presidents to declare that their working papers and correspondence are not subject to freedom of information requests. The argument is that premature disclosure of "presidential papers" might stifle discussion and feedback, reduce valid consideration of alternatives, and potentially ruin delicate negotiations. As a former college president I understand these arguments, and to a point I believe that they are well taken. They do not, however, justify permanently removing such papers from the public eye. Ultimately, we need to know how decisions were made and what the alternatives were if we are to assess the virtue of those decisions.

In fact, many presidents have hidden their long-term decisions to expand programs, purchase land, negotiate public/private partnerships, and increase costs behind the curtain of permanent presidential privilege. Except in unusual cases, all presidential papers should become public within one year of a decision having been rendered or action taken. Institutions, their presidents, and their boards ought to have processes in place that enable them to make careful decisions, but not permanently to hide the basis for those decisions.

I admit that the notion of disclosure of presidential papers would not always be easy to enforce (who would know?), but the principle should constitute a guiding administrative light. Public colleges and universities are entities that ideally should operate in the best interests of the citizenry. Only if those operations (including those of related foundations) are open to public inspection can we know if that has been the case.

Whoa, you might say! Are not many elements of the essential data I have mentioned already available? Yes, a knowledgeable individual often can find many of the data mentioned on the College Navigator website of the National Center for Education Statistics (https://nces.ed.gov/collegenavigator), or on stylized sites such as *U.S. News and World Report*, the *Princeton Review*, and the Brookings Institution (for alumni earnings), or on the site of the United States Department of Education (especially for loans and student debt). Unfortunately, many students and their parents do not know that these sites exist and instead rely upon the websites of specific institutions for data. Only a small proportion of institutions actually offer such data on their websites, and when they do, one often must click on a series of links to find them. Institutions do not wish to trumpet the fact that, say, the undergraduate products of their basket-weaving program don't earn much money, are burdened by large student debt, and perhaps are still living at home with their parents.

Some states now do require their public colleges and universities to provide a range of relevant data on their websites, but as just noted, these data often are not easy to find and interpret. Nor are the data refreshed on a timely basis.

Consequently, the asymmetric-information situation continues. Legislative action and governing board monitoring can improve this circumstance, yet reality is that higher education is both an experience market and a trust market, and no legislative or board fiat can do much about this. Mandatory provision of information will improve the circumstances of consumers in public higher education, but is unlikely to eliminate information asymmetry entirely.

State governing and coordinating boards have important roles to play in this arena. They can ensure that appropriate data are posted, refreshed on a timely basis, and permit realistic comparisons among institutions.

Nevertheless, I reluctantly conclude that while the provision of additional accurate information to consumers is a necessary condition to making higher-education consumers more knowledgeable (and thereby more cost sensitive), it is not a sufficient condition for this to happen. Accurate consumer information does discipline the higher-education marketplace, but it does not eliminate the basic motivating influences that push colleges and universities in the direction of cost-inflating behaviors.

Keep Open the Proverbial Doors of Opportunity

Flagship institutions in particular develop cleverly scripted and labeled narratives to justify to their governing boards what they wish to do and their need for tuition and fee increases that vastly exceed growth rates of prices and incomes. For example, the College of William and Mary, which may be the most expensive public institution in the United States for in-state undergraduates, euphemistically terms its tuition program the "William and Mary Promise."[20]

In defense of the College of William and Mary, it must be underlined that it is a superb academic institution. Further, as I have noted in previous chapters, it offers attractively low net prices to its lower-income students. The problem is that not very many lower-income students end up taking advantage of these lower prices—we have seen above that only 11 percent of William and Mary students were Pell Grant recipients in 2016–17. William and Mary, and dozens of other state universities, are becoming increasingly expensive to attend and progressively less inclusive in terms of the family incomes of their undergraduate student bodies. Their governing boards have bought into what have been gradual, evolutionary changes, with only a rare negative vote cast by a board member who has expressed concern.

Flagship institutions offer essential ladders of opportunity to ambitious, talented individuals, yet those ladders gradually have become increasingly out of the reach of ordinary citizens. The number of hours of work required for a median wage earner to earn enough to pay the average tuition at a flagship state university has doubled over the last fifteen years. Financial aid has not kept up with cost increases (including room and board as well as tuition and fees). The result is that many flagship state universities gradually have been transformed into institutions that arguably increase economic inequality rather than reduce it and sharpen class and social divisions rather than ameliorating them.

When the June 2018 cover story of the *Atlantic* is entitled "The Birth of a New Aristocracy," and the cover picture shows a baby clothed in a college T-shirt, it is fair to conclude that there is reality attached to allegations that our system of higher education often exacerbates economic inequality rather than reducing it.[21] Sadly, examples such as "Fighting Bob" LaFollette, who truly was born in a log cabin in Wisconsin, ended up graduating from the University of Wisconsin, and eventually became a highly notable United States senator; or Donna Brazile, who was enrolled in a high school Upward Bound program in Louisiana and graduated from Louisiana State University; or Mike Mansfield, who dropped out of high school in Montana at age fourteen and enlisted in the United States Navy, yet later graduated from the University of Montana and became the U.S. Senate majority leader, have become less common.

It isn't that opportunities for social mobility via public higher education have disappeared, but instead that, relatively speaking, they have diminished. It is a matter of degree. In any case, even assuming admission, there is a matter of a student's "fit" at an institution. Only 21.7 percent of undergraduate students at Georgia Tech come from families with incomes in the lowest

60 percent of the income distribution. At the University of North Carolina at Chapel Hill (UNC) it is only 20.7 percent, and at the University of Virginia (UVA) only 15.0 percent. At UNC, only 8 percent of undergraduates are African Americans, at Georgia Tech only 7 percent, and at UVA only 6 percent.[22] Would the modern equivalents of Bob LaFollette, Donna Brazile, or Mike Mansfield feel comfortable at these institutions today, even if they were admitted and could afford to attend them?

The ladders of opportunity are more accessible and economic and social disparities less dramatic in non-elite, non-flagship institutions, where the masses of American college students are educated. Racial and ethnic representations at these institutions come closer to reflecting the population of high school graduates in the United States. The problem is that the post-college opportunities available to graduates of these institutions frequently are less attractive than those confronting graduates of the elites and the flagships. Further, some of the non-elite institutions are surprisingly expensive in terms of their net costs of attendance.

How and why has public higher education been transformed in this fashion? There are multiple reasons, but important among them is the misguided performance of public college and university governing boards. *Quite simply, many members of the boards of these institutions have been co-opted by those institutions and their presidents. Too often, they act as if their primary duty is to find ways for their institution, its administrators, and its faculty to prosper as opposed to representing citizens, taxpayers, students, and families.*

I understand this process, having served as a president at two state universities for a total of fifteen years and additionally having been a consultant at almost fifty institutions. I've observed dozens of skillful college presidents fill the ears of board members with enticing, institution-centered narratives; watched them cleverly present their boards with leading questions and topics that demonstrated the "need" for their initiatives; observed them showing board members their institution's points of pride (even while identifying strategic challenges that could be surmounted if only additional resources could be found); saw them feed and entertain board members sumptuously; listened to board members being flattered concerning the value of their service; and, finally, watched skilled, charismatic presidents send their board members home happy with the thought that "their" institution was on the right track.

Seldom do board members ever question the fundamental rationale for administrative proposals, often because they don't have the knowledge to do so. Negative votes usually can be counted on a single hand. For example, an exemplary database exists of the 2016 and 2017 tuition and fee increase votes of trustees of the public university governing board members in Virginia. Approximately 160 board members were present for tuition and fee votes in each of these two years. Only two negative votes were recorded over the two years (both cast by the same board member), and there were only two abstentions. All other board members (99 percent) voted yes, even though state financial support for public higher education increased in 2016 and 2017 while head-count enrollment was declining.[23] Indeed, leading board members tend to chastise or shun fellow members who deviate from this scenario. Between board meetings, talented presidents ensure that board members are kept current with university developments; they and their vice presidents meet with members to articulate their positions and answer questions before public board sessions so that the public sessions are models of harmony. Many is the time I have heard board chairs and presidents instruct new board members that difficult, potentially delicate, or divisive questions should be dealt with in private.

Board members nearly always receive the modern equivalent of dashboard indicators that measure quantitative aspects of institutional performance. If anything, they are deluged with mountains of information, nearly always positive. Seldom are data concerning affordability and access part of this data smorgasbord.

Once they are a member of the "team," board members are asked to intervene with legislators and regulators on carefully prescribed issues for "their" institution and of course are asked for financial gifts once they have become a member of the club.

In fewer than 20 percent of cases have I ever witnessed a meaningful board discussion (public or private) that either explored the basic purpose of the institution or elucidated the public responsibilities of governing board members. Questions regarding affordability and access seldom arise, and let's admit it—they simply are not as fetching to most board members as are new research grants to fight cancer, spiffy new digital laboratories, or sessions with students who have scored at the ninety-ninth percentile on the Law School Admissions Test.

This oft-replicated approach to governance has contributed significantly to our current public-institution cost malaise. *To reverse the affordability crisis in public higher education, we require governors to appoint board members who first of all have been educated to understand what has been going on in higher education, and second who view their major responsibility as being to citizens, taxpayers, and students rather than to a specific institution and its charismatic president.* If prospective board members do not agree to such provisos, then they should be ineligible for appointment. This does not mean that big donors to political campaigns, candidates, and parties never should be appointed to boards. It does imply, however, that their willingness to learn about higher education and understand their duties must be more important than their political and financial clout.

A portion of the education of board members must include a demystification of the string-quartet simile and the notion that the labor-intensive nature of modern colleges and universities prevents them from doing things a different way. Another part of their education should be coldly statistical— not simply talking enrollment, research funding, and fundraising, but also apprising board members of what has been happening to higher-education costs, student characteristics, and student debt. In addition, board members need an evidentiary look at trends such as administrative proliferation, the financial tradeoff between instruction and research, and the expansion of amenities. Clearly, a very important part of their education must focus on their ultimate duties and responsibilities.

However, even well-educated and trained board members ultimately must possess courage. They must be willing to ask probing questions at opportune times and look beyond institutional narratives and the rhetoric of administrators and faculty. As Patrick Callan, the highly regarded president of the Higher Education Policy Institute and an individual with considerable administrative experience, has pointed out, on occasion they must have the mettle to simply "say no."[24]

By no means does this imply that board members should devote themselves to opposing presidential initiatives on a ritual basis, because most presidents possess an unmatched view and mastery of their institution. Presidents deserve the attention and respect of board members, but they are not infallible. Appropriately incentivized and evaluated presidents can inspire and move institutions in positive directions. No other actor in the process comes close to an institution's president in this regard.

These prescriptions for board members may make it sound as if I am implicitly endorsing micromanagement on the part of board members. Absolutely not! Board members should stick to goal setting, policymaking, monitoring performance, and evaluating their president.

Except in emergency circumstances, they should not be involved in making individual administrative decisions. The relevant point is that boards need to establish the right set of goals for their institution and its president and fashion their policies accordingly. Boards must monitor and evaluate their institution and their presidents on the basis of metrics that include citizen- and student-oriented concerns, not simply enrollment, fundraising, and research funding. Bigger may not be better.

Wise board members should assess institutional and presidential proposals initially from the standpoint of what is best for citizens, taxpayers, and students. On occasion, this means their decisions will make some of the long-term constituencies at the institution (including their president) unhappy. However, this will not occur repeatedly if boards invite public discussion before adopting enlightened goals and subsequently set appropriate evaluative criteria and metrics for their president. These criteria should be accompanied by incentives that correspondingly reward the president.

The appointment and education of board members is an ongoing, long-term process. While one governor or statewide board may excel in this arena, another may not. Legislative views also can change, sometimes with amazing rapidity. Hence, the quality of governance may ebb and flow over time. In some cases, progress may be reversed completely.

What's more, key administrators, faculty, staff, and some presidents have staying power. Most will be present on campus next year, and many ten years from now as well. State governors and board members, on the other hand, disappear. As they do, their reforms may evaporate along with them.

Thus, we must return to the metaphor that suggests we may be punching a massive cube of Jell-O if we attempt to change how public institutions of higher education conduct their business. It is not entirely clear that the governing board evolution I have prescribed can be accomplished, primarily because public higher education is a complicated enterprise that involves multiple parties whose self-interests often point them in disparate directions. Many of these trends are not consistent with the views I enunciate here. Candor requires that all interested parties acknowledge that the concerns and priorities of presidents, administrators, faculty, and board members do not always coincide with those of students and families.

Place Prices on Previously Free Resources

Earlier in this chapter, I noted that many public colleges and universities have acquired more space than they need; this is expensive behavior. Foundational to the "space problem" is the persistent custom of most colleges and universities to consider institutional space a free good. Departments and programs seldom pay for their use of space and therefore often attempt to control as much space as they can and demand incremental space whenever possible. The more, the better, especially if you don't have to pay for it.

When zero prices attach to any good or service, that good or service typically is used inefficiently. *A portion of the solution to the collegiate cost conundrum, therefore, is to have institutions begin to price heretofore free resources such as space, utilities, and computer support.* While institutions must be careful that they do not introduce pricing systems that cost more to implement than they receive in return in efficiency gains, it also is true that department chairs, deans, and vice presidents (to say nothing of students) are unlikely to give a second thought to how much of a scarce resource they use unless there is a price on that resource that forces them to choose what is most important to them.

Faculty and students often are repelled by the notion of running a college or university "like a business," and not without reason. The University of New Mexico is not General Motors, and the University of Nebraska is not a Subway franchise. Still, many processes inside modern institutions of higher education exhibit businesslike characteristics. Nearly all members of the academic community accept this principle when we talk about pricing tickets to football games, and most understand and do not complain when campus food services and university automobiles have market-based prices attached to their use. If prices were not attached to these items, then they would be used unwisely.

Even so, there is less consensus on campuses concerning the pricing of scarce educational inputs such as computer services and hardly any agreement over pricing resources such as space. However, the pricing of such resources ultimately is an important way to restrain tuition and fee inflation. Departments do not exhibit their voracious appetites for space when they must pay the equivalent of rent for the space they use. All of us think twice about purchasing expensive new software when we must bear the cost, but deliberate far less when we request, if not demand, a free technician whom we believe should show up promptly to minister to our needs.

Pricing of a different sort also can influence the behavior of college and university presidents. *Rather than presidential evaluative criteria focusing only on traditional "bigger is better" metrics such as enrollment, fundraising, and programmatic growth, these criteria need to be supplemented by measures of cost control and student access.* Am I baying at the moon here? After all, how many presidents ever have been rewarded for *not* growing and *not* building? Cost containment and student access seldom constitute the ingredients that motivate great post-presidential memoirs, or cause institutions to shoot upward in national rankings. Even so, they are essential ingredients in an opportunity-oriented society.

But let's return to the basic pricing principle. *Prices and incentives are capable of modifying (though not eliminating) the impact of Bowen's rule.* For this to occur, however, many board members, administrators, and faculty must overcome their anathema to pricing resources. One cannot place a price on everything, nor should one even try. There are, however, identifiable and easily tracked resources such as utilities, space, office supplies, copying-machine usage, automobiles, grants and contracts, library resources, and food services that have been successfully priced on many campuses. Note that I did not include long-distance telephone usage. Today, except where international calls are concerned, it no longer is cost efficient for most institutions to track and bill long-distance telephone charges. More interesting, however, is the question of office telephones. Now that virtually every administrator or faculty member owns a cell phone, is it necessary for the university to place a land line in every office enclosure?

There is yet another resource that often appears to constitute a free good to institutions, though it certainly does not to society: federal student financial aid. As we have seen, the most recent rigorous empirical evidence suggests that institutions often extract a portion of that aid and, because of the fungible nature of funds inside a college or university, use those dollars for other purposes.

Federal student financial aid formulas are based upon institutional costs. When an institution's costs rise, per-student federal financial aid to that institution's students rises. To some institutions, it must seem as if the federal government is validating their cost increases. Hence, they may encourage students to assume additional debt and may care little whether those students can pay back that debt.

One somewhat controversial way to alter this dynamic is to require that institutions acquire a piece of the action. Thus, if an institution's former students do not pay back their federal student loans, the institution will be assessed a financial penalty. The working hypothesis is that this will provide dual incentives—first for institutions to discourage students from assuming excessive debt, and second to encourage institutions to work with their current and former students so that they can successfully pay off their federal student loans. They have little or no reason to do either currently, other than avoiding an occasional bit of bad publicity.

The circumstances of each campus usually differ. What seldom if ever fluctuates, however, is the throbbing tendency of institutions to increase their costs of operations. The internal pricing of resources, and requiring institutions to assume a portion of the financial responsibility for the federal student loan debts their students incur, represent two often ignored ways to discourage excessive cost increases.

Reorient University Foundations

Rare is the public college or university that does not have its own foundation that focuses on fundraising for the institution, invests donated assets, and provides the institution with the ability to make certain expenditures that might be forbidden by state laws and regulations. Some flagship state universities have fifty or more foundations, each dedicated to a portion of these multifaceted institutions.

The Parable of the Football Field Lights. In one of my state university presidencies, the football field, located in the center of the campus, was less than fifty yards from my office windows. The field lights often would still be burning at midnight, though the field was empty of participants. Ever the economist, I asked the athletic director why this was so, and in so many words he replied that he did not have to pay the electric bill, so it was not much of a concern to him. I changed this. The next budget year, I allocated a sum of money to the athletic director for electricity and told him that if he turned off the lights within his domain, he could keep the money he saved. Voila! The lights at the football field soon were turned out a few minutes after the players left the field.

In many states, the activities of these foundations are not subject either to open meetings laws or to freedom of information laws. This has enabled the foundations to undertake transactions substantially outside of the public eye and on occasion to make expenditures that are ethically challenged or unprofitable. The University of Michigan, for example, which has an endowment of more than $10 billion dollars, has invested more than $400 million in hedge funds managed by alumni who advise Michigan on its investments.[25] This raised eyebrows for two reasons. First, an apparent conflict of interest existed. Second, the rate of return earned by the average hedge fund has trailed the Standard and Poor 500 Index over the past fifteen years. Simply put, university foundation hedge fund investments typically have underperformed, not the least because of the high fees they charge.[26]

We should not equate the University of Michigan with the diverse universe of public college and universities that exists in the United States. Even so, the Michigan experience is a reminder that public university foundations are increasingly important, though imperfectly understood, participants in a complex higher-education world in which non-state funding often now is dominant. Public-university foundation actions should be transparent and easily accessible.

In most instances, achieving this status will require changes in state laws. One can count upon many, perhaps most, foundations and institutions resisting the sunlight that such changes would produce. They will argue that greater visibility will reduce their ability to raise funds, because anonymity can be important to a few donors. I agree, though most welcome publicity. The anonymity of a donor, however, should not translate into anonymity of the conditions surrounding gifts. These should be publicly disclosed, not hidden, and be subject to the rigors of the academic marketplace. So also should be the salaries of foundation personnel, its expenditures, the composition of the foundation's portfolio, the fees it pays to those who manage its funds, and the performance of its portfolio.

Governing boards must recognize that the nature of higher-education finance has changed dramatically. The increased size, importance, and influence of university foundations now require that their activities be open to public scrutiny and that it be possible for external observers to observe and critique the choices they make. Note that scrutiny and evaluation do not mean control. Universities have established foundations primarily for good reasons, including the legitimate desire to avoid noxious state laws and regulations and reduce the possibility of state confiscation of donated assets. These protections must continue, albeit with significantly increased transparency.

Finally, every public-university foundation ought to be asked why the affordability of higher education does not rank among its highest expenditure priorities. What is deemed more important and why? That said, we need to recognize that foundation support for reducing undergraduate costs can be a complex consideration. Universities and their foundations may perceive that any support they provide for lowering tuition and fees represents an invitation for governors and legislators to reduce state financial commitments to higher education. There are ways around this potential problem, however, that include matching-dollar arrangements: "We'll do X if you'll match it." Purdue University's Back a Boiler program (which is managed by the Purdue Research Foundation) also represents a novel way to avoid the problems just noted.

Take Legislative Action

Instinctively, healthy proportions of individuals want their legislators to pass laws that, for example, restrict the proportion of out-of-state students an institution may enroll, or limit the size of tuition and fee increases, or require institutions to utilize accumulated fund balances to diminish tuition and fees. Versions of these and similarly minded laws have been passed in several states with some subsequent success at restraining costs.

Nevertheless, such laws and regulations at either the state or federal levels have their limitations. One must be careful to avoid instituting new rules that generate unintended side effects or hamstring institutions and boards so that they have no freedom of action when they (and society) really need it. Consider a limit on the number of out-of-state students who may enroll at an institution. Because out-of-state students are a major source of revenue to many colleges and universities, limiting their ranks constitutes a budget cut for institutions. Plausibly, they could react by increasing tuition, fees, and other charges on the now larger proportion of in-state students.

Or suppose a rule is devised that limits tuition and fee increases for in-state students to the previous year's growth in median household income. Alas, median household income can be a highly variable metric. It declined in absolute terms in the United States in both 2009 and 2010, and fell in real terms in eleven of fifteen years between 2001 and 2015. Attaching tuition and fee changes to it would have produced a massive implosion in higher education, given the decreases in public general fund tax support that were occurring at the same time. Yes, there should be a relationship between household income and tuition and fees, but it is not easy to specify a rule for all seasons.

Ideally, any rule relating tuition and fee increases to metrics such as the Consumer Price Index, the Higher Education Price Index, or median household income should be phrased in terms of a tie to a rolling average of previous years, with a three-year rolling average perhaps making the most sense.* (Review figure 1-3 in chapter 1 to see what this would look like.) Even so, it would be wise to recall years such as 1975, 1981, and 1982, when the Consumer Price Index rose more than 10 percent. Tuition and fee increases in response to such price inflation would not have taken effect immediately, but then would have persisted for several years after the price inflation had dissipated.

Many senior administrators are experienced survivors who are capable of finding alternate ways to skin financial cats. If we impose rules that constrain tuition and fee increases, then they may raise the same funds by means of user and course fees not covered by the general rule, or by invoking special discipline-specific tuition charges for students.

Limitations on accumulation of fund balances may lead institutions to spend such funds prematurely and foolishly, or to find places to hide those balances (for example, in foundations and affiliated organizations, including those relating to research and hospitals).

Further, enterprising institutions often have the flexibility to alter their overhead charges for activities ranging from computer services to security, or to change the menu of items for which they levy those overhead charges. This means that colleges and universities possess a surprising ability to shift funds from one institutional area to another and thereby evade price controls or fund balance controls.

The bottom line? New laws and rules can work, but in most cases only if boards, presidents, and administrators want them to work. Bluntly, members of governing boards not only must believe they bear a responsibility to citizens and students as well as to their institutions, but must also be aware of

---

*One year (matching tuition and fee increases to the previous year's metric) is too short and would result in highly variable signals and behavior. Five years probably is too long a period because it would either prevent institutions from adjusting quickly to new realities or enable them to take advantage of conditions that since have disappeared.

the considerable potential of wily administrators to alter or even derail what they are trying to accomplish. An appropriate place to start is to appoint a president who agrees with their views and to evaluate and compensate her accordingly. Otherwise, legislative and board efforts may emulate punches into the massive cube of Jell-O.

Promote Stronger versus Weaker Statewide Boards

New majors and degree programs nearly always drive up costs despite claims to the contrary. New academic and services centers (usually advertised as improving verities such as public outreach and interdisciplinary activity) similarly are accompanied by higher expenditures.

What is the best way to restrain curricular and programmatic bloat? *An intellectually respectable position in this fray is to endorse the existence of a powerful statewide higher-education board such as those that exist in California.* In such a world, a very respectable institution such as California State University, Stanislaus is restricted in terms of the breadth and level of academic programs that it may offer. For example, except in areas such as education, it may not offer doctoral degrees. The same restrictions do not apply at the University of California, San Diego. Still another academic tier exists in the community college system in California.

This approach to identifying and limiting programs and missions has achieved some success in restraining institutional aggrandizement in the Golden State and therefore has been imitated in several other states, including New York and Illinois. There are downsides, however. It cannot be implemented without incurring significant costs, which include the expenses associated with the higher-education regulatory body itself. Higher-education boards and coordinating bodies are not exempt from Bowen's rule, and a perusal of IPEDS data reveals that in many cases their budgets have increased more rapidly than the budgets of the institutions they regulate.

Further, *powerful statewide bodies may not create environments that stimulate innovation and unconventional approaches to problems.* The State Council of Higher Education for Virginia (SCHEV) is, as statewide boards go, a weaker body in a national context because each four-year public institution in Virginia has its own board that sets tuition and fees and adopts policies for that institution. This model has produced a set of highly differentiated institutions that range from the elite, small, but public College of William and Mary to a 34,000-student metropolitan institution such as George Mason University (GMU). Building on the nearby Washington, D.C., power structure, GMU has pursued and attained academic ranking and recognition in highly focused areas such as law and economics, and it seems unlikely that this would have been permitted in many other states.

This is the positive side of the "weak" regulatory-body ledger. One also can argue, however, that Virginia institutions have utilized their freedom to add expensive programs and complexity beyond what has been appropriate, and this is a reason why tuition and fees in that state not only are high but have increased more rapidly than the national average since the turn of the century. Witness the gradual spread of doctoral program granting authority across Virginia's smaller regional institutions and HBCUs, and the high net cost of student attendance at many Virginia publics.* The same scenario has played out in many other states as well.

Once again, we find that we live in a world of tradeoffs. More of one thing often requires less of another. For that reason, a *definitive answer to the question of whether stronger or weaker state boards are better for citizens in an overall sense is not at hand. One must balance the costs of operating strong or weak statewide boards against their benefits.* What is true for one

---

*Consider Christopher Newport University (CNU), in Newport News, Virginia. Under the leadership of former U.S. senator Paul Tribble, CNU, which enrolled 5,042 students in 2016–17, has developed a very attractive campus and become an institution of choice. In the process, it also has become an expensive institution, whose average net price for an in-state undergraduate student was a hefty $22,637 in 2015–16 ($15,500 for in-state students coming from families with annual incomes $0–30,000). Compare these numbers to Elite 28 member Virginia Tech's $17,190 and $11,998 (College Navigator, National Center for Education Statistics, http://nces.ed.gov/collegenavigator). In this evolutionary process, the percentage of CNU's undergraduates that received Pell Grants declined to 14 percent, and the *New York Times* reported that only 18 percent of CNU's students came from families whose incomes placed them in the bottom 60 percent of the income distribution (Gregor Aisch and others, "Some Colleges Have More Students from the Top 1 Percent than the Bottom 60," *New York Times,* January 18, 2017). However, the seventy-fifth percentile SAT score of CNU's entering freshmen rose to 1,850. Does this institutional evolution represent the exercise of sound public policy? In CNU's favor, it has met the "market test" and succeeded in transforming itself from a small, very regional institution into one that has the luxury of denying admission to many applicants and charging premium prices to those who do attend. Virginia's decentralized control of higher education (Florida bears some similarities) makes possible such an evolution, which in terms of the conventional academic hierarchy is a success story. At the same time, this approach to the world is symptomatic of the escalating costs of higher education. Query whether Virginia or any other state can afford to field and subsidize very many CNUs.

state with a peculiar geography and history may not hold for another. Thus, while many opinions have been expressed, a definitive answer remains elusive.

FINAL THOUGHTS

I end on a personal note by telling you that I am one of four sons of a Lutheran pastor, and my wife is the daughter of a letter carrier. As undergraduates, we matriculated at Illinois State University, which neither one of us could have afforded to attend except for its then low costs. Those were days when students could work full-time during the summer, hold a part-time job while on campus, and pay their higher-education bills with the proceeds. Alas, today this scenario is a virtual impossibility for anyone emanating from our backgrounds.

We have four grandsons. Ten years ago, I was confident that with a little bit of help, these thriving young people could afford to attend a strong public university. Today, I am less confident. If current trends continue, then they will need to either earn substantial academic scholarships or go deep into debt to earn bachelor's degrees.

Between the 2001–02 and 2016–17 academic years, the average *real* net price paid by an in-state undergraduate at the typical four-year public college or university rose 66 percent. (Net price is the sum of tuition and fees plus on-campus room and board for in-state students minus any grants received by students, but not including their loans). This means that the net cost of attending a typical four-year public institution rose 66 percent faster than the Consumer Price Index.

One result of this unsustainable pricing regime has been the stratification of college and university student bodies by income and race. In January 2017, as mentioned in earlier chapters, the *New York Times* published sobering data concerning the incomes of the families of students who attend more than 2,000 colleges and universities in the United States. Students whose family incomes placed them in the *bottom* 60 percent of the income distribution were revealingly rare at most public flagship universities. Only one in about six undergraduate students at the University of Virginia and the University of Michigan came from the bottom 60 percent of the income distribution, while it was one in five at both the University of North Carolina at Chapel Hill and the University of Colorado. As described earlier in this chapter, at several flagship public institutions the percentage of undergraduates who are African American is in the single digits.

It is difficult to pose such institutions as truly public universities when progressively they are becoming sufficiently stratified on the basis of income and race. Someone from another country might mistake this incarnation of higher education for an informal caste system. Despite the flowery rhetoric of institutions concerning inclusiveness and diversity, and significant expenditures said to support such, the enrollment numbers speak for themselves.

These circumstances constitute a recipe for additional economic and social stratification and societal discord. Slowly, inexorably, significant aspects of public higher education have become part of an emerging problem rather than part of the solution. The sons of pastors and daughters of mail carriers today must travel a much more demanding financial path to achieve social and economic mobility than they did even a decade previous.

This is a harsh judgment, and it should not distract us from acknowledging that many public colleges and universities continue to offer invaluable ladders of opportunity to the citizens and taxpayers who support them. Even so, the employment avenues that become available to the graduates of the non-elite state colleges and universities generally are less promising and remunerative than those provided by the elite flagship institutions. Wall Street financial firms and Silicon Valley giants do not habitually recruit at Typical 49 institutions. When graduates of Typical 49 institutions obtain positions at such firms, it usually signals either that they have proven their worth by working their way up through the industry ranks, or that they have connections.

The advantages of the elite institutions do not stop there. The average taxpayer subsidy per student is higher at the flagships than at other public institutions, and they benefit from considerably higher levels of voluntary gifts to support their activities.

What does this have to do with higher-education cost inflation? The elite institutions are the leaders. Their brand magnetism enables them to set the pace (if they wish) in implementing tuition and fee increases. They lead and other institutions follow, whether with respect to tuition and fee increases per se, additional cost-accelerating amenities, faculty teaching loads, or administrative bloat. The non-elite like nothing better than to imitate the elite and to rationalize their inflationary actions on the basis that they must do so to compete with what their state's flagship institution is doing.

While all might not agree, I believe a workable vision of an equitable society is one that is opportunity-based rather than outcome-based. Opportunities and encouragement are provided, though outcomes are not guaranteed. Critical to this view, however, is the notion that opportunities will exist.

It is shrewd and unifying, and economically productive as well, for society to provide generous opportunities and support for individuals to climb the ladders that lead to economic and social mobility and subsequent success. Nonetheless, if we truly wish to nurture a society that is rich in individual opportunity, and one in which a person's birth circumstances do not constitute an insuperable barrier, then we must ensure that our public higher-education system is accessible and affordable. It must not become a regressive engine.

Unfortunately, the loops of current higher-education behavior described in this book, while fascinating, often turn out to be dysfunctional insofar as an opportunity-based society is concerned. The current system incorporates practices and incentives that consistently generate spiraling costs of attendance. The result has been diminished economic and social prospects for an increasingly large swath of individuals in our society.

The good news is that this battle has not been irretrievably lost. Determined action on the part of the members of institutional governing boards, enlightened leadership by presidents presented with a different set of performance criteria and incentives, targeted funding by influential major foundations, and differing governmental approaches can turn the tide.

We must walk a different path in public higher education. There is no better time to start than today.

Notes

Chapter 1

1. *Consumer Reports* 81 (August 2016), cover.

2. While Ms. Krowen attended an independent institution, the University of Rochester, her comments were echoed repeatedly by public college graduates. In its August 9, 2016, issue, *Forbes* magazine reported a survey indicating that more than one-third of individuals aged eighteen to thirty-five who went to college wished they had not done so. This theme is revisited by *Forbes* multiple times.

3. Student Loan Hero, "A Look at the Shocking Student Loan Debt Statistics for 2018," StudentLoanHero.com, May 1, 2018.

4. College Board, *Trends in Student Aid 2017*, table 3 (https://trends.collegeboard.org/sites/default/files/2017-trends-student-aid_0.pdf). For the total number of student debtors, see Student Loan Hero, "A Look at the Shocking Student Loan Debt Statistics for 2018."

5. Susie Poppick, "Here's What the Average Grad Makes Right Out of College," *Money*, April 22, 2015.

6. Rajashri Charkrabarti, Nicole Gordon, and Wilbert van der Klaauw, "Diplomas to Doorsteps: Education, Student Debt, and Homeownership," *Liberty Street Economics* (blog), Federal Reserve Bank of New York, April 3, 2017; Meta Brown and Sydnee Caldwell, "Young Student Loan Borrowers Retreat from Housing and Auto Markets," *Liberty Street Economics* (blog), April 17, 2013. On lower retirement contributions, see Shahar Ziv, "5 Reasons to Stop Prioritizing Student Loan Payments," *Forbes*, May 16, 2016, and "Student Loans Rising: An Overview of Causes, Consequences, and Policy Options," *Economic Studies at Brookings*, Urban-Brookings Tax Policy Center, May 2014. On negative household wealth, see Olivier Armantier and others, "Which Households Have Negative Wealth," *Liberty Street Economics* (blog), August 1, 2016. On credit scores, see Brown and Caldwell, "Young Student Loan Borrowers Retreat from Housing and Auto Markets." On the lower level of new business formation, see Brent W. Ambrose, Larry Cordell, and Shuwei Ma, "The Impact of Student Loan Debt on Small Business Formation," Working Paper 15–26 (Federal Reserve Bank of Philadelphia,

July 2015). On living at home and not forming households, see Lisa J. Dettling and Joane W. Hsu, "Why Boomerang? Debt, Access to Credit, and Parental Co-residence among Young Adults" (Board of Governors of the Federal Reserve System, October 1, 2015). On evidence of debt effects, see Kim Justice, "Declining Support for Education Threatens Economic Growth" (Seattle: Washington State Budget and Policy Center, November 16, 2011).

7. Association of Governing Boards of Universities and Colleges, *The AGB 2017 Trustee Index: Trustees and Higher Education's Value Proposition* (Washington, D.C., 2017).

8. Mark Huelsman, "The Unaffordable Era: A 50-State Look at Rising College Prices and the New American Student," Demos.org, February 22, 2018.

9. Bryan Caplan, *The Case against Education: Why the Education System Is a Waste of Time and Money* (Princeton University Press, 2018).

10. Doug Lederman, "Is Higher Education Really Losing the Public?," *Inside Higher Education*, December 15, 2017.

11. Jane Wellman, "Technology and the Broken Higher Education Cost Model: Insights from the Delta Cost Project," *Educause Review*, September 5, 2012.

12. Bill Destler, "What Isn't Broken in Higher Education?," *Huffington Post*, May 17, 2014.

13. Deanna Pan, "The Business Model in Higher Education Is 'Not Sustainable,' Warns S.C. Commission," *Post and Courier*, February 16, 2018.

14. Jon Marcus, "Polls: Americans Increasingly Mistrustful of College Costs, Leadership and Value," *Hechinger Report*, November 7, 2016.

15. Josh Verges, "Minnesota State University Presidents Say Tuition Freezes Aren't Working," *St. Paul Pioneer Press*, April 17, 2018.

16. Grapevine, College of Education, Illinois State University, table 1 (https://education.illinoisstate.edu/grapevine/tables).

17. Minnesota State University, "Student Full Year Equivalent (FTE) FY 2008–2020" (www.minnstate.edu/system/finance/budget/enrollment/docs/FY2008-2020%20Master%20FYE%20Sept%202017.pdf); and Greta Kaul, "Enrollment in Minnesota's Higher Education Institutions Is Down—and It May Be for a While," *MinnPost*, May 22, 2018.

18. "Tuition and Fees, 1998–99 through 2016–2017," *Chronicle of Higher Education* (www.chronicle.com/interactives/tuition-and-fees?cid=wcontentgrid).

19. Marcus, "Polls."

20. "Current Term Enrollment Estimates: Fall 2017," National Student Clearinghouse Research Center, December 19, 2017.

21. Douglas A. Webber, "The Lifetime Earnings Premia of Different Majors: Correcting for Selection Based on Cognitive, Noncognitive and Unobserved Factors," *Labour Economics* 28 (June 2014), pp. 14–23; Jonathan James, "The College Wage Premium" (Federal Reserve Bank of Cleveland, August 8, 2012); Claudia Goldin and Lawrence Katz, "The Race between Education and Technology: The Evolution of U.S. Educational Wage Differentials, 1890 to 2005," Working Paper 12984 (Cambridge, Mass.: National Bureau of Economic Research, March 2007).

22. A usable summary and references are available at "Signalling," *Wikipedia* (https://en.wikipedia.org/wiki/Signalling_(economics)), accessed March 15, 2018.

23. U.S. Department of Education, College Scorecard Data, last updated March 29, 2018 (https://collegescorecard.ed.gov/data).

24. Timothy J. Bartik and Brad Hershbein, "Degrees of Poverty: Family Income Background and the College Earnings Premium," *Upjohn Institute Employment Research* 23 (July 2016), pp. 1–3.

25. "Colleges with the Best Salary Outcomes, Based on 3 Analyses, 2015," *Chronicle of Higher Education*, August 19, 2016.

26. For unemployment rates and higher incomes for college graduates, see Bureau of Labor Statistics (http://www.bls.gov/emp/ep_chart_001.htm). See also "Employment Rates and Average Starting Salaries by Discipline for Bachelor's-Degree Recipients from the Class of 2015, by Academic Discipline," *Chronicle of Higher Education*, August 19, 2016.

27. Goldman Sachs Equity Research, "What If I Told You . . . College May Not Be Worth It?," December 2, 2015; Douglas Belkin, "Recent Grads Doubt College's Worth," *Wall Street Journal*, September 29, 2015; Goldie Blumenstyk, "Just Half of Graduates Strongly Agree Their College Education Was Worth the Cost," *Chronicle of Higher Education*, September 29, 2015; Piyush Mangukiya, "Is College Worth the Cost?," *Huffington Post*, December 2, 2015.

28. David O. Lucca, Taylor Nadauld, and Karen Shen, "Credit Supply and the Rise in College Tuition: Evidence from the Expansion in Federal Student Aid Programs," Staff Report 733 (New York Federal Reserve Bank, March 2016).

29. Tamara Hiler and Lanae Erickson Hatalsky, "What Free Won't Fix: Too Many Public Colleges Are Dropout Factories," ThirdWay.org, August 11, 2016.

30. Ibid. See also Susie Poppick, "Here's What the Average Grad Makes Right Out of College," *Money*, April 22, 2015.

31. Michael Bugeja, "Take Charge of Curricular Glut," *Inside Higher Education*, June 13, 2016.

32. Josh Freedman, "Why American Colleges Are Becoming a Force for Inequality," *Atlantic*, May 16, 2013. See also Carolyn M. Hoxby and Christopher Avery, "The Missing 'One-Offs': The Hidden Supply of High-Achieving, Low-Income Students," Working Paper 18586 (Cambridge, Mass.: National Bureau of Economic Research, December 2012).

33. Robert B. Archibald and David H. Feldman, *Why Does College Cost So Much?* (Oxford University Press, 2011); Archibald and Feldman, "The Anatomy of College Tuition" (Washington, D.C.: American Council on Education, 2012); Archibald and Feldman, "Federal Financial Aid Policy and College Behavior" (Washington, D.C.: American Council on Education, 2016).

34. College Board, *Trends in College Pricing 2017*, table 3 (https://trends.collegeboard.org /college-pricing). CPI-U data come from the Bureau of Labor Statistics, Series CUUR0000SEEB01, computed from July 1997 to July 2017 (www.bls.gov).

35. Danielle Allen, "Tuition Is Now a Useless Concept in Higher Education," *Washington Post*, August 19, 2016.

36. The Commonfund HEPI: www.commonfund.org/commonfund-institute/higher -education-price-index-hepi.

37. Melissa Korn, "College Enrollment Drops 1.4% as Adults Head Back to Work," *Wall Street Journal*, December 19, 2016.

38. For machinists' wages, see Bureau of Labor Statistics, National OES estimates for occupation 51-4040 in 2000 and 2016, National Occupational Employment and Wage Estimates (www.blg.gov/oes/current/oes_nat.htm). For tuition and fees, College Board, *Trends in College Pricing 2017*, table 3.

39. Dylan Mathews, "The Tuition Is Too Damned High," parts I through X, *Washington Post*, beginning August 26, 2013.

40. Thomas Frank, "Colleges Are Full of It," *Salon*, June 8, 2014; Henry E. Riggs, "The Price of Perception," *New York Times*, April 13, 2011; Richard Vedder, "Twelve Inconvenient Truths about American Higher Education," *Center for College Affordability and Productivity* (blog), March 2012; the James G. Martin Center for Academic Renewal, www.jamesgmartin.center.com.

41. College Board, *Trends in Student Aid 2017*, figure 15A.

42. Ibid., tables 2 and 3. On a full-time equivalent student basis, student loans increased 48.6 percent between 1996–97 and 2016–17, but approximately 69 percent if we focus only on the approximately 70 percent of undergraduate students who actually did borrow according to the College Board, *Trends in Student Aid 2017*, figure 9, https://trends.collegeboard.org/sites/default/files/2017-trends-student-aid_0.pdf. The 70 percent estimate is conservative because it does not include those who borrow from nonfederal sources.

Chapter 2

1. College Board, *Trends in College Pricing 2017*, figure 9 (https://trends.collegeboard.org/college-pricing).

2. Federal Reserve Economic Data, "Real Median Household Income in the United States" (graph), Series MEHOINUSA672N (http://fred.stlouisfed.org), updated September 13, 2017.

3. Kim Peterson, "How Much Does It Cost to Own a Car in 2014?," *CBS Money Watch*, May 13, 2014.

4. College Board, *Trends in Student Aid 2017*, table 2 (https://trends.collegeboard.org/student-aid). Josh Mitchell, "Federal Student Lending Swells," *Wall Street Journal*, November 28, 2012, reported that 93 percent of all loans received by undergraduates in 2012 came from the federal government.

5. Federal Reserve Economic Data, "Real Median Household Income in the United States" (graph).

6. Sarah A. Donovan, Marc Labonte, and Joseph Dalaker, *The U.S. Income Distribution: Trends and Issues* (Congressional Research Service, 2016).

7. Gregor Aisch and others, "Some Colleges Have More Students from the Top 1 Percent than the Bottom 60," *New York Times*, January 18, 2017.

8. Charlie Javice, "The 8 Most Confusing Things about Fafsa," *New York Times*, December 19, 2017.

9. U.S. Department of Education, "Federal Student Loan Programs," StudentAid.gov, September 2017 (https://studentaid.ed.gov/sa/sites/default/files/federal-loan-programs.pdf).

10. U.S. Department of Education, "Federal Student Aid," StudentAid.gov (https://studentaid.ed.gov/sa/types), accessed August 2018.

11. College Navigator, National Center for Education Statistics (http://nces.ed.gov/collegenavigator); U.S. Department of Education, Federal Student Aid, "Official Cohort Default Rates for Schools" (www2.ed.gov/offices/OSFAP/defaultmanagement/cdr.html), updated September 2017.

12. National Association of Student Financial Aid Administrators, "2017 Tax Year: Federal Tax Benefits for Higher Education" (www.nasfaa.org/2017_tax_year).

13. W. Lee Hansen and Burton Weisbrod, *Benefits, Costs, and Finance of Public Higher Education* (Chicago: Markham Publishing, 1969).

14. Jon Marcus and Holly K. Hacker, "The Rich-Poor Divide on America's College Campuses Is Getting Wider, Fast," *Hechinger Report*, December 17, 2015.

15. For information about Georgia's HOPE scholarship program, see the website GAFutures.org (www.gafutures.org/hope-state-aid-programs).

16. Susan M. Dynarski, "Hope for Whom? Financial Aid for the Middle Class and Its Impact on College Attendance," Working Paper 7756 (Cambridge, Mass.: National Bureau of Economic Research, June 2000), and Dynarski, "Does Aid Matter? Measuring the Effect of Student Aid on College Attendance and Completion," Working Paper 7422 (Cambridge, Mass.: National Bureau of Economic Research, November 1999).

17. Greg Rossino and Ryan Kruger, "New Analysis Shows HOPE Scholarship to Run Out of Money by 2028," www.11alive.com, August 10, 2016.

18. Kati Lebioda, "A Gamble with Consequences: State Lottery-Funded Scholarship Programs as a Strategy for Boosting College Affordability," *Policy Matters*, September 2014 (www .aascu.org/policy/publications/policy-matters/StateLotteryScholarships.pdf).

19. Rossino and Kruger, "New Analysis Shows HOPE Scholarship to Run Out of Money by 2028."

20. William Bennett, "Our Greedy Colleges," *New York Times*, February 18, 1987.

21. Meredith Kolodner, "States Moving College Scholarship Money Away from the Poor, to the Wealthy and Middle Class," *Hechinger Report*, June 22, 2015.

22. Aisch and others, "Some Colleges Have More Students from the Top 1 Percent than the Bottom 60." The *U.S. News and World Report* rankings are for 2017, while the *New York Times* income distribution data relate to 2013.

23. Jason Delisle and Kim Dancy, "Do State Subsidies for Public Universities Favor the Affluent?" (Brookings Institution, July 28, 2016).

24. Tax Policy Center, "Household Income Quintiles, 1967 to 2015" (May 2017) (www .taxpolicycenter.org/statistics/household-income-quintiles).

25. College Navigator, National Center for Education Statistics (https://nces.ed.gov /collegenavigator/?q=university+of+georgia&s=all&id=139959). Income distribution data come from Aisch and others, "Some Colleges Have More Students from the Top 1 Percent than the Bottom 60." Net price data come from College Navigator, National Center for Education Statistics (https://nces.ed.gov/collegenavigator/?q=pittsburgh&s=all&pg=2&id =215293#finaid).

Chapter 3

1. Josh Mitchell, "Nearly 5 Million Americans in Default on Student Loans," *Wall Street Journal*, December 13, 2017.

2. Danielle Douglas-Gabriel, "There Are a Lot of People Lowering Their Student Payments, but Also a Lot of People Who Are Behind," *Washington Post*, August 22, 2016.

3. Center for Microeconomic Data, "Household Debt and Credit Report," charts 13 and 14 (New York Federal Reserve Bank, August 2016).

4. Judith Scott-Clayton, "What Accounts for Gaps in Student Loan Default, and What Happens After" (Brookings Institution, June 21, 2018).

5. Daniel Pianko, "Writing Off Student Debt Is Only a Matter of Time," *Wall Street Journal*, August 15, 2016.

6. Consumer Financial Protection Bureau, *Student Banking: Annual Report to Congress* (Washington, D.C., 2016), p. 2.

7. Beth Akers and Mathew Chingos, "Is a Student Debt Crisis on the Horizon?" (Brookings Institution, June 24, 2014) and Beth Akers and Mathew Chingos, *Game of Loans: The Rhetoric and Reality of Student Debt* (Princeton University Press, 2016)

8. Judith Scott-Clayton, "The Looming Student Debt Crisis Is Worse Than We Thought" (Washington, DC: Brookings Institution, January 11, 2018).

9. Scott-Clayton, "What Accounts for Gaps in Student Loan Default, and What Happens After."

10. Fernanda Zamudio-Suaréz, "A New Academic Year Brings Fresh Anxiety at Illinois's Public Colleges," *Chronicle of Higher Education*, August 23, 2016. For those students who graduated with student debt, the average size of that debt was $28,288 in 2017. However, the variance among states was large: only $18,435 in Utah but $33,462 in New Hampshire ("Student Loan Debt by School by State," Lendedu [https://lendedu.com/blog/average-student-loan-debt-statistics]). Reflective of this were the average net prices the National Center for Education Statistics' College Navigator says were paid by undergraduates in 2014–15 at the University of Utah ($12,136) and the University of New Hampshire ($21,995). College Navigator, National Center for Education Statistics (http://nces.ed.gov/collegenavigator).

11. Jill Barshay, "Federal Data Show 3.9 Million Students Dropped Out of College with Debt in 2015 and 2016," *Hechinger Report*, November 6, 2017.

12. Danielle Douglas-Gabriel, "Want College to Pay Off? These Are the 50 Majors with the Highest Earnings," *Washington Post*, October 17, 2016.

13. Jeffrey Selingo, "Where Student Debt Is a Real Problem," *Washington Post*, January 5, 2018.

14. "Women's Student Debt Crisis in the United States," American Association of University Women, May 2018.

15. Adam Looney and Constantine Yannelis, "Most Students with Large Loan Balances Aren't Defaulting: They Just Aren't Reducing Their Debt" (Brookings Institution, February 16, 2018).

16. "Despite Lower Rates, More than 650,000 Defaulted on Federal Student Loans," press release, Institute for College Access and Success, September 24, 2014.

17. Melissa Korn, "Federal Aid Kept ITT Afloat," *Wall Street Journal*, September 6, 2016.

18. Kim Clark, "The 5 Colleges That Leave the Most Students Crippled with Debt," *Money*, September 14, 2014. Additional work performed by American Enterprise Institute economist Jason Delisle, but published in 2016 by Brookings (Jason Delisle, "The Coming Public Service Loan Forgiveness Bonanza" [Brookings Institution, September 22, 2016]) has raised probing questions about the federal government's Public Service Loan Forgiveness (PSLF) program. The PSLF program enables student debtors who subsequently take jobs in "public service" and make ten years of regular loan payments to write off their remaining federal student loan

debt. It is a politically popular program that has proven to be substantially more popular than originally forecast, not the least because it covers jobs that account for one-quarter of all employed individuals in the United States. Delisle reports that the cost of the program was revised upward "by a staggering amount," which translated to costs that were twenty to fifty times higher than originally forecast. Under relaxed PSLF standards, borrowers pursuing certain graduate programs in certain professions can have the entire cost of their program paid for and forgiven under the PSLF.

Between fourth quarter 2011 and second quarter 2016, the number of PSLF program enrollees increased from 0 to 431,853. Problematic has been the very high outstanding loan balances of many participants and their graduate student status. The median loan balance of participants (62 percent of whom were working for government agencies in 2015) was more than $60,000, and more than 30 percent of participants had loan balances exceeding $100,000.

Delisle demonstrated that students who enter graduate school with a typical level of undergraduate student debt could go to graduate school free if they enroll in the PSLF and complete its terms. His conclusion is that the PSLF program creates major student employment distortions that are undesirable and should be reduced in size or terminated. It does not seem likely that this will occur because of the considerable political appeal of the program and the number of individuals involved. However, it does appear that limits on the amounts that can be borrowed and a stricter interpretation of what constitutes public service are in the cards.

19. Rajashri Chakrabarti, Nicole Gorton, and Wilbert van der Klaauw, "Diplomas to Doorsteps: Education, Student Debt, and Homeownership," *Liberty Street Economics* (blog), Federal Reserve Bank of New York, April 3, 2017.

20. Meta Brown and Sydnee Caldwell, "Young Student Loan Borrowers Retreat from Housing and Auto Markets," *Liberty Street Economics* (blog), Federal Reserve Bank of New York, April 17, 2013.

21. Daniel H. Cooper and J. Christina Wang, "Student Loan Debt and Economic Outcomes," Current Policy Perspectives No. 14-7 (Federal Reserve Bank of Boston, 2014); Olivier Armantier and others, "Which Households Have Negative Wealth?," *Liberty Street Economics* (blog), Federal Reserve Bank of New York, August 1, 2016.

22. Beth Akers, "Reconsidering the Conventional Wisdom on Student Loans and Home Ownership" (Brookings Institution, May 8, 2014).

23. Olivier Armantier and others, "Which Households Have Negative Wealth?," *Liberty Street Economics* (blog), Federal Reserve Bank of New York, August 1, 2016.

24. Cooper and Wang, "Student Loan Debt and Economic Outcomes."

25. Y. Yuh, "Assessing Adequacy of Retirement Income for U.S. Households: A Replacement Ratio Approach," *Geneva Papers on Risk and Insurance: Issues and Practice*, 36, no. 2 (2011), pp. 304–23; Joyce A. Cavanagh and Deanna L. Sharpe, "The Impact of Debt Levels on Participation in and Discretionary Retirement Savings," *Journal of Financial Counseling and Planning Education* 13, no. 1 (2002), pp. 47–60.

26. Brown and Caldwell, "Young Student Loan Borrowers Retreat from Housing and Auto Markets."

27. Lisa J. Dettling and Joanne W. Hsu, "Why Boomerang? Debt, Access to Credit, and Parental Co-Residence among Young Adults" (Board of Governors of the Federal Reserve System, October 1, 2015).

28. Brent W. Ambrose, Larry Cordell, and Shuwei Ma, "The Impact of Student Loan Debt on Small Business Formation," Working Paper 15-26 (Federal Reserve Bank of Philadelphia, July 2015).

29. Jesse Rothstein and Cecilia Elena Rouse, "Constrained after College: Student Loans and Early-Career Occupational Choices," *Journal of Public Economics* 95, no. 1 (2011), pp. 149–63; Erica Field, "Educational Debt Burden and Career Choice: Evidence from a Financial Aid Experiment at the NYU Law School," *American Economic Journal: Applied Economics* 1, no. 1 (2009), pp. 1–21; William Gale, Benjamin Harris, and Bryant Renaud, "Student Loans Rising: An Overview of Causes, Consequences, and Policy Options" (Washington, D.C.: Tax Policy Center [Urban Institute and Brookings Institution], May 2014).

30. Jeffrey Dew, "Debt Change and Marital Satisfaction Change in Recently Married Couples," *Family Relations* 57, no. 1 (2008), pp. 60–71; Dora Gicheva, "Does the Student-Loan Burden Weigh into the Decision to Start a Family?" UNCG Economics Working Papers 11-14 (University of North Carolina at Greensboro, Department of Economics, 2011).

31. Sandy Baum and Marie O'Malley, "College on Credit: How Borrowers Perceive Their Education Debt," *Housing Studies* 33, no. 3 (2003), 7–19.

32. Catherine Millett, "How Undergraduate Loan Debt Affects Application and Enrollment in Graduate or First Professional School," *Journal of Higher Education* 74, no. 4 (2003), pp. 386–427.

33. Back a Boiler Program, Purdue University (https://purdue.edu/backaboiler).

34. Anne Kim, "Innovating Out of Student Debt" (Washington, D.C.: Progressive Policy Institute, May 2018).

Chapter 4

1. Gordon C. Winston, "College Costs: Subsidies, Intuition and Policy," paper presented at the National Commission on the Cost of Higher Education (Boston, November 6, 1997). See also his "Subsidies, Hierarchy and Peers," *Journal of Economic Perspectives* 13 (Winter 1999), pp. 13–26, for the precise subsidy estimates.

2. Peter Schmidt, "Where Even Experts Can't Figure Out Tuition Costs," *Chronicle of Higher Education*, December 16, 2016.

3. Purdue University, "Estimated Cost of Attendance, 2016–2017" (www.admissions .purdue.edu/costsandfinaid/tuitionfees.php); updated August 2018 to reflect costs for 2018–19.

4. "2011 Survey of Differential Tuition at Public Higher Education Institutions," ILR School, Cornell University.

5. Wendy Nelson Espeland and Michael Sauder, *Engines of Anxiety: Academic Rankings, Reputation, and Accountability* (New York: Russell Sage Foundation, 2016).

6. Frank Bruni, "Why College Rankings Are a Joke," *New York Times*, September 17, 2016.

7. "Best Colleges, 2017," *U.S. News and World Report* (www.usnews.com/info/blogs/press -room/articles/2016-09-13/us-news-releases-2017-best-colleges-rankings).

8. Cody Davidson, "Changes to Federal Pell Grant Eligibility: The Effect of Policy and Program Changes on College Students at Public Institutions in Kentucky," *Journal of Student Financial Aid* 43, no. 3 (2013), pp. 111–31.

9. "State Holds the Line on Higher Education Tuition Increases, but Fees Lead to Higher Costs," Office of Missouri State Auditor, August 30, 2016.

10. Brian Jacob, Brian McCall, and Kevin M. Stange, "College as Country Club: Do Colleges Cater to Students' Preferences for Consumption?" Working Paper 18745 (Cambridge, Mass.: National Bureau of Economic Research, January 2013).

11. Robert Kelchen, "An Analysis of Student Fees: The Roles of States and Institutions," *Review of Higher Education* 39, no. 4 (2016), pp. 597–619, and the Delta Cost Project (www .deltacostproject.org).

12. Author's calculations from the Delta Cost Project (www.deltacostproject.org).

13. Two brief surveys of the evidence are Hanover Research, "Tackling Tuition: Research-Drive Solutions," August 28, 2014 (www.hanoverresearch.com/insights-blog/tackling-tuition -research-driven-solutions); and Reed College Economics, "Case of the Day: Elasticity of Demand for Higher Education," n.d. (www.reed.edu/economics/parker/f10/201/cases/elasticity .html).

14. Rajashri Chakrabarti, Michael Lovenheim, and Kevin Morris, "The Changing Higher Education Landscape," *Liberty Street Economics* (blog), Federal Reserve Bank of New York, September 8, 2016.

15. College Navigator, National Center for Education Statistics (https://nces.ed.gov /collegenavigator); Danette Gerald and Kati Haycock, "Engines of Inequality: Diminishing Equity in the Nation's Premier Public Universities" (Washington, D.C.: Education Trust, 2006).

Chapter 5

1. College Navigator, National Center for Education Statistics (https://nces.ed.gov /collegenavigator).

2. Ibid.

3. Ibid.

4. To access the Integrated Postsecondary Education Data System, go to https://nces.ed .gov/ipeds.

5. Deirdre N. Mc Closkey, "'You Know, Ernest, the Rich Are Different from You and Me': A Comment on Clark's *A Farewell to Alms*," *European Review of Economic History* 12, no. 2 (August 2008), pp. 138–48.

6. Robert Hiltonsmith, "Pulling Up the Ladder" (New York: Demos, May 5, 2015).

7. Douglas Webber, "Fancy Dorms Aren't the Main Reason Tuition Is Skyrocketing," FiveThirtyEight.com, September 13, 2016; Webber, "State Divestment and Tuition at Public Institutions," *Economics of Education Review* 60 (October 2017), pp. 1–4.

8. Neal McCluskey, "Not Just Treading Water: In Higher Education, Tuition Often Does More than Replace Lost Appropriations," Policy Analysis No. 810 (Washington, D.C.: Cato Institute, February 15, 2017).

9. Karin Kapsidelis, "Colleges' Spending, Not Just Decreased State Support, Have Spurred Tuition Increases, Panel Hears," *Richmond Times Dispatch*, November 16, 2016.

10. College Navigator, National Center for Education Statistics.

11. Ibid.

12. "Tuition and Fees, 1998–99 through 2017–18," *Chronicle of Higher Education*, November 28, 2017 (www.chronicle.com/interactives/tuition-and-fees?cid=wcontentgrid).

13. Jeff Groen and Michelle White, "In-State versus Out-of-State Students: The Divergence of Interest between Public Universities and State Governments" (Working Paper, Cornell University ILR School, July 2003).

14. College Board, *Trends in College Pricing 2017*, table 2 (https://trends.collegeboard.org /college-pricing).

15. "Real Median Household Income in the United States," Federal Reserve Bank of St. Louis (https://fred.stlouisfed.org/series/MEHOINUSA672N).

16. Nick Anderson and Danielle Douglas-Gabriel, "Nation's Prominent Public Universities Are Shifting to Out-of-State Students," *Washington Post*, January 30, 2016.

17. Laura Pappano, "How the University of Alabama Became a National Player," *New York Times*, November 3, 2016.

18. Anderson and Douglas-Gabriel, "Nation's Prominent Public Universities Are Shifting to Out-of-State Students."

19. College Navigator, National Center for Education Statistics; "Tuition and Fees, 1998–99 through 2017–18."

20. Ibid.

21. CPI-U data come from the Bureau of Labor Statistics, Series CUSSR0000SA0 (www .bls.gov); median household income data come from the Federal Reserve Bank of St. Louis (https://fred.stlouisfed.org/series/MEHOINCUSVAA646N).

22. "Tuition and Fees, 1998–99 through 2017–18," *Chronicle of Higher Education*, November 28, 2017 (www.chronicle.com/interactives/tuition-and-fees?cid=wcontentgrid).

23. Gregor Aisch and others, "Some Colleges Have More Students from the Top 1 Percent than the Bottom 60," *New York Times*, January 18, 2017.

24. College Navigator, National Center for Education Statistics; "Tuition and Fees, 1998–99 through 2017–18."

25. Andrew Howard Nichols, "The Pell Partnership: Ensuring a Shared Responsibility for Low-Income Student Success" (Washington, D.C.: Education Trust, 2015).

26. "Tuition and Fees, 1998–99 through 2017–18."

27. College Navigator, National Center for Education Statistics; "Tuition and Fees, 1998–99 through 2017–18."

28. "University of Michigan Unveils Five-Year Strategic Plan for Diversity, Equity and Inclusion," *Michigan News*, October 6, 2016; Mark J. Perry, "More on My Efforts to Advance Diversity, Equity, and Inclusion and End Gender Discrimination in Michigan," *AEIdeas*, May 17, 2018.

29. Perry, "More on My Efforts to Advance Diversity, Equity, and Inclusion."

30. Purdue's website (www.purdue.edu) contains information on the tuition freeze, early graduation, competency-based credit, and income-share initiatives. For net prices, see College Navigator, National Center for Education Statistics.

31. College Navigator, National Center for Education Statistics.

32. Pappano, "How the University of Alabama Became a National Player."

Chapter 6

1. National Association of College and University Business Officers (www.nacubo.org /-/media/Nacubo/Documents/EndowmentFiles/2017-Endowment-Market-Values.ashx?la =en&hash=E71088CDC05C76FCA30072DA109F91BBC10B0290).

2. Ibid.

3. "Faculty: The Cornerstone of Academic Excellence," University of North Carolina at Chapel Hill (https://giveto.unc.edu/impact/what-to-support/faculty/), and conversations with administrators.

4. "Dow Jones Industrial Average," Yahoo.com (https://finance.yahoo.com/quote/%5EDJI/history?period1=1199170800&period2=1473919200&interval=1wk&filter=history&frequency=1wk).

5. Janet Lorin, "Seven College Endowments Report Annual Losses in Choppy Markets," *Bloomberg*, September 12, 2016.

6. Nick Anderson, Susan Svrluga, and Danielle Douglas-Gabriel, "Lawmakers Want to Know Why U-Va. Stockpiled Billions, but Still Boosted Tuition," *Washington Post*, August 25, 2016.

7. College Navigator, National Center for Education Statistics (http://nces.ed.gov/collegenavigator).

8. Ibid.

9. Sandy Baum, Catharine Bond Hill, and Emily Schwartz, "College and University Endowments: In the Public Interest?" (New York: Ithaka S+R, 2018); emphasis added.

10. College Affordability and Transparency Center, U.S. Department of Education (https://collegecost.ed.gov/catc/#).

11. Tuition and fee data come from "Tuition and Fees, 1998–99 through 2017–18," *Chronicle of Higher Education*, November 28, 2017 (www.chronicle.com/interactives/tuition-and-fees?cid=wcontentgrid); enrollment data come from the College Navigator, National Center for Education Statistics.

12. College Navigator, National Center for Education Statistics.

13. The Princeton Review, *The Best 381 Colleges, 2017 Edition* (www.princetonreview.com).

14. Brian Jacob, Brian McCall, and Kevin Stange, "College as Country Club: Do Colleges Cater to Students' Preferences for Consumption?," Working Paper 18745 (Cambridge, Mass.: National Bureau of Economic Research, January 2013).

15. College Navigator, National Center for Education Statistics.

16. Rich DeMillo, as quoted in Margaret Tate, "Is College Worth It?," *How to Pay for College*, website of Georgia Tech University, n.d. (www.news.gatech.edu/features/college-worth-it). See also Richard DeMillo, *Abelard to Apple: The Fate of American Colleges and Universities* (MIT Press, 2011).

17. Sarah Butrymowicz, "An Unprecedented Look at Pell Grant Graduation Rates from 1,149 Schools," *Hechinger Report*, September 24, 2015.

18. College Navigator, National Center for Education Statistics; "Tuition and Fees, 1998–99 through 2017–18."

19. John A. Byrne, "Arizona State, EdX to Offer Entire Freshman Year of College Online," *Fortune*, April 22, 2015.

20. "Remarks of Helen E. Dragas to Higher Education Subcommittee of the House Appropriations Committee of the Virginia House of Delegates and to the Senate Finance Committee," quoted in Nick Anderson and Susan Svrluga, "A Debate over U-Va.'s Investment Fund, and the University's Role in Virginia," *Washington Post*, August 26, 2016.

21. Nick Anderson, "Lawmakers Want to Know Why U-Va. Stockpiled Billions but Still Boosted Tuition," *Washington Post*, August 25, 2016.

22. "Debate over 'Slush Fund' Distracts from the Real Issue," editorial, *Cavalier Daily*, August 23, 2016.

23. Matthew Dolan and David Jesse, "U-M Socks Away Millions in Endowment as Families Face Rising Tuition," *Detroit Free Press*, February 2, 2018.

24. James A. Bacon, "UVA Fund Is Legal and Proper, State Auditor Finds," *Bacon's Rebellion* (blog), August 26, 2016.

25. Gregor Aisch and others, "Some Colleges Have More Students from the Top 1 Percent than the Bottom 60," *New York Times*, January 18, 2017.

Chapter 7

1. The percentages are derived from figure 7-1.

2. Douglas A. Webber, "State Divestment and Tuition at Public Institutions," *Economics of Education Review* 60 (October 2017), pp. 1–4.

3. A good, brief, nontechnical review of some of these issues can be found in Rick Seltzer, "State Funding Cuts Matter," *Inside Higher Education*, July 24, 2017.

4. Karin Kapsidelis, "Colleges' Spending, Not Just Decreased State Support, Have Spurred Tuition Increases, Panel Hears," *Richmond Times-Dispatch*, November 16, 2016.

5. Neal McCluskey, "Not Just Treading Water: In Higher Education, Tuition Often Does More than Replace Lost Appropriations," Policy Analysis 810 (Washington, D.C.: Cato Institute, February 15, 2017).

6. Robert Hiltonsmith, "Pulling Up the Higher-Ed Ladder" (New York: Demos, May 5, 2015).

7. Ozan Jaquette and Edna Parra, "The Problem with the Delta Cost Project Database," *Research in Higher Education* 57 (2016), pp. 630–51.

8. College Navigator, National Center for Education Statistics (http://nces.ed.gov/college navigator).

9. College Board, *Trends in College Pricing 2017*, table 2 (https://trends.collegeboard.org /college-pricing).

Chapter 8

1. William Bennett, "Our Greedy Colleges," *New York Times*, February 18, 1987.

2. "College Tuition 101," *Wall Street Journal*, September 15, 2003.

3. "Definition of 'Moral Hazard,'" *Economic Times* (https://economictimes.indiatimes.com /definition/moral-hazard).

4. Sam Peltzman, "The Effects of Automobile Safety Regulation," *Journal of Political Economy* 83, no. 4 (1975), pp. 677–726.

5. Robert B. Archibald and David H. Feldman, "The Anatomy of College Tuition" (Washington, D.C.: American Council on Education, 2012); Donald E. Heller, "Does Financial Aid Drive Up College Prices?" (Washington, D.C.: American Council on Education, 2013).

6. Robert B. Archibald and David H. Feldman, "Federal Financial Aid Policy and College Behavior" (Washington, D.C.: American Council on Education, 2016).

7. Wikipedia, "Students Loans in the United States" (https://en.wikipedia.org/wiki/Student _loans_in_the_United_States), accessed June 1, 2018.

8. Libby Nelson, "'Our Greedy Colleges': Why Financial Aid Might Make College More Expensive," *Vox*, August 12, 2015. Given the controversy that surrounds the financial aid/tuition

issue, a few words about Nelson's background are appropriate. Her appraisal of the evidence appeared on vox.com, a general-interest Internet news site founded by onetime *Washington Post* reporter Ezra Klein. The *Vox* site is dedicated to explaining the news in terms that can readily be understood by an educated adult. *Vox* generally advocates liberal or progressive points of view. Nelson also contributes to *Inside Higher Education*, another higher-education website, and her work has appeared in the *New York Times* and the *Chronicle of Higher Education*.

9. David O. Lucca, Taylor Nadauld, and Karen Shen, "Credit Supply and the Rise in College Tuition: Evidence from the Expansion in Federal Student Aid Programs," Staff Report 733 (New York: Federal Reserve Bank of New York, 2015).

10. Grey Gordon and Aaron Hedlund, "Accounting for the Rise in College Tuition," Working Paper 21967 (Cambridge, Mass.: National Bureau of Economic Research, 2016).

11. Ibid.

12. Michael McPherson and Morton Schapiro, "Keeping College Affordable: Government and Educational Opportunity" (Brookings Institution, 1991).

13. John Wirt and others, "The Condition of Education 2001" (Washington, D.C.: National Center for Education Statistics, 2001); Larry D. Singell and Joe A. Stone, "For Whom the Pell Tolls: The Response of University Tuition to Federal Grants-in-Aid," *Economics of Education Review* 26 (June 2007), pp. 285–95.

14. M.J. Rizzo and Ronald Ehrenberg, "Resident and Nonresident Tuition and Enrollment at Flagship State Universities," National Bureau of Economic Research, 2004 (www.nber.org /chapters/c10103.pdf).

15. David Archibald and David H. Feldman, *Why Does College Cost So Much?* (Oxford University Press, 2011).

16. Kyle Zinth and Matthew Smith, "Tuition-Setting Authority for Public Colleges and Universities," Education Commission of the States, October 2012 (www.ecs.org/clearinghouse /01/04/71/10471.pdf).

17. Stephanie Riegg Cellini and Claudia Goldin, "Does Federal Student Aid Raise Tuition? New Evidence on For-Profit Colleges, *American Economic Journal: Economic Policy* 6 (November 2014), pp. 174–206.

18. Lesley J. Turner, "The Road to Pell Is Paved with Good Intentions: The Economic Incidence of Federal Student Grant Aid," 2014 (http://econweb.umd.edu/~turner/turner _FedAidIncide). See also Dennis Epple, Richard Romano, and Holger Sieg, "Admission, Tuition and Financial Aid Policies in the Market for Higher Education," *Econometrica* 74 (July 2006), pp. 885–928, and Dennis Epple, Richard Romano, Sinan Sarpca, and Holger Sieg, "The U.S. Market for Higher Education: A General Equilibrium Analysis of State and Private Colleges and Public Funding Policies," Working Paper 19298 (Cambridge, Mass.: National Bureau of Economic Research, 2013).

19. Rick Seltzer, "HOPE for Whom?," *Inside Higher Ed*, September 16, 2016.

20. Susan Dynarski, "Hope for Whom? Financial Aid for the Middle Class and Its Impact on College Attendance," *National Tax Journal* 53 (September 2000), pp. 629–62, and Susan Dynarski, "Does Aid Matter? Measuring the Effect of Student Aid on College Attendance and Competition," *American Economic Review* 93 (March 2003), pp. 279–88.

21. Jonathan D. Cohen, "The Democratic Program That Killed Liberalism," *Washington Post*, March 28, 2018.

22. Jennifer Levitz and Scott Thurm, "Shift to Merit Scholarships Stirs Debate," *Wall Street Journal*, December 19, 2012.

23. Danielle Douglas-Gabriel, "Top Public Universities Are Shutting Out Poor Students, Report Says," *Washington Post*, October 26, 2017.

24. Cohen, "The Democratic Program That Killed Liberalism."

25. For national data: College Board, *Trends in College Pricing 2017*, table 3 (https://trends .collegeboard.org/college-pricing); for Georgia institutional data: College Navigator, National Center for Education Statistics (http://nces.ed.gov/collegenavigator).

26. Bridget Long, "How Do Financial Aid Policies Affect Colleges?," *Journal of Human Resources* 39, no. 4 (Fall 2004), pp. 1045–66; James V. Condon, Lori H. Prince, and Erik B. Stuckhart, "Georgia's HOPE Scholarship Program after 18 Years: Benefits, Unintended Consequences and Changes," *Journal of Student Financial Aid* 41, no. 1 (2011), pp. 17–27.

27. Lindsay Street, "S.C. Disproportionately Funds Merit-Based Scholarships, Bucking National Trend," *Statehouse Report*, November 20, 2017.

28. Raj Chetty and others, "Mobility Report Cards: The Role of Colleges in Intergenerational Mobility" (Washington, D.C.: U.S. Treasury, July 2017).

29. Andrew Gillen, "Introducing Bennett Hypothesis 2.0" (Washington, D.C.: Center for College Affordability and Productivity, February 2012).

30. Libby A. Nelson, "Warnings of Unintended Consequences," *Inside Higher Ed*, January 26, 2012. See also Matthew M. Chingos, "End Government Profits on Student Loans: Shift Risk and Lower Interest Rates" (Brookings Institution, April 30, 2015).

31. Jordan Weissmann, "Is Financial Aid Really Making College More Expensive?," *Atlantic*, February 16, 2012.

32. Patrick Brendel, "What Colorado Can Teach Other States about College Vouchers: Not Much," *Colorado Independent*, April 5, 2011; Archibald and Feldman, *Why Does College Cost So Much?*

33. James L. Fisher, *The Board and the President* (New York: American Council on Education, 1991); James L. Fisher and James V. Koch, *Presidential Leadership: Making a Difference* (Phoenix: Oryx Press, 1996).

Chapter 9

1. William J. Baumol and William G. Bowen, *Performing Arts: The Economic Dilemma* (MIT Press, 1966).

2. Robert B. Archibald and David H. Feldman, *Why Does College Cost So Much?* (Oxford University Press, 2011); Archibald and Feldman, *The Anatomy of College Tuition* (Washington, D.C.: American Council on Education, 2012); Archibald and Feldman, "Federal Financial Aid Policy and College Behavior" (Washington, D.C.: American Council on Education, 2016).

3. See, among many sources, Adrianna Kezar, Daniel Maxey, and Judith Eaton, "An Examination of the Changing Faculty: Ensuring Institutional Quality and Achieving Desired Student Learning Outcomes" (Washington, D.C.: Council for Higher Education Accreditation, January 2014); William G. Bowen, "The 'Cost Disease' in Higher Education: Is Technology the Answer?," Tanner Lectures (Stanford University, October 2012).

4. Jay Schalin, "Faculty Teaching Loads in the UNC System" (Raleigh, N.C.: John William Pope Center for Higher Education Policy, August 2014).

5. Roberta Spalter-Roth and Janene Scelza, "What's Happening in Your Department: Who's Teaching and How Much?" (Washington, D.C.: American Sociological Association, March 2009).

6. David C. Levy, "Do College Professors Work Hard Enough?," *Washington Post*, March 23, 2012.

7. National Center for Education Statistics, "Percentage Distribution of Full-Time Faculty: Fall 2003," table 315.30 (https://nces.ed.gov/programs/digest/d15/tables/dt15_315.30 .asp).

8. Jeffrey F. Milem and others, "Faculty Time Allocation: A Study of Change over Twenty Years," *Journal of Higher Education* 71 (July–August 2000), pp. 454–75; John Ziker, "The Long, Lonely Job of Homo Academicus," *Blue Review*, March 31, 2014 (https://thebluereview.org /faculty-time-allocation/); Alexa Silverman, "Get a Clearer Picture of Faculty Workload," EAB, August 30, 2017 (www.eab.com/research-and-insights/academic-affairs-forum/expert-insights /2017/get-a-clearer-picture-of-faculty-workload).

9. Peter Hinrichs, "Trends in Expenditures by U.S. Colleges and Universities, 1987–2013," *Economic Commentary* (September 2016).

10. Archibald and Feldman, *Why Does College Cost So Much?*; Archibald and Feldman, *The Anatomy of College Tuition*; Archibald and Feldman, "Federal Financial Aid Policy and College Behavior."

11. CPI-U data come from the Bureau of Labor Statistics, Series CUUR0000SA0 (www.bls .gov); data about legal services come from the Producer Price Index of the CPI-U.

12. Richard Arum and Josipa Roksa, *Academically Adrift: Limited Learning on College Campuses* (University of Chicago Press, 2011).

13. "CLA+ National Results, 2015–16" (New York: Council for Aid to Education, 2016).

14. National Center for Education Statistics, "National Assessment of Adult Literacy (NAAL): Performance in 2003" (https://nces.ed.gov/naal/kf_dem_edu.asp).

15. William G. Bowen and others, "Interactive Learning Online at Public Universities: Evidence from Randomized Trials" (New York: Ithaka S+R, May 22, 2012).

16. For information about the online master's degree in computer science from Georgia Tech, see www.gatech.edu/academics/degrees/masters/computer-science-online-degree-ms.

17. Subhash Kak, "Universities Must Prepare for a Technology-Enabled Future," *Conversation* (blog), January 9, 2018.

18. Sophie Quinton, "Georgia State Has Improved Its Graduation Rate by 22 Percent in 10 Years," *Atlantic*, September 23, 2013. See also Beth McMurtrie, "Georgia State U. Made Its Graduation Rates Jump. How?," *Chronicle of Higher Education*, May 25, 2018.

Chapter 10

1. Howard R. Bowen, *The Costs of Higher Education: How Much Do Colleges Spend per Student and How Much Should They Spend?* (San Francisco: Jossey-Bass, 1980).

2. Robert E. Martin and R. Carter Hill, "Measuring Baumol and Bowen Effects in Public Research Universities," Departmental Working Papers 2012–05, Department of Economics (Louisiana State University, December 2012).

3. Ronald G. Ehrenberg, *Tuition Rising: Why College Costs So Much* (Harvard University Press, 2002).

4. See the work of Jagdish Bhagwatti, Anne Krueger, Fred McChesney, Gordon Tullock, and James Buchanan, all of whom have written prolifically on this topic.

5. Men-Andri Benz, *Strategies in Markets for Experience and Credence Goods* (Wiesbaden: Springer, 2017).

6. See the work of Michael Jensen, William Meckling, Barry Mitnick, William Niskanen, and Stephen Ross, all of whom have written prolifically on this topic.

7. "Trust-Based Marketing," *Wikipedia* (https://en.wikipedia.org/wiki/Trust-based_marketing), accessed July 15, 2018.

8. State Council for Higher Education in Virginia, "2016–17 Tuition and Fees at Virginia's State-Supported Colleges and Universities," July 31, 2016 (www.schev.edu/docs/default-source/Reports-and-Studies/2016-reports/2016-17tuitionandfeereport.pdf).

9. George Stigler originally made this argument in "The Theory of Economic Regulation," *Bell Journal of Economics and Management Science* 2 (Spring 1971), pp. 3–18.

10. Donna M. Desrochers and Steven Hurlburt, *Trends in College Spending: 2003–2013*, Delta Cost Project, 2016 (www.deltacostproject.org/sites/default/files/products/15-4626%20Final01%20Delta%20Cost%20Project%20College%20Spending%2011131.406.P0.02.001%20. . . .pdf).

11. As quoted in Jon Marcus, "New Analysis Shows Problematic Boom in Higher Ed Administrators," *HuffPost*, February 6, 2014 (www.huffingtonpost.com/2014/02/06/higher-ed-administrators-growth_n_4738584.html).

12. For room and board charges at four-year public institutions: College Board, *Trends in College Pricing 2016* (https://trends.collegeboard.org); for the food price index: U.S. Department of Labor, Bureau of Labor Statistics, CPI-All Urban Consumers, CUUR0000SAF (https://data.bls.gov/cgi-bin/surveymost).

13. James V. Koch, "No College Kid Needs a Water Park to Study," *New York Times*, January 9, 2018.

14. College Navigator, National Center for Education Statistics (http://nces.ed.gov/collegenavigator).

15. "Edifice Complex," *Urban Dictionary* (www.urbandictionary.com/define.php?term=edifice complex).

16. "Oregon State University," *Oregon Encyclopedia* (https://oregonencyclopedia.org/articles/oregon_state_university).

17. College Navigator, National Center for Education Statistics, and University of Central Florida website (guides.ucf.edu).

18. David Laurence, "Preliminary Report on the MLA Job Information List, 2016–17," *The Trend* (blog), Modern Language Association Office of Research, October 17, 2017; Colleen Flaherty, "Withering Humanities Jobs," *Inside Higher Ed*, November 21, 2017.

Chapter 11

1. American Council on Education web page (www.acenet.edu/Pages/default.aspx).

2. Association of Governing Boards web page (www.agb.org).

3. Robert B. Archibald and David H. Feldman, *Why Does College Cost So Much?* (Oxford University Press, 2011); Archibald and Feldman, "The Anatomy of College Tuition" (Washing-

ton, D.C.: American Council on Education, 2012); Archibald and Feldman, "Federal Financial Aid Policy and College Behavior" (Washington, D.C.: American Council on Education, 2016).

4. Donald Heller, "Does Federal Financial Aid Drive Up College Prices?" (Washington, D.C.: American Council on Education, 2013).

5. State Higher Education Executive Officers Association, "State Higher Education Finance" (www.sheeo.org/projects/shef-%E2%80%94-state-higher-education-finance).

6. Amazon Machine Learning (https://aws.amazon.com/machine-learning).

7. For more on these initiatives by Georgia State University, see chapter 9.

8. David O. Lucca, Taylor Nadauld, and Karen Shen, "Credit Supply and the Rise in College Tuition: Evidence from the Expansion in Federal Student Aid Programs," Staff Report 733 (New York Federal Reserve Bank, March 2015).

9. Dennis Epple and others, "The U.S. Market for Higher Education: A General Equilibrium Analysis of State and Private Colleges and Public Funding Policies," Working Paper 19298 (Cambridge, Mass.: National Bureau of Economic Research, August 2013).

10. College Navigator, National Center for Education Statistics (http://nces.ed.gov/collegenavigator).

11. University of Maryland, Office of the President, "Proposal for Affordable Excellence, Access and Economic Growth," press release, May 1, 2015.

12. College Navigator, National Center for Education Statistics.

13. Ibid.

14. See "UNC Continues Rigorous Examination of Degree Program Productivity," May 27, 2015 (www.northcarolina.edu/news/2015/05/unc-continues-rigorous-examination-degree-program-productivity), and discussion by Jesse Safron, "What's to Be Done about 'Low Productivity' Degree Programs?," James G. Martin Center for Academic Renewal, September 22, 2014.

15. Ad Astra Information Systems, "Executive Summary: The Higher Education Scheduling Index" (Overland Park, Kans., July 2016).

16. University of North Carolina System, "Fall Utilization Reports" (https://old.northcarolina.edu/ira/fac_util/dashboard.html). See Duke Cheston, "Students in Space," James G. Martin Center for Academic Renewal, October 30, 2012 (www.jamesgmartin.center/2012/10/students-in-space/), for a discussion of these data.

17. American School and University, "38th Annual Maintenance & Operations Cost Study for Colleges" (April 2009) (www.asumag.com/maintenance/38th-annual-maintenance-operations-cost-study-colleges).

18. The Good Jobs Project, November 13, 2017 (https://goodjobsdata.org/resources).

19. Old Dominion University, "Operating Budget and Plan, 2017–2018" (Norfolk, Va.).

20. "The W&M Promise," College of William and Mary website (www.wm.edu/sites/wmpromise/index.php).

21. Matthew Stewart, "The Birth of a New Aristocracy," *Atlantic*, June 2018.

22. Gregor Aisch and others, "Some Colleges Have More Students from the Top 1 Percent than the Bottom 60," *New York Times*, January 18, 2017.

23. Partners for College Affordability, Trustee Votes Project–Virginia (database) (www.pcapt.org/initiatives/trustee-vote). The two negative votes were cast by Robert Holsworth, a

member of the Board of Visitors at Virginia Commonwealth University (VCU), with 30,000 students. Ironically, Dr. Holsworth formerly was Dean of VCU's College of Humanities and Sciences. It is fair to say he knew more than most board members about the inner workings of the University.

24. Patrick Callan, "Five Ways Trustees Can Help Make College Affordable," *Real Clear Education*, May 2, 2018.

25. Marjorie Valbrun, "Questions on Michigan's Investment Tactics," *Inside Higher Education*, June 5, 2018.

26. Mark Perry, "More Evidence That It's Very Hard to 'Beat the Market' over Time, 95% of Finance Professionals Can't Do It," *AEIdeas* (blog), American Enterprise Institute, March 20, 2018.

Index